Explorations of the Far Right (EFR)

vol 6

ISSN 2192-7448

GENERAL EDITOR: Dr. Anton Shekhovts

CW00815894

)

Explorations of the Far Right

edited by Anton Shekhovtsov

ISSN 2192-7448

Péter Krekó, Attila Juhász

THE HUNGARIAN FAR RIGHT

Social Demand, Political Supply, and International Context

ibidem-Verlag
Stuttgart

Bibliographic information published by the Deutsche Nationalbibliothek

Die Deutsche Nationalbibliothek lists this publication in the Deutsche Nationalbibliografie; detailed bibliographic data are available in the Internet at http://dnb.d-nb.de.

Bibliografische Information der Deutschen Nationalbibliothek

Die Deutsche Nationalbibliothek verzeichnet diese Publikation in der Deutschen Nationalbibliografie; detaillierte bibliografische Daten sind im Internet über http://dnb.d-nb.de abrufbar.

Cover picture: © VT at Hungarian Wikipedia. Licensed under CC BY-SA 1.0 (s. https://creativecommons.org/licenses/by-sa/1.0/deed.en)

Büro Budapest

Supported by the Friedrich-Ebert-Stiftung—Budapest Office

ISSN: 2192-7448

ISBN-13: 978-3-8382-1184-8

© *ibidem*-Verlag / *ibidem* Press

Stuttgart, Germany 2017

Printed in the United States of America

Contents

List of tables and figures

Figures

Tables

Preface

Hungary has made a lot of headlines in the international media over the last ten years. The reasons for this international interest are two-fold: the Hungarian far right and the illiberal tendencies in the country. Needless to say, the two phenomena are strongly interconnected. In this book, we try to explain why.

In April 2015, an unprecedented event happened in Hungary: during the mid-term parliamentary elections, Jobbik—the Movement for a Better Hungary (*Jobbik Magyarországért Mozgalom*, Jobbik), once the most extreme ultranationalist party in European parliaments, gained its first ever individual mandate, in a district in Tapolca, western Hungary, where previously Viktor Orbán's governmental party Alliance of Young Democrats (*Fiatal Demokraták Szövetsége*, Fidesz) had enjoyed strong support. This victory was indicative of Jobbik's spectacular political successes. Jobbik has had a meteoric rise in the last ten years. A political party established in 2003 that barely gained 2 percent votes in 2006 during the parliamentary election collectively with Hungarian Justice and Life Party (*Magyar Igazság és Élet Pártja*, MIÉP) gained 15 percent votes in 2009 during the European Parliament (EP) elections and received 17 percent votes a year later during consecutive parliamentary elections. Then, in the 2014 parliamentary elections, Jobbik gained 21 percent of the votes (excluding votes outside Hungary), and in the summer of that year, at the EP elections, Jobbik took over the position of the second largest party—and has continued to hold it since then. Jobbik's politicians hope that a continuation of this trend will play a major role in the party's further rise to power.

However, it would be premature to call this prophecy: tensions within Jobbik and policies of a radicalizing Fidesz implementing Jobbik's program have hindered party support since then. While it seems that Jobbik will remain a major player in the Hungarian political scene, an electoral breakthrough at the 2018 elections will be difficult.

The Hungarian far right is the rule and the exception at the same time: the rule because it fits to the features of the "Populist Zeitgeist" and because it is an essentially European and Eastern European phenomenon. Its original revisionist, anti-Semitic ideology built on a strong nostalgia toward the 1920s and 1930s, along with its soft irredentist rhetoric and harsh critique of the political transition in 1989–1990, makes it similar to many far-right organizations in the region, from the Bulgarian Attack (*Ataka*) to Marian Kotleba's People's Party Our Slovakia (*Ľudová strana Naše Slovensko*). The way the party tries to turn more moderate is following European cookbooks. Gábor Vona, the leader of the party since 2006, has done his best in the last four years to moderate the party and bring it to the "mainstream" of the European populist radical right, using recipes from, among others, parties in France and Serbia. The most extreme party of the European scene before Golden Dawn (*Laïkós Sýndesmos—Chrysí Avgí*) emerged with a strong heritage from the Hungarian fascist movements and gradually became the centrist challenger to an increasingly authoritarian and chauvinist Fidesz from 2013 onward. And this is a completely open move: Gábor Vona openly admitted recently that he "took the spirit of the party" (Vona, 2016a), betraying its original principles, to make a centrist, modern conservative force capable of governing from an extreme one: a real "mature adult" from a rebellious "adolescent."

As a result of this policy, which leads to a leadership challenge in the party that Vona could overcome, Jobbik can be, in the long run, an exception to the rule (see, for example, Minkenberg, 2015) that radical-right parties in Eastern Europe are more volatile, and have lower life cycles than the mainstream parties. Jobbik can rather become more similar to their Western counterparts in France, Austria, and the Netherlands, for example, parties that are integral parts of the party system for decades. Jobbik became an important part of the political system, a relatively stable middle-size party. And its quick moderation makes it an exception for one more reason as well. The strategy to become a soft, mild centrist party obviously paid off until 2014 and 2015; it became problematic afterward—with the beginning of the refugee crisis. While in most of the European countries—let's take Austria, Germany, France, Slovakia as examples—radical-right parties could rise at the expense of mainstream governmental parties, in

Hungary the case was the very opposite. Fidesz, with its law-and-order policy steps (e.g., raising a fence on the southern border of Hungary) and strong xenophobic rhetoric (running billboard campaigns against refugees and initiating a referendum against the mandatory refugee allocation mechanism with very harsh anti-Brussels and xenophobic tone) could gain popularity, while Jobbik rather lost support as it could not, and did not want to, exceed Fidesz in radicalism. But the simple fact that right-wing radicalism could become even more mainstream clearly shows that there is massive social demand for it in Hungary.

In this book, overviewing the available literature, but mainly relying on accumulated knowledge and analyses of Political Capital Institute on the subject, we make an attempt to explain the "demand," or social, and "supply," or political, factors responsible for the rise and popularity of Jobbik, the leading force of the genuine Hungarian far right after the regime change. When analyzing Jobbik's policies and politics, we cannot ignore the domestic political context in general and Jobbik's relations to current governmental party Fidesz in particular: how Fidesz influenced Jobbik and vice versa. We think that the general simplifying explanation that Jobbik pushed Fidesz more to the extreme position is simplifying and misleading. What we can see instead is that the problems with post-transitional Hungary and the general disillusionment from the democratic ideals and Western models and approaches, hand in hand with political opportunism, led to very similar political and policy approaches in both parties. While they definitely had an impact on each other, their direction was not determined by each other. Furthermore, we highlight the international context of the Hungarian far right. Jobbik and Fidesz, political parties with a nationalist, authoritarian approach, a pro-Russian orientation, and strong anti-Western stance, are products of the problematic transformation period that is specific to postcommunist countries. But they are products of a general "populist Zeitgeist" on the West as well, with declining trust in representative and international institutions, politicians, experts, and the mainstream media and rise of politicians such as Heinz-Christian Strache, Marine Le Pen, Geert Wilders, and Donald Trump as a consequence. The rise of this "Populist Internationale," as Anne

Applebaum calls it, is a consequence of a strong anti-intellectual revolution and deep feelings of a "center-periphery" conflict. This perceived dichotomy behind the resurgence of populist forces all over the world that can manifest itself in many forms (capital vs. countryside, urban vs. rural, elite vs. people) seems to be much more important than the objective socioeconomical status. And this tension is a strong driving force of political conflicts in Hungary as well.

The story of Jobbik and Fidesz will not be told as separate case studies, but as representatives of broader Central European and European trends. Telling their story from this perspective, we will rely on Cas Mudde's (2007) *pathological normalcy* thesis. Populist radical-right parties such as Jobbik (and increasingly, Fidesz) are not pathologic and extraordinary, but instead the opposite: seemingly pathological manifestations of normal, mainstream political tendencies and attitudes. The radical right is not the opposite of the mainstream. This is a sharp caricature of the mainstream.

In this book, we do not aim to give an extensive overview of the literature on the far right. We only use the existing literature to give a theoretical framework for our investigation. Also, our approach is not entirely value neutral. When talking about players and policies of the far right, we talk about solutions that often openly go against political values and human rights standards, the pillars of Western civilization.. We do think that authoritarian, nationalistic populist rhetoric and policies are posing a threat to liberal democracies and social peace.

We never thought that the far right and their ideology should be banned or silenced. But political forces and rhetoric that aim to capitalize from the sharpened social conflicts need special attention—because they can provoke violence. But making a distinction between the political force and its voters remains important. Voters' views may differ in many ways from the policies of their party of choice—and this is the case of Jobbik as well. Jobbik's supporters are often more moderate on many issues than Jobbik party members (Bíró, Boros, and Varga, 2012). For many, Jobbik is like a political Rorschach test on which they can project their disillusionment, political desires, and hopes. Furthermore, voters with extremist attitudes don't necessarily vote for the far right; they frequently support mainstream parties.

As it is mentioned above Jobbik changed its political and policy stance substantially in the last few years, as parts of a strategy to gravitate towards the mainstream—while we can observe an opposite trend regarding Fidesz. These two trends might highlight the most dynamic tendencies of the last decade in Hungarian domestic politics, causing significant change in voters' attitudes as well. But it also means that analyzing the far-right in Hungary is like shooting to a constantly and quickly moving target. We analyze, for example, Jobbik's political programs and manifestos written in 2010 and 2014, but some of these elements have already been softened and moderated by the party. But we think it is still important to give a retrospective analysis of Jobbik's symbolic politics and policies as well, for two simple reason. First, they are deeply rooted in the Hungarian nationalist and far-right traditions (e.g. Paksa, 2012), therefore their relevance goes beyond the party. Second, the moderation strategy is mainly coming from the party leader, Gábor Vona. If he is being replaced as the party leadership in the coming years (e.g. as a consequence of worse-than-expected election results), a hardliner can take back the party and bring back the more radical political line. While party positions can change relatively quickly, the traditional ideology of the Hungarian far-right and its topics seem rather ethernal.

Acknowledgments

This book would not have been possible without the help and support of Friedrich Ebert Stiftung office in Budapest. We extend our appreciation to Jan Niklas Engels and János Molnár for their support and recommendations—and also for their patience. We are grateful to founders of Political Capital Institute, Zoltán Somogyi and Krisztián Szabados, for their encouragement and support for these researches from the very beginning. We also thank Csaba Molnár, László Róbert, Kálmán Kiss, Gergely Gimes, Bulcsú Hunyadi, Lóránt Győri, and Patrik Szicherle, former or current analysts at Political Capital Institute, whose research served as the foundation for chapters of this book. Our intern, Pálinkás Réka, was of utmost help organizing the literature. Katya Dunajeva helped a lot in improving the text during the months he spent at Political Capital. Pál Salamon helped with the translation of some chapters. All errors and omissions remain the responsibility of the authors.

Our approach in the book

What are we talking about? The concepts

As such the concept of the *far right* is not suitable for a description of consistent and inert political phenomena; instead, it simply attempts to define a set of dynamically shifting ideas, groups, organizations, parties, and other political actors and practices sharing a number of common features. Consequently, a precise definition of our topic is a daunting task. However, we are far from being alone with this predicament; a review of European professional literature shows that twenty years ago Cas Mudde in his study "The war of words: Defining the extreme right party family" (1996) considered in detail the difficulties of applying various terms and definitions, while Elisabeth Carter in her book *The Extreme Right in Western Europe* plainly referred to a "deluge of terminological experiments" (2005, p. 21). In other words, political science has yet to come up with proper terminology describing the political phenomenon in question. We have no established terminology in respect of Europe, let alone global developments taking place outside our continent.

Of course, one can ask whether it makes any sense to squeeze all far-right or "right-radical" (by their own definition) political ideas, players, and practices into a single label when they themselves do not constitute a uniform and consistent category. Political phenomena regularly lumped into this category are rather diverse and may show a wide range of differences across time and place alike. In the cases discussed here, an unusual level of heterogeneity can be attributed to the fact that great emphasis has been placed on country- and region-specific developments. While the European far right represents an increasingly international phenomenon (see, for example, Vejvodova, 2014), all political players, in the need for targeting their own constituency, have to deal with local answers for social problems, which means that in developing their programs and policies, specific conditions of their country come to play an important role.

While the topics, rhetorical styles, and ideological cornerstones of the far-right ideologies, in most of the cases, have very similar features, there can be an important difference between how these forces define their enemies (see, for example, Mudde, 2007). While xenophobia as the rejection of the universal stranger is often a central component of far-right dogma and rhetoric, in some places, like Western and Northern Europe, where immigration from the East creates tensions, xenophobia is accompanied with incitement against East Europeans. In the nativist tones of the Brexit campaign, for example, the voices against Eastern Europeans were much louder than the islamophobic ones. In Eastern Europe, on the other hand, in many cases for historical reasons, anti-Tziganism and anti-Semitism dominate the nativist discourses—with a new wave of xenophobia as a consequence of the refugee crisis. As a consequence of the rivaling nationalisms and differing enemy images, the European far-right parties are traditionally facing difficulties to creating a broad-based alliance reaching across countries, similar to that established by the continent's conservative, liberal, green, or left-wing party families. A good example is when a former far-right group in the European Parliament (EP) split up in 2007 when Alessandra Mussolini, a descendent of Benito Mussolini, claimed that Romanians are "habitual law-breakers" and the Greater Romania Party (*România Mare*) left the group as a response (Spiegel Online, 2007).[1] But we can see a more coherent radical-right narrative emerging in Europe as a consequence of three factors: (1) islamophobia is becoming a common denominator as a consequence of the refugee crisis; (2) the European Union (EU), especially since the economic crisis in 2008, is becoming an increasingly important enemy for the far-right parties; and (3) the common friends of populist radical-right parties, such as Russia, are creating the possibilities of a joint platform. While the far-right groups in Europe are getting closer to each other, we cannot see a real pan-European far-right movement:

---

[1]   Spiegel Online. (2007). Cat Fight on the Far Right: Mussolini's Romania Comments Split Extremist MEP Group. [online] SPIEGEL ONLINE. Available at: http://www.spiegel.de/international/europe/cat-fight-on-the-far-right-mussolini-s-romania-comments-split-extremist-mep-group-a-516407.html [Accessed April 12, 2017].

the relatively strong populist radical-right group in the EP, Europe of Nations and Freedom (ENF) is dominated by Western European political parties, incorporating politicians from Eastern Europe (two Polish members of parliament [MPs] from the ex-party of Korwin Mikke and an expelled Romanian Social Democrat) only to increase the number of member states within the caucus. At the same time, this radical-right group is not lacking its Eastern European models: Viktor Orbán has been cheered as a European leader by politicians of the three most prominent parties represented in the European group: Front National (FN), the Dutch Freedom Party (*Partij voor de Vrijheid*), and the Austrian Freedom Party (*Freiheitliche Partei Österreichs*, FPÖ).

The fact that one may identify a number of shared theoretical principles pointing to the common origin of otherwise divergent ideologies followed by far-right political forces may still afford a more or less comprehensive definition. In the most general terms, political ideas advocating the primacy of various communities, described as traditional or organic, positioned against the individual and other communities provide a shared theoretical basis. This is what Cas Mudde (2007) labeled as "nativist," to be the minimal definition of populist radical-right groups. The radical right's discriminative ideology is based on ethnocentric, cultural, or religious foundations. In other words, a *national collectivist ideology* is a unifying principle underlying all political phenomena that may be described as far right.

There have been many terminological debates in Hungary as well in the academic and analyst communities about how to call the Hungarian far right (for a summary, see Filippov, 2011). And this is not only a theoretical debate: Jobbik, one of the main subjects of this book, went to court and won several cases against those describing it as a "far-right" party. Jobbik has sued a private television, ATV, for using the term "far right" in a news piece—and finally, a Constitutional Court verdict claimed that this is an opinion that has no room in the news programs (Index, 2016). Also, much effort has been made to distinguish—primarily in the legal sense—"radicalism" from "extremism." This is based on the argument that radicals accept the political framework of a liberal democracy and challenge it only at the rhetorical level, while extremists aim at its elimination (Norris, 2005; Kurtán, 2007). However, this distinction may be challenged on several grounds:

1. From the perspective of the institutional system, the rules of a liberal democracy may be accepted not only out of conviction but also under duress (or for tactical reasons); that is, if the democratic framework is sufficiently solid, the far right has no choice but to play by its rules. However, history has shown that political parties with parliamentary seats gained in democratic elections continue to reject the parliamentary system and are unlikely to abandon their extremist views and practices. Let's just recall the National Socialist German Workers' Party (*Nationalsozialistische Deutsche Arbeiterpartei*) or the Hungarian Arrow Cross Party (*Nyilaskeresztes Párt*) between the two world wars.

2. With respect to political communication or the dimensions of policy making, and since the publication of Austin's (1990) theory of speech acts, making a distinction between words and actions has become highly questionable. This means that a party's policies can no longer be assessed and defined based on its resolutions or agenda alone; in our approach, political action is given a wider interpretation and includes ideas, speeches, statements, and symbols.

3. Making a clear distinction between the terms "extremism" and "radicalism" is highly questionable from a normative aspect as well: while justified in a legal context, political science can hardly be expected to make a sharp distinction between phenomena with no clear lines of demarcation, where the investigation involves the potential overlapping and convergence of the two terms. In this context, the argument that the term "radicalism" is more likely to meet objective scientific criteria than the term "far right" is difficult to justify. For one thing, the latter may be used in a descriptive way, and the former may also be seen as stigmatizing. Moreover, one does not have to take a neutral position with respect to far-right politics to make an analysis. For instance, following World War II, few analyzed Nazism with cool detachment or empathy. The same can be said about the atrocities of communism. Be that as it may, most of our knowledge of these historical events comes from authors taking a firm position against these systems. Hannah Arendt investigated the totalitarian phenomenon from a humanistic point of view, and yet her obviously "biased" works and the debate they generated helped rather than hindered our understanding of the nature of totalitarian systems. In Hungarian public discourse, from time to time, it comes up that reference to the "far-right" definition is politically incorrect. However, the same can be said if one uses the terms "right-wing radicals" and "national radicals" to describe Jobbik. The only difference is that the former term is used by the enemies of Jobbik, while the latter is used by Jobbik for self-definition.

Occasionally, the following question also comes up in Hungarian public discourse: is the use of the term "far right" justified at all, or should we talk about a "far-left" aberration. The issue is not new; the term "green Bolshevism" had already been used in 1941 with respect to the Arrow Cross Party (Máthé, 2013). There are some who believe that emphasizing the far-left character of the Hungarian far right is justified even today, and they refer to Jobbik's ideology as "national Bolshevism" (Gerő, 2010). However, the fact that far-right and far-left ideolo-

gies overlap at some points does not provide sufficient ground for blur-
ring the distinction between the two ideologies.[2] Furthermore, a number of differences may be identified even with respect to these con-
verging points, such as the issue of anticapitalism. As mentioned earlier, (national) collectivism as understood by the right has nothing in
common with the phenomenon defined by the left using the same
term.

Regarding the classification of Jobbik, the opinions are quite diverse. Pál Tamás (2007) considers it as a neopopulist party, which, at
the same time, carries certain aspects of neofascism. István Grajczjár
and András Tóth (2012, p. 87) say that Jobbik is the representative of
a new party family, which managed to turn radical nationalism into a
modern ideology that is digestible for the masses but still manages to
incorporate those favoring an extremist right ideology. Róna (2014)
believes that Jobbik's antisystem beliefs are an important building
block of the party's policies. He believes that although Jobbik has not
questioned the legitimacy of the elections since 2006 and they accepted the court ruling that banned the Hungarian Guard (*Magyar
Gárda*), the reorganization of it under new names and the promise that
the Guard would be made part of policing and territorial defense
openly question the state's monopoly on the use of force; therefore,
Jobbik confronts the system through the Hungarian Guard (Róna,
2014, pp. 32–33). The antidemocratic acts of party members have not
been condemned by the leadership so far, and Jobbik also disap-
proves of universal suffrage (Róna, 2014). Róna (2014) categorizes
Jobbik as an extreme-right party, as it is antidemocratic and opposes
the current system in the areas of legality, the obedience of rules, and
the state's monopoly on the use of force. Minkenberg (2015, p. 32)
puts the party in the autocratic-fascist, radical-right category, while he
categorizes the MIÉP as a member of the milder, ethnocentrist group.
Pytlas (2015, p. 32) believes that Jobbik is a representative member
of the Eastern European far-right party family, the ideology of which is
built upon pre- and postcommunist issues alike, which, on the one

---

[2]   While obviously all discursive strategies aimed at this are more than
understandable and analyzable, each major political and ideological movement
aims to rid itself of its extremists and push them to the opponent's side.

hand, puts it on the same platform as its Western counterparts, while, on the other hand, also divides the two blocks.

An important question arises, several aspects of which are to be discussed later: what social groups are susceptible to far-right ideologies and who votes for the parties classified in this category. The left tends to emphasize the role of the lower middle class, while conservative and liberal circles identify members of the working class as the most likely to line up behind the far right. In other words, while the issue divides various schools of thought in social science, it is all but evident that social groups losing their sense of status are the staunchest supporters of the far right.

On our part, we wish not to enter the debate over terminology or discuss the one-dimensional issue of social base and, based on the arguments set out earlier, would simply indicate that we consider the use of the term "far right" as a general concept fully justified with respect to the ideas, players, and phenomena under investigation. At the same time, we think that anyone who is doing research on the radical right nowadays has to realize the imperfections of terminologies and the difficulty of capturing such complex phenomena with one or two words.

The supply and demand model

While in political discourse it is common to trace the recurring ascendance of the far right to a single cause (i.e., economic crisis, immigration, etc.), social science literature appears to provide a plethora of explanations (for an overview, see, for example, Mudde, 2007). Due in part to the large numbers and in part to the rich content, even a classification of the various theories would be a daunting task that goes beyond the ambitions of this book.

Although a research of extremist movements should not differ fundamentally from an analysis of other political trends and players (see, for example, Mudde, 2010), attitude toward the far right is considered to be a particularly sensitive area even within the world of politics. Theories carry not simply scientific but also political relevance, such as the following: Who and what to blame for the tendency? Who are voting for the far right? The different explanations always have ideological and political relevance, and ideologically heated explanations have a tendency to ignore the truth. Just two examples follow: critics of globalization have a tendency to blame the "neoliberal political system" (see Tamás Gáspár, 2015), ignoring Jobbik's anticapitalist position, and political analysts close to the right-wing Fidesz party try to prove that Jobbik's voters did not come from the right (Századvég, 2012), despite serious researches that prove the opposite (see, for example, Karácsony and Róna, 2011). However, this should not come as a surprise since the discussed political phenomenon is truly heterogeneous, lending itself to analysis along many criteria. A grand synthesizing theory is missing due to the profusion of country-specific factors.

In the scholarly literature, one finds a number of attempts at classifying theories dealing with the far right. Along scientific disciplines, Hagtvet (1994) distinguishes psychological, historical, sociological, and political explanations, and Knigge (1998) categorizes those into economic, social, and political categories. In Rydgren's classification (2007), the two major categories are represented by supply- and demand-based theories. Mudde (2007) gave a comprehensive list of the supply- and demand-side factors that can explain the rise and decline of populist radical-right actors. In the latter case, voter attitudes and behavior, along with their assumed preconditions such as crises, ethnic conflicts, and economical problems, are identified as the factors most likely generating social demand for far-right ideas, political actors, and practices. The other approach, focusing on political supply, deals with far-right politics and context, such as the political balance of power, the election system, and the far-right's leadership, organizational strength, political strategies lined up against them, the power of institutional restraints, as well as the media environment.

We think that in order to understand the far right, the two approaches must be examined side by side. The professional literature is particularly critical of exclusively demand-side theories because they say nothing about the underlying causes of this tight relationship and fail to identify the reasons why similar circumstances lead to the rise of a far-right force in some cases while they do not in others. But even so, most critics seem to acknowledge that there is a close relationship between far-right preferences and specific voter attitudes (Enyedi, 2005; Mudde, 2007). Our position is that the social demand is necessary, but far from a sufficient precondition for a resurgence of a strong far right. It is necessary because in a society where voters are not susceptible to some aspects of the far-right ideology (criticism of the establishment elite, prejudice, etc.), the advocates of far-right policies have little chance of building a substantial social base. While political players, to some extent, can, in a voluntaristic manner, shape the structure of the political system and the demand of the voters (see, for example, Enyedi, 2004), the room of such action is not unlimited. And the existence of a social need for such political forces, rhetorical solutions, and ideologies is definitely not sufficient because right-wing extremism does not automatically create a far-right political supply— or at least not necessarily on the radical-right end.

It is also evident that strong demand for right-wing extremism may not simply manifest itself in the emergence of a stronger far-right party, but may also have an impact on other areas of the political and institutional system. For instance, a low level of public trust may erode the democratic system and undermine the legitimacy of democratic institutions. Furthermore, strong antiestablishment attitudes and demand for economic isolation may compromise the investment-friendly climate and encourage those in power to apply excessively protectionist, paternalistic, and discriminative economic policy. Xenophobia may also push all political actors into increasingly extreme positions and incite ethnic conflicts within society and between nations. The Eastern European political landscape provides a perfect illustration of this trend. Usually, far-right parties are weaker here because mainstream (often governmental) parties are incorporating strongly nationalistic, often racist agendas, and generally, there is higher permeability between the radical right and the mainstream right (Minkenberg, 2015). In Eastern Europe, no parliamentary far-right party has such a high support as Jobbik has.

Generally, following the extension of universal suffrage, modern politics has essentially become demand driven, that is, the political sphere is shaped by the electorate and its ballots, and politicians, familiar with voters' needs, vie for winning votes (Johnson, 1999); it is thus easy to conceive that demand for a high level of extremism will definitely have an impact on the political players and the system as a whole. We give an overview on the demand- and supply-side theories later, without aiming to give an exhaustive taxonomy on all the literature in the field (for a more detailed analysis, see, for example, Mudde, 2007; Norris, 2005).

Theories focusing on the demand side include the anomie-based explanations, relative deprivation, and the modernization losers hypothesis (e.g., Betz, 1993; Jackman and Volpert, 1996; Golder, 2003b). According to the anomie concept, atomized individuals isolated from society are more likely to support ethnocentrist and populist parties and policies. While this explanation is pretty widespread and offered as a standard explanation for fascism and national socialism, it does not enjoy the support of empirical evidence (Rydgren, 2007). Arendt's (1963) works, on the other hand, underline a very important notion: acts that are regarded to be deviant under normal circumstances can become "normal" under different (extranormal) circumstances, contributing to the "banality of evil." The relative deprivation and the modernization losers hypotheses both focus on frustration and a sense of threat. The former points to a decline relative to one's former status or to a reference group, and the latter refers to the theory of Betz (1993), arguing that far-right parties are supported by losers of a transition to postindustrial society. Typically, these assumptions are based on economic indicators, such as the rate of unemployment. However, an analysis limited to economic indicators alone does not provide a conclusive explanation regarding the support for the far right. Generally, "losers" can prefer mainstream opposition parties as well or abstain from vote, and the perception of economy matters much more than the real indicators of economy.

Rydgren (2007) discusses theories of ethnic competition and xenophobia, both concepts mainly related to immigration. While the first focuses on the economic threat attributed to immigrants, such as competition for resources, the second mainly deals with threats involving cultural and national identity. Generally, according to most researches, cultural factors seem to overweigh economic ones.

Lucassen and Lubbers (2012) made an attempt to separate economic and cultural threats and, in most (eight out of eleven) countries, their effort proved to be successful.[3] They found that cultural threats provide a much better indicator of support for populist parties, calling into question the common-sense assumption that aversion to immigrants may simply be traced to economic interests and fear of unemployment. Economic factors are not negligible, however: the authors also show that a higher GDP (gross domestic product) corresponds to a lower preference for the far right and a higher level of perceived ethnic threat.

In 2008, for example, Oesch found that in two countries under review the presence of immigrants mobilized support for far-right populist parties not tied primarily to competition for the scarce resources, but to the preservation of national identity and cultural protectionism (Oesch, 2008a). Mudde (2010), looking for an explanation for the fall of the "three last bastions" of tolerance (Denmark, Holland, and Sweden), found that while anti-Islam sentiments have significantly increased in these countries, the overall level of tolerance, surprisingly, remained stable. The paradox may be resolved if one assumes that tolerance is one of the causes behind the opposition to Islam: in these countries, openness, secularization, and women's rights, among other issues, are top priorities. According to Mudde, these values are perceived to be threatened by Islam, leading to the "intolerance of the tolerant." This theory also underlines the primacy and importance of symbolic threats over economic ones.

It is not that only immigrants can raise symbolic fears, though. According to Minkenberg (2015), the radical right should be understood as a manifestation of the political rejection of modernity. Modern supranational institutions, threatening the national sovereignty, and leading to the visions of the "death of nation-states" can also be targets

---

[3]   These countries were Austria, Belgium, Switzerland, Germany, Denmark, France, Italy, Holland, Norway, Poland, and Slovenia, while they failed to prove their theory in Austria, France, and Holland.

of political fears. Minkenberg and Perrineau (2007) explain the support for far-right parties by globalization and tensions generated by EU integration. In their analysis, far-right parties appeal to Euroskepticism and apprehensions associated with multinational Europe. In the new member states, such as in Romania, for example (Sum, 2010), supporters of the radical right tend to be suspicious and ambivalent about the EU institutions. The authors suggest that addressing voters opposed to the EU integration may be a successful strategy for a far-right party striving to expand its base. In their analysis, the main fears are also about losing identity, and not about losing money. Boomgaarden and Vliegenhart (2007) successfully demonstrated that news coverage of immigration issues and not economical ones raised the support for far-right parties.

Despite general findings that economic factors can poorly explain the support for the far right (see, for example, Mudde, 2007), these economic reductionist explanations prevail stubbornly. These explanations can be divided into two groups. On the one hand, consolidation of the far right is tied to a higher level of welfare services, suggesting that high taxes needed to sustain welfare benefits sap the competitiveness of the local economy that, in turn, strengthens the appeal of far-right parties demanding protectionism and slashing of welfare spending. On the other hand, this approach also features a version that accounts for immigration, arguing that during elections the electorate opts for extremist solutions, fearing that migration may overburden the welfare system. One school of thought representing the "universal welfare" concept claims that welfare benefits mitigate global competitive disadvantages, and followers of this theory maintain that, in fact, a high level of benefits works against extremism (Jesuit, Paradowski, and Mahler, 2009, p. 281). We are rather skeptical about explanations on the role of social transfers in reducing the threat for the far right, because, as it happens in the case of Hungary, and in many other countries as well, the myth that the immigrants/Roma receive most of the public funds and are positively discriminated in welfare transfers can easily prevail despite contradicting evidence (see, for example, Marketing Centrum, 2011).

According to some other authors, political disaffection can also work as a driving force for the success of the far right (e.g., Lubbers, Gijsberts, and Sheepers, 2002). They argue that antiestablishment messages and criticism of the entire system make the electorate susceptible to far-right ideas. According to some authors, this is precisely the feature that links otherwise quite dissimilar far-right parties in Europe (e.g., Ivarsflaten, 2008). This hypothesis also explains that the success of far-right parties is not limited to countries with high levels of immigration and high levels of prejudices in the public opinion. As noted by Knigge (1998), an analysis of the far right inevitably covers the concepts of political culture and democracy. In this context, a number of studies have shown that those unhappy with the way democracy is working or who have a low confidence in politicians and democratic institutions are more likely to become supporters of far-right parties (see, for instance, Lubbers, Gijberts, and Scheepers, 2002; Norris, 2005). In his analysis of the Central European region, Tupy (2006) concluded that the spread of corruption and poor economic decisions have discredited the elite and simultaneously increased the appeal of populist parties. Indeed, if one considers Jobbik, it is the most dispirited camp: they are dissatisfied with conditions in the country and the political elite, as well as the institutions of the democratic state (Grajczjár and Tóth, 2010; Krekó, Juhász, and Molnár, 2011; Róna and Sőrés, 2012).

The support base of far-right parties

Closely tied to theories focusing on social demand—and often burdened by ideological debate—is the question regarding which social class or strata constitute the support base of the far right. The political left and the academic representatives (see, for example, Adorno, 1950 tend to emphasize the role of the lower middle class, while conservative and liberal circles and some academics (e.g., Lipset, 1981) identify members of the working class as the most likely to line up behind the far right. In other words, even as the issue is divisive politically as well as academically, one common element behind the explanations is that social groups losing their status (or afraid of this possibility) can become supporters of the far right. The importance of status uncertainty had already been pointed out in research following World War II, and the term "extremism of the center," coined by Seymour Martin Lipset, refers to this as well (Lipset, 1981). In his view, rightist, leftist, and centrist positions all feature moderate and extremist strains, which may be identified by ideological and social background examination of the group (Lipset, 1981, p. 127). The left may also be characterized by "working-class fascism" or "Peronism," typically in the underdeveloped and poor countries experiencing rapid industrialization (Lipset, 1981, p. 135). This ideology conveys antiparliamentary and nationalist characteristics, while it supports "class war" by workers. Thus, the primary supporters of this ideology are impoverished industrial and farm workers (Lipset, 1981, p. 130 and p. 176).

Looking at the right, extreme political movements emerge in economically underdeveloped countries, where the traditionally conservative power of the "throne" and "altar" continues to hold sway, as in Francisco Franco's Spain or in Charles De Gaulle's France (Lipset, 1981, p. 135). As opposed to extremism in the center and the left, this version of extremism is less inclined to create a new political order, or as Lipset put it, as it is "more conservative than revolutionary." Instead, this ideology is more likely to remain supportive of the institutional and ideological status quo. The extreme versions of conservative movements are supported primarily by upper and traditional classes, industrialists, property owners, and church institutions (Lipset, 1981, pp. 128–130). However, according to Lipset, "classic fascism" is harbored by the political center in countries with a strong industrial base and a working class, such as Nazi Germany (Lipset, 1981, p. 135). The movement relies primarily on the lower middle class that simultaneously rejects the working class (as well as trade unions and communism), the upper middle class, and the elite (representatives of big business and the former aristocracy).

Classic fascism is antiliberal when it supports the role of the state, and liberal when it rejects big business, the trade unions, the socialist state model, religion, and other traditional phenomena. Simultaneously repudiating big business and the working class, the extreme right's anticenter struggle attempts to restore the "old middle class." These movements rely primarily on the frustration of the self-employed urban and rural middle class that see themselves as the "losers of modernization," with declining social prestige and influence. Most of the support comes from white-collar middle-class workers, anticlerical professionals, and especially, small business owners and farmers (Lipset, 1981, p. 129). Given that Jobbik's supporters are mainly from the middle class, it can be regarded as a "centrist" radical movement in Lipset's classification.

Scholars emphasizing economic causes of far-right parties' popularity have also argued that a predisposition for far-right populist messages may be correlated to one's position in society, notably the fear of finding oneself on the periphery or threatened by that prospect, as suggested by "losers of modernization" expression. This postulation has been demonstrated by a number of empirical studies, and the characteristics of those showing preference for such parties have been examined by a number of authors. In most cases, populist parties' support base is made up of unemployed and poorly educated young men (see, for instance, Minkenberg and Perrienau, 2007; Lubbers, Gijsberts and Sheepers, 2002; Betz, 1993). In Hungary, the situation is obviously different, as the core electorate of Jobbik voters are rather "winners" and not losers of the society, even if such a huge electorate is difficult to be described with simplifying sociological patterns.

In her 2005 book, Norris made an attempt to compare fifteen countries to study the radical right. According to her main findings, members of the lower middle class, skilled and unskilled workers, were overrepresented, while officeholders were underrepresented. There were clear differences among countries: for instance, the "losers" argument did not hold true in the case of Hungary, Italy, and Israel. Moreover, there were variations with respect to age: in some postcommunist countries young people are supporters, while in other countries members of the older generation are more likely to be supporters. In Hungary, with respect to specific features of the far-right camp, Grajczjár and Tóth (2010) concluded that the appeal of Jobbik may have been helped by the tension between the planned and the achieved social position and the need for status building. Typically, Jobbik's supporters define themselves as coming from the middle class. Overall, this theory stresses that the populist far-right ideology may be appealing to the losers and the winners alike, which in turn undermines the narrow class-based approaches. We have also found in our research (Bernat et al., 2012, p. 7) that the fear over losing social status is an important fear in the Jobbik camp, which can explain the prejudices of Jobbik's voters as well:

> The middle-class voters of Jobbik may feel that their social status is simultaneously endangered from below, by those who are dragging down the better-off (i.e., the "parasites" who live off state handouts, an ethnicized symbol of which are gypsies), and from above, by a tight-knit liberal and cosmopolitan elite group (symbolized by the Jews), which takes over all positions of leadership in the fields of the economy, finance, culture, the media, and politics, and pushes those who want to become part of this elite downward.

The relevance of explaining electoral support based on class is still the subject of continued debate. Oesch (2008b) maintains that through the separation of social and economic dimensions and the application of a more detailed model made up of more classes, one may demonstrate certain systematic party preferences. In his study, he defined an economic fault line manifested in the social fabric, based on access to resources, and a cultural fault line, based on schooling and receptiveness to cultural diversity. (He found that the social structures of Great Britain and Germany could be best described using traditional terms, while the application of cultural criteria is more effective in the case of Switzerland.) One of the conclusions challenging the standard class-based explanation was precisely the finding that in many cases support for far-right parties comes from social groups with access to fewer resources, primarily workers, who, one would assume, should identify with a left-wing party (Oesch, 2008b).

The difficulty in explaining electoral behavior in terms of party affiliation may be caused in part by the heterogeneity of working and middle classes (Güveli, 2007, cited in Oesch 2008a and 2008b). Even so, radical right-wing parties are often referred to as a new breed of workers' parties (Arzheimer, 2012; Oesch, 2012). According to Arzheimer, the "proletarization" of the far-right support base may also have to do with the fact that the majority of immigrants are skilled or somewhat skilled workers, posing a threat primarily to workers with similarly low levels of education.

Coffé (2013) focused on gender differences in the support base and found that masculine personality traits were more robust predictors of support for the far-right and radical anti-immigration policies than biological sex. In his view, this is related to the phenomenon of political individualization: individual characteristics (schooling and income status) have become more relevant than socioeconomic factors. Earlier, Kessler and Freeman (2005) arrived at a similar conclusion. While they demonstrated in seven EU member states that young men with less education are more likely to become supporters of far-right ideologies, political attitudes (opposition to immigration and dissatisfaction with the political system) proved to be stronger predictors. As a result, the authors concluded that the latter factors are more important than socioeconomic and demographic conditions.

All this goes to prove that it's time to move beyond earlier sociological models and shift the focus to attitudes, value preferences, and the supply side, that is, how demand for support of far-right policies is generated. We generally assume that attitudes can better describe and differentiate voters of the far right than economic and sociological explanations.

Supply-side theories

In his overview, Rydgren (2007) divides supply-driven approaches into three major groups: political opportunity structure (POS) theories, literature dealing with the organizational structure, and ideology and discourse of parties. The POS model focuses on such potential sources of support as the election system and threshold, convergence of parties in the political arena, and the role of the elite in the media. In sum, the model looks at the external causes of a party's success and a given system's receptiveness to new political variables. In the inter-pretation of Koopmans and Muis (2009), supply side is represented by political opportunity, while the demand side by various "grievances." Koopmans supplemented the original POS theory with the concept of visibility: it is not enough to have conditions conducive to the success of a radical right-wing party in place, but it must also be explained why it may take years or even decades for the factors mentioned earlier to bear fruit. Koopmans argues that for this to happen there is a need for "discursive opportunities." In the case of Jobbik, the rising anti-Roma discourses after two deadly violent incidents (a lynching of a non-Roma teacher by a Roma mob in Olaszliszka in 2006 and the murder of a handball player by Roma youngsters at a disco fight in 2009) can be identified as the main discursive opportunities that helped the party to exploit their messages nationally (Juhász, 2010).

In her 2005 study, Carter also investigated various supply-side aspects, such as party ideology, organizational structure, party com-petition, and electoral systems. Based on her findings, the most im-portant predictor is the closing gap between right- and left-wing par-ties, which corresponds to Kitschelt's earlier suggestion (1995, cited in Rydgren, 2007) about convergence in the political arena. However, Norris (2005) did not find evidence for this hypothesis. Arzheimer and Carter (2006) found that the degree of the "rightness" of a mainstream right-wing party also has an effect: the further to the right, the better for the radical right, due to legitimization effect. In the Hungarian polit-ical scene, the shift to the right was an obvious tendency since 2006 that helped Jobbik's growth (see, for example, Political Capital, 2009).

Spies (2013) examined the issue of the economic versus cul-tural support (discussed earlier) from the perspective of party compe-tition. In his argument, the overrepresentation of workers among far-right voters can be explained with the competition between the parties, and not by any shift in this group's political preferences. Political com-petition, the author argues, takes place on two planes: cultural and economic. According to the author, the slightest polarization of the economic dimension has an influence on the success of far-right par-ties, offering these parties an excellent opportunity to mobilize their voters along cultural rather than economic issues. In the case of Hungary, the cultural and symbolic aspects always played a very important role in the mobilization of the far right, while economic messaging was always less important.

Aside from the position of competing parties, the effect of the electoral system is also a frequently investigated area. The exact impact of the proportional and the majoritarian systems has yet to be determined. While some studies (e.g., Jackman and Volpert, 1996) concluded that support for radical right-wing parties tends to be higher in the proportional system, others (e.g., Van der Brug, Fennema, and Tillie, 2005) found no supporting evidence for this claim. The Hungarian electoral system, combining more majoritarian than proportional elements, has led to the spectacular underrepresentation of Jobbik in the parliament compared to its ratio of votes in both 2010 and 2014—in the latter case, even more, as some changes in the electoral system further amplified this distortion: Jobbik gained more than 20 percent of the votes and received less than 12 percent of the mandates (see Table 1).

Table 1:   The electoral results and parliamentary mandates of Jobbik, 2010 and 2014

	A: Votes received on party list (%)	B: Mandates in the parliament (%)	C: Underrepresentation (C = B/A)
2010	16.7	12.2	0.73
2014	20.2	11.6	0.57

Demand for the ideology
of the far right in Hungary

In this chapter, we are trying to give a general picture on the social climate in Hungary that helped the resurgence of the most powerful far-right force of Central Eastern Europe. The Hungarian figures will be examined in international context.

A tool for measuring social demand for the far right: The DEREX index

In order to assess the general social demand for the radical right in Hungary and beyond, analysts of Political Capital Institute invented a measurement tool called Demand for Right-Wing Extremism index (DEREX, for the detailed description, see Krekó, Juhász, and Molnár, 2011). DEREX is a percent-based indicator: it shows the percentage of respondents who in a given society are psychologically (based on their attitudes and values, not their personality) predisposed to adopt traditionalist, chauvinist, authoritarian, and antiestablishment ideologies and related political acts. This is to say the potential percentage of supporters of the far right whom we even called "attitude radicals." Political Capital Institute designed its structured DEREX index using its own theoretical model and data from the European Social Survey (ESS), a biannual study that tracks changes in societal attitudes and values in thirty-three countries in Europe. The hierarchical structure of the index can be seen in Figure 1, the detailed methodology of which is provided the Appendix.

**Figure 1:   Structure of the Demand
for Right-Wing Extremism index**

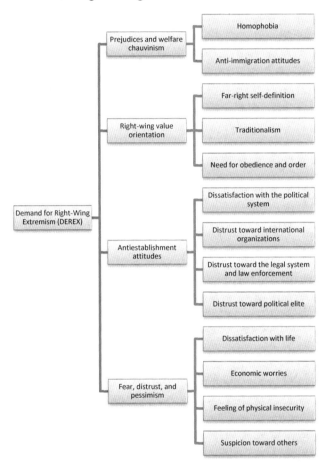

Our definition of right-wing extremism is thus based upon both ideological and psychological elements. In the opinion of practically all researchers of the subject, the first three subindices (prejudice and welfare chauvinism, right-wing value orientation, and antiestablishment
attitudes) are inherent parts of far-right ideology. These are practically
the demand-side aspects of the three ideological components on the
supply side of the populist radical right according to Mudde (2007):
nativism, populism, and authoritarianism. The fourth component (fear,

distrust, and pessimism) includes emotional factors that typically fuel the first three components, according to previous research.

A country's DEREX score is determined by the rate of respondents who belong to at least three of the four categories: for example, respondents who express anti-immigrant sentiments, antiestablishment attitudes, and right-wing values all at once. Using these strict criteria, the DEREX index examines the percentage of people whose extremist views could destabilize a country's political and economic system—if these views continue to gain credence.

The four subindices are the following.

Prejudice and welfare chauvinism

This subindex includes respondents who, based on the established set of criteria, would limit the rights of homosexuals, would deny immigrants from other countries and poor countries to enter Hungary and/or those convinced that for at least two out of three reasons (economic, cultural, and general "livability" considerations) immigration would be highly detrimental to their country. This includes two key components: opposition to immigration and homophobia. For all practical purposes, according to the far-right concept, the first of the two is an integral part of all extreme right-wing ideologies. Mudde (2000) describes this factor as "racism" and "xenophobia," and then "nativism" (Mudde, 2007). Meijerink, Mudde, and Van Holsteyn (1998) refer to the same as "exclusionism" and Falter and Schumann (1988) as "ethnocentrism." While most approaches focus on far-right discrimination based on race, a number of authors emphasize that this is intrinsically linked to a predisposition to discriminate other groups as well. Regarding the conceptual/ideological correlation, belonging to an ideal far-right community requires not only racial but also a set of additional "exclusivity" and "inclusivity" criteria (Minkenberg, 2009); the desire to discriminate is not limited to other racial/national groups, but extends to people with different religious or sexual orientation as well (Muižnieks, 2005). A number of studies have shown that there is a widespread proclivity—some kind of prejudice factor—underlying the rejection of outside groups. A general bias against outside groups, the desire to create a racial and cultural uniformity and preserve a hierarchical social order, plays a major role in the latest conceptual and operational approach to authoritarianism (e.g., right-wing authoritarianism [Altemeyer, 1981] or social dominance orientation [Sidanius and Pratto, 2005]).

Right-wing value orientation

This index is similar in attitudinal content than what Mudde (2007) described as "authoritarianism." This subindex is reserved for respondents who, based on the selected questions, position themselves along the right end of the left-right scale, may be described as having strong religious/traditionalist values, or subscribe to strong law-and-order and authoritarian policies. In this category, we collect all typical attitudes we consider to form an inherent part of a traditional right-wing/conservative worldview, that is, lending the rightist character the concept of "right-wing extremism" (beyond prejudice and chauvinism). This subindex is made up of four components: far-right self-definition, traditionalism, preference for law and order, and culture of compliance.

Far-right self-definition implied that the more "conscious" members of the radical right firmly stand by their far-right ideological orientation even at the level of self-definition. The standard left-right scale used in ESS as well is an excellent tool in making this position visible. Those positioning themselves at the far right of this continuum can be considered to be far right by "self-definition." Most studies find that a large percentage of the voters are familiar with the relevance of this dimension and the tool is an excellent measure of voters' ideological orientation and a reliable predictor of several social attitudes regarding a number of topics (Huber, 1984; Inglehart, 1987). Moreover, those accepting this position may be susceptible to ideological messages formulated by parties defining themselves as far right and may identify with parties that emphasize their radical-right orientation. The identification of far-right supporters using the left-right scale is standard practice in domestic research as well (Tamás, 2007).

In the component of traditionalism we integrated tenets related to religiosity, religious practices, and the following of traditions. In the definition of Karl Mannheim (1994, p. 59), traditionalism is a psychological predisposition, "a common human spiritual proclivity expressed in a stubborn adherence to tradition and a reluctant acceptance of all innovation." A number of authors agree that this trait is an integral part of right-wing extremism. According to Minkenberg (2009, p. 17), right-wing radicalism represents a radical political attempt to counter modernity and social changes itself; it is some kind of "romantic and populist ultra-nationalism opposed to the values of liberal and pluralistic democracies, as well as attendant individualism and universalism, while emphasizing the role of traditionalism." The same author also writes extensively on the role of religion in the ideology of the radical right and refers to fundamentalist bodies as one type of radical right-wing organization.

Finally, for the preference for law and order and the culture of compliance, one must acknowledge that the emphasis of the power and relevance of "law and order" is a shared attribute of both classic fascist and contemporary far-right parties (Hagtvet, 1994). This conclusion is supported by psychological theories and empirical studies as well. In the all but unanimous conclusion of research initiated by Adorno's circle (see their summary, for example, Fábián, 1999), predisposition for law and order and compliance constitute part and parcel of the "authoritarian syndrome." According to Altemeyer's right-wing authoritarianism concept, the three major "factors" of authoritarianism are authoritarian aggression, submission to authority, and conventionalism. The present component focuses primarily on the two latter factors with the help of the four questions of Schwartz's (2003) value questionnaire—without following Schwartz's methodology to the letter—studying the relationship to authority and adherence to rules and conventions offering security.

Antiestablishment attitudes

This category is the demand-side equivalent of Mudde's (2007) populism. It is made up of respondents who express extreme distrust of the political elite (politicians and the parliament), the legal system and law enforcement (the police and the law of the land), international organization (institutions of the EU and the United Nations [UN]), and the political system (the government and democracy). According to the majority of authors, antiestablishment attitudes form an integral part of far-right ideologies. From an ideological perspective, Ignazi (1992) refers to a negative attitude to the political establishment (*attitudinal-systematic criterion*) as one of three factors defining the "new right" in Europe. System criticism and opposition to political institutions may be manifested in various ways in the ideology and rhetoric of far-right parties: as antiparty sentiments (Mudde, 1996), antipolitics and antiestablishment, and open opposition to the political system (Cappoccia, 2002). Antielitism is shared by all new populist movements and parties (Canovan, 1981), and populism is a common attribute of new far-right movements (Mudde, 2000, 2007). It is not uncommon that international institutions are rejected as well, which, according to many, poses a serious threat to national sovereignty—and antielitism and Euroskepticism are cases in point (Kopecky and Mudde, 2002). In an analysis of antiestablishment, we defined four components (the classification of institutions into these four categories has also been confirmed by a correlation study): involving mistrust with respect to the political system, the legal system and law enforcement agencies, the political elite, as well as international organizations.

Fear, distrust, and pessimism/anxiety
This category includes respondents who are distrustful of other people ("horizontal" trust), are fundamentally dissatisfied with their life, or look at the financial prospects of the country or their own household with pessimism. This subindex, based on earlier research and theory, contains emotional factors that predispose individuals to prejudicial, authoritarian, or conservative attitudes or to support such beliefs. In one way or another, the variables studied here are related to the emotional state of fear and anxiety. According to several studies and theories, a sense of fear and danger may reinforce prejudice, encourage the individual to grasp onto traditional values, and increase a yearning for figures of authority (Simon et al., 1997; Jost, Glaser, Kruglanski, and Sulloway, 2003).

We identified four essential components of this subindex: dissatisfaction with life, financial uncertainty and concerns, fears related to public security, and suspicion of others. In combination, all these factors contribute to fear and pessimism, in turn leading to higher susceptibility to far-right ideology and various forms of prejudice.

According to some theories, pessimism and dissatisfaction with life are closely related to right-wing ideologies (Tomkins, 1963) and to authoritarianism (Stenner, 2005). Furthermore, an analysis of the ESS database shows that dissatisfaction with one's life is closely related to dissatisfaction with the functioning of the political institutions. .

Fears related to the state of the economy and the sense of existential threat reinforce dissatisfaction with general conditions and opposition to the establishment. In periods characterized by strong economic and social uncertainty, authoritarian tendencies tend to intensify (Sales, 1973; Fromm, 2002; Doty, Peterson, and Winter 2006).

Concerns about public security may easily turn a large segment of society to authoritarian political formations promising justice and order. Law and order and authoritarianism have always constituted an integral part of far-right groups (Mudde, 2000, 2007). As early as 1950, the classic theory and research of Adorno et al. related fear of a "dangerous world" to right-wing authoritarianism, and recent studies also show a correlation between the perceived threat of crime and a heightened desire to severely punish criminals, and right-wing authoritarianism (Altemeyer, 2006).

According to some theories, the increasing individualization, atomization of society, and the dissolution of traditional ties play into the hands of the far right; it may become attractive through its symbolic creation of a community with strong and clear contours. Joining the "total" community of the far right, part of the electorate may come to believe that it can reduce its sense of isolation and lose itself in the intense experience of collectivism. Accordingly, a higher level of social capital (Putnam, 1995) may offer protection against the ideology of extremist, chauvinist, and discriminatory groups (Ignazi, 2003), while individuals less integrated into society and harboring suspicion against others may be more susceptible to extremist rhetoric (Arendt, 1951; Kornhauser, 1960; Ignazi, 2003; Lubbers, Gijberts, and Scheepers, 2002).

Social demand for the far right in Hungary, 2002–2015

In Hungary, the political rise of the radical right in 2009 was preceded by a sharp rise of the demand for right-wing extremism (see Figure 2 and Table 2), then, with fluctuations, remained on a high level. In the following pages, we give an overview on the trends in the attitudes of the voters that made the far right attractive in Hungary.

A period of rapid rise in demand for the far right (2002–2009)
In Hungary, while in 2002 the percentage of voters expressing far-right attitudes meeting the rather strict criteria of the DEREX stood at "only" 10 percent, in 2009 the percentage of voters' index nearly doubled and grew to 21 percent. It means that ideologically and psychologically more than one-fifth of the population over the age of fifteen became susceptible to far-right thinking. The growth could have been observed in practically every sub-dice except right-wing value orientation.

Figure 2:   DEREX scores in Hungary, 2002–2015

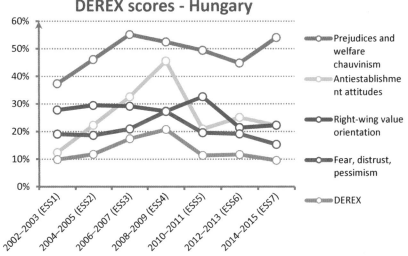

Table 2:   DEREX scores in Hungary, 2002–2015

DATA TABLE	Prejudices and welfare chauvinism	Antiestablishment attitudes	Right-wing value orientation	Fear, distrust, pessimism	DEREX	Fieldwork
2002–2003 (ESS1)	37%	12%	28%	19%	**10%**	2002.10.29. 2002.11.26.
2004–2005 (ESS2)	46%	22%	29%	19%	**12%**	2005.04.02. 2005.05.31.
2006–2007 (ESS3)	55%	33%	29%	21%	**17%**	2006.11.21. 2007.01.28.
2008–2009 (ESS4)	52%	46%	27%	27%	**21%**	2009.02.20. 2009.04.20.
2010–2011 (ESS5)	49%	21%	33%	20%	**11%**	2010.10.19. 2010.12.10.
2012–2013 (ESS6)	45%	25%	21%	19%	**12%**	2012.11.10. 2013.02.17.
2014–2015 (ESS7)	54%	22%	22%	15%	**10%**	2015.04.24. 2015.06.26.

Prejudice and *welfare chauvinism* are traditionally strong in Hungary. As both domestic (e.g., Csepeli, Fábián, and Sík, 1998) and comparative (e.g., Bernát, 2010) studies indicate, strong prejudice against minority groups is a dominant trend in Hungarian public opinion. This is partially a characteristic of the entire Central and Eastern European regions, but Hungary seems to be a champion of the region in this aspect. This is related to an increased sense of threat in society, as in general we are intolerant of groups we perceive as posing a threat (Enyedi, 2004). In contrast to improving trends seen in a number of Western countries, it is alarming that in Hungary prejudice against minorities has rather intensified in the past few years and norms that may domesticate and dampen openly professed prejudice have had no effect.

The DEREX index unambiguously demonstrated this trend as well, especially in the 2002–2009 period—in a period where left-wing governments were leading the country. Homophobia and/or prejudice against immigrants indicated by the DEREX index characterized only 37 percent of the public in 2002, although by 2005 and 2007 that ratio increased to 46 percent and 55 percent, respectively. While in 2009 the subindex value showed a slight decline (52%), Hungary still had the third most prejudiced public in Europe after Turkey and Latvia. With respect to prejudice against homosexuals, the number of those wishing to encroach on the civil rights of homosexuals has not significantly increased in this period. The percentage of respondents holding discriminative and homophobic ideas (those who completely disagree with the statement "gay men and lesbians should be allowed to live their lives as they wish") account for less than one-third of all prejudiced persons (15%). However, this is considered rather high by international standards, a figure exceeded in the 2009 survey in only a few countries (e.g., Ukraine, Bulgaria, and Russia). And this is an extremely discriminatory opinion against the gay people that points toward the criminalization of homosexuality.

Anti-immigration attitudes "spiced" with welfare chauvinism are much more attractive in Hungary than homophobia (i.e., generally more widespread in orthodox countries). The ratio of respondents who would deny nonethnic Hungarians from other countries to immigrate is 33 percent, and their number is exceeded only by those saying that residents of poor countries outside Europe should be banned from settling in Hungary (41%). These indicators represent the two highest values in the 2009 survey. The data also show that Hungarian xenophobia is motivated strongly by economic considerations (e.g., fear of job loss and "subsidy-envy"). While 9 percent of the Hungarian population believes that immigrants have an adverse effect on Hungarian culture, twice as many—22 percent—maintain that immigrants have a devastating effect on the economy. At the same time, the high rate of xenophobia is reinforced by the fear of the unknown. It is important to note that the rate of immigrants in Hungary is but a fraction of that in Western countries with a more tolerant population: less than 2 percent, according to the statistics of the Central Statistical Office in Hungary. What is important is that in Hungary, xenophobic attitudes were already strong in the society before the refugee crisis, in a period where even the danger of immigration did not exist. This is what we call *platonic xenophobia*: anti-immigration sentiments without immigrants.

Right-wing value orientation rather stagnated in Hungary. In politics, the former equilibrium toppled, but it was not followed by the shift of the values and attitudes. While following regime change the right and the left represented relatively equal forces in the country, that equilibrium toppled in 2006; by 2010 (when Fidesz received a two-thirds majority and right-wing forces, Fidesz and Jobbik altogether, received almost 70 percent of the votes) the political system had undergone significant transformation: centralization and demolition of checks and balances. The resulting shift to the right may be explained primarily with the growing public rejection of left-wing liberal governments, pushing an increasing number of voters to the other end of the political spectrum. With all that, Hungarian public opinion and values did not fundamentally change or make a sharp turn in the direction of a conservative right-wing ideology. Between 2002 and 2009, the rate of voters characterized by right-wing attitude and value orientation has essentially remained unchanged, fluctuating between 27 percent and 29 percent (representing but a negligible change), which is not considered high by any means compared to other European countries. The rate of respondents positioning themselves at the right end of a left-right scale (identifying with the two extreme-right values on an eleven-grade scale) stands at 10 percent, which represents a slight increase since 2002 (at that time the rate stood at 6%). Traditionalism (comprising religious faith, the following of religious customs and traditions) characterizes no more than 7 percent of the respondents. This is considered to be a low-to-median level, and it has not shown any increase in the past few years.

Furthermore, in Hungary, 17 percent of the respondents can be described as highly law abiding and supporting law-and-order policies, a relatively high ratio by international standards, although this indicator showed a slight decline in the period under review. (This component reached its peak in 2005, at 21 percent.) Within this set of values associated with authoritarianism (yearning for a strong leader and security, rigid adherence to rules and norms), demand for a strong state and a high level of security remains rather high. This is important, as opinions questioning democracy, referred to earlier, may easily morph into demand for authoritarian solutions.

Authoritarianism has an interestingly ambivalent nature: demand for authoritarian figures may be reinforced by the fact that today's Hungarian society is bereft of figureheads and authorities. Since the collapse of communism, we can rather observe an "authority vacuum," which creates a fertile ground for the emergence of authoritarian populist leaders (Krekó, 2012). The regime change abolished all vestiges of state socialism's power structures and led to the general collapse of trust in the sources of authority (Hunyady, 1996), and neither new institutions nor new players have managed to earn genuine respect or set standards for the general public. In Hungary, religion has no effective role in communicating values or authority. The steep decline in the assessment of political actors enjoying considerable respect after the regime change (e.g., the president, as indicated by the researches of Medián Institute) and a general loss of confidence in institutions in the past few years point to the waning authority of political figures (to some degree independent of the individuals personifying power). The decline of trust in institution, therefore, adds to the potential of authoritarian politics—aiming to reestablish law, order, and respect in a perceived decline and chaos.

The steepest rise in *antiestablishment attitudes* was seen in the period under review, compared to preceding years. Between 2002 and 2009, the rate of respondents critical of the political system increased from 12 percent to 46 percent. We analyzed lack of confidence in official institutions in four categories: distrust of the political elite, dissatisfaction with the political system, dissatisfaction with the legal system and law enforcement agencies, and loss of confidence in international institutions.

The index value of "distrust of the political elite" component is extremely high: based on 2009 data, the percentage of those distrustful of the parliament and politicians is 34 percent (in 2000, the same rate stood at 7%). As a general rule, confidence in the political elite and that in the supreme representative body go hand in hand, and through the directly elected representative body, the parliament, waning confidence in politicians seeps through the entire system.

While all institutions have been affected by the erosion of trust, distrust in the government and distrust in democracy have been the most pronounced in the seven years under review. In early 2009 (toward the end of the Gyurcsány administration and at the time of the change in government), the percentage of those extremely critical of the government stood at 53 percent, while those expressing strong criticism of democracy came to 29 percent (in 2009, higher values were measured only in Bulgaria, and values measured in all other countries fell far short of these figures). The percentage of respondents simultaneously dissatisfied with the government in office and democracy in general is 26 percent, which also indicates a sharp increase, especially if one considers that in 2002 the same value stood at only 4 percent. However, it is important to note that the criticism of institutions doesn't necessarily come with an equally strong rejection of the system. The large majority of respondents dissatisfied with democracy do not expect the resolution of problems by "system-toppling" riots supported by the most militant fringe of the far right. Distrust is not equal to antiestablishment attitude but is a precondition for that.

Regarding the dissatisfaction with the legal system and law enforcement agencies, in 2009 the percentage of respondents who are simultaneously strongly distrustful of the legal system and the police charged with enforcing the law stood at 13 percent, while 22 percent were extremely distrustful of the courts and 17 percent were of the police alone. These numbers show an increase compared with the 2002 figures. While in comparison with other components these may appear to be low figures, in the European context they are considered rather high, with higher values seen only in Russia and Bulgaria. Aside from the research findings, distrust of the legal system and the police is clearly demonstrated by the reappearance of the Hungarian Guard after its 2007 dissolution, and the explosive increase in the membership of its splinter organizations. Among other factors, due to a widespread disappointment in law enforcement, part of the population has turned to nonstate organizations expecting them to perform public duties.

Finally, when assessing the "loss of confidence in international institutions" component, it is important to mention that in the past few

years confidence has declined not only in the institutions of the constitutional state but also in democratic institutions. In 2009, 18 percent
of the respondents were highly distrustful of the EP, 15 percent were
distrustful of the UN (in 2002 this was only 5%), and 12 percent were
suspicious of both institutions. While the reasons behind a loss of confidence in the EU may be investigated separately, it is striking that the
population's assessment of the EU and its organizations since the accession has essentially moved in tandem with that of the government;
that is, the EU has shared in the loss of confidence involving the government and democratic institutions in general. The undifferentiated
character of Hungarian public sentiment also shows that essentially
the national attitude that "everything is cursed" spreads to outside organizations, such as the EU and the UN. As least, it would be difficult
to make a link between the actions of the UN and the fact that between
2002 and 2009 the number of respondents highly distrustful of the organization tripled from 5 percent to 15 percent.

Finally, in the period under review, the value of "fear, distrust,
and pessimism" subindex also increased from 19 percent to 27 percent. This is fundamentally explained by a rising level of anxiety about
the economy. In 2009, 49 percent of the respondents believed that the
country's economic health was extremely fragile (10 percent in 2002),
and 14 percent said that their income made it extremely hard to make
ends meet (12 percent in 2002). Characteristic of Hungarian public
thinking, popular despair over the state of the economy is more intense than in countries facing more severe economic problems and
lower standard of living (see Keller, 2009).

Typically, Hungarian pessimism is rather passive and diffident
and is unlikely to turn into active mass protest—with very few examples, such as the protest against the Internet tax in early 2015, with
more than 100,000 participants. At the same time, in the past few
years (especially following 2006) and due in part to the economic crisis, pessimism related to the assessment of one's personal circumstances and the economic/political climate increased sharply, and
morphed into a strong antigovernment-protest mood, clearly reflected
in the election results of the past two years (2006 municipal election,
2008 referendum, and the 2009 EP election). Considering the current

state of the parliamentary opposition, an increasingly institutionalized far right also managed to profit.

The period of normalization (2009–2015)

Between 2009 and 2013, the percentage of those with extremist views increased slightly in Hungary; in 2012, 12 percent of the adult population could be described as susceptible to far-right ideologies. The DEREX index values for Hungary here show the precise trend in prejudice and welfare chauvinism, antiestablishment attitudes, right-wing value orientation, fear, as well as distrust and pessimism.

While the proportion of those who discriminate against minority groups (homosexuals and immigrants) has steadily declined over the last three surveys, a large part of the population (45%) continues to harbor such sentiments. Against this improving trend there are deteriorating ones: since the consolidation of power toward the end of 2010, at the turn of 2012-2013, the percentage of those expressing antiestablishment attitudes started to rise again. By the evidence of the latest survey, every fourth respondent was extremely distrustful and dissatisfied with the political institutional system. Of all the components in the subindex, the proportion of respondents strongly dissatisfied with the performance of government increased substantially (from 13% to 24%), as well as the proportion of those extremely distrustful of the EU (from 10% to 14%).

In addition, following the 2010 election, the proportion of those expressing typically right-wing sentiments jumped to a record high in Hungary. In comparison, in two years the number dropped significantly and reached the lowest value to date. The spectacular decline may be explained by a number of simultaneous developments, connected to the reelection of a populist nationalist government: the proportion of those describing themselves as standing on the far right, devoted to traditions, and expressing a preference for law-and-order and authoritarian attitudes all declined. Also, in the last two years the proportion of those either distrustful of others or strongly dissatisfied with their lives or having a dim view of the country's or their household's finances has stagnated.

As a consequence of the refugee crisis and the Hungarian xenophobic campaign, it was mainly the prejudices and welfare chauvinism subindex of DEREX that was showing a rise. Exclusionary attitudes rose from 45 percent to 54 percent in Hungary. This was not an exclusive case though: in 10 countries out of the twenty in the sample, the share of those who would not allow a single immigrant to settle down rose significantly. In the other two Visegrad countries, we can see some rise as well: from thirty-two to thirty-nine in the Czech Republic and from eighteen to twenty-five in Poland.

International comparison

In Western European societies, the general level of DEREX is lower. It is true for practically all subindices, but the difference is lower in the case of ethnic prejudices. We can observe high level of prejudice and welfare chauvinism in many Western European countries, including France, the UK, and even Portugal. Antiestablishment attitudes are on the rise, especially because of the rising Euroskepticism. With all that, anti-immigration continues to be a popular line with the West European far right, and while it may be accompanied by other topics the discourse of these parties rarely turns against the established order that guarantees the stability of these systems.

On the other hand, in Eastern Europe prejudice and anti-Roma sentiment are closely tied to an antiestablishment attitude, distrust, and malaise. All these have been clearly manifested on the supply side in the "Guard" phenomenon to be discussed later, where parties creating alternative paramilitary organizations challenging the state's monopoly on violence and, in fact, for all practical purposes promise the creation of alternative state structures. With the exception of Italy, in Western Europe we have seen few examples for this; the stability of the system is barely threatened by the far right, while East European democracies appear to be much more fragile right now. The refugee crisis, though, led to the emergence of the vigilante groups all over Europe.

If we take a look at all the countries that have been surveyed in the last rounds,[4] we can come to the following key conclusions. First, the proportion of those with extremist views is the highest in the Balkan countries, in Albania (32%) and Kosovo (30%). The first six places are occupied exclusively by countries located to the east and southeast of Hungary. We found above 20 percent DEREX values in Cyprus (28%), Ukraine (23%), and Bulgaria (22%). With respect to extremist attitudes, Hungary has the tenth highest value (12%). The ratio of those with extremist views is slightly higher in Israel (13%), Italy (13%), and Slovakia (13%). In Portugal, the DEREX index value essentially matches that in Hungary, 12 percent. This group was followed far behind by the Czech Republic and Poland with a DEREX index of 8 percent in each. Northern countries (Norway, Finland, Sweden, Iceland, and Denmark) and Switzerland are at the end of the scale with 1 percent attitude extremism.

In five countries, "prejudice and welfare chauvinism" exceeds 50 percent; in other words, at least every other respondent holds extremist views about homosexuals, lesbians, and/or immigrants. Unsurprisingly, in Kosovo and Cyprus—countries suffering from severe ethnic tensions—we measured 65 percent for this subindex. In the samples taken in Israel, Russia, and Albania as well, we measured high values (55–56%), while in Ukraine the first subindex has a value of 49 percent. Hungary stands in the seventh place, and among twenty-one EU member states it is second after Cyprus. In other words, looking at the EU as a whole, the Hungarian value of 45 percent is considered rather high. Sweden, Iceland, and Norway are the least prejudiced (4 percent, 7 percent, and 8 percent, respectively). The prevalence of anti-immigrant attitude is well illustrated by the fact that only in these three countries we measured values below 10 percent for the "prejudice and welfare chauvinism" subindex.

---

[4]   Twenty-nine countries participated in the ESS conducted in 2012–2013. These countries were Albania (AL), Belgium (BE), Bulgaria (BG), Cyprus (CY), Czech Republic (CZ), Denmark (DK), the United Kingdom (UK), Estonia (EE), Finland (FI), France (FR), Holland (NL), Ireland (IE), Iceland (IS), Israel (IL), Kosovo (XK), Poland (PL), Lithuania (LT), Hungary (HU), Germany (DE), Norway (NO), Italy (IT), Russia (RU), Portugal (PT), Slovakia (SK), Slovenia (SI), Spain (ES), Sweden (SE), Switzerland (CH), and Ukraine (UA).

Based on the six waves of the ESS to date, it can be concluded that of all subindices "antiestablishment attitudes" shows the largest variation within each country. In other words, the current political situation, and in some cases the proximity of the upcoming elections to the date of the survey, may have effected indicators measuring confidence in the political institutional system identified in the subindex. Consequently, it is not surprising that we measured the strongest antiestablishment attitude in Ukraine, where 60 percent of the respondents met the criteria set for the second subindex. We measured high index values in Bulgaria (51%), Albania (48%), and Portugal (41%) as well. Similarly, in countries swept up by the second wave of the economic crisis (Portugal, Cyprus, Slovenia, Italy, and Spain), we typically measured high values. With a 25 percent subindex value, Hungary is in the middle of the field. The proportion of those expressing extreme antiestablishment attitudes is the lowest in Northern countries; the value is 3 percent in Norway, Denmark, and Finland.

Based on "right-wing value orientation," Kosovo (60%), Cyprus (46%), and Albania (43%) occupy the first three places. In Hungary, every fifth respondent (21%) met the criteria established for the third subindex, and similar to the previous subindex, the country is thus on the fifteenth place. It is interesting to note that countries with the lowest value orientation are geographically remote: the lowest sub-index value was measured in Iceland (9%), Germany (11%), Portugal (11%), Holland (12%), and Estonia (13%).

The "fear, distrust, and pessimism" subindex was high in Bulgaria (47%), Albania (44%), Ukraine (31%), Cyprus (30%), and Kosovo (30%). In Hungary, close to one-fifth of the respondents (19%) gave extremist responses regarding indicators included in this category. The country ranked ninth; consequently, in addition to high level of prejudice, Hungary is in the upper third of the European community made up of twenty-nine countries in terms of fear and distrust. In West European countries, less affected by the economic crisis, fear, distrust, and pessimism were lower, and the proportion of respondents meeting this criteria was below 10 percent (see Table 3).

Table 3: DEREX and subindex values in the sixth ESS wave (2012) / the values for Hungary are indicated in grey

Ranking	1. Subindex: Prejudice and welfare chauvinism (%)	2. Subindex: Anti-establishment attitudes (%)	3. Subindex: Right-wing value orientation (%)	4. Subindex: Fear, distrust, and pessimism (%)	DEREX (%)
1	XK (65)	UA (60)	XK (60)	BG (47)	AL (32)
2	CY (65)	BG (51)	CY (46)	AL (44)	XK (30)
3	IL (56)	AL (48)	AL (43)	UA (31)	CY (28)
4	RU (55)	PT (41)	IL (38)	CY (30)	UA (23)
5	AL (55)	XK (38)	IT (36)	XK (30)	BG (22)
6	UA (49)	CY (35)	PL (36)	RU (22)	RU (16)
7	HU (45)	RU (35)	SK (34)	SK (20)	SK (13)
8	PT (40)	SI (34)	BG (33)	IT (20)	IT (13)
9	LT (39)	IT (33)	SI (27)	HU (19)	IL (13)
10	EE (39)	ES (33)	UA (24)	PT (18)	HU (12)
11	SK (39)	SK (31)	ES (24)	PL (15)	PT (12)
12	CZ (32)	CZ (31)	RU (23)	FR (15)	CZ (8)

Ranking	1. Subindex: Prejudice and welfare chauvinism (%)	2. Subindex: Anti-establishment attitudes (%)	3. Subindex: Right-wing value orientation (%)	4. Subindex: Fear, distrust, and pessimism (%)	DEREX (%)
13	BG (31)	PL (29)	CZ (22)	CZ (14)	PL (8)
14	UK (27)	IL (25)	IE (22)	IE (14)	FR (7)
15	FR (26)	HU (25)	HU (21)	ES (14)	SI (7)
16	SI (25)	LT (25)	FR (20)	EE (13)	IE (7)
17	IE (23)	IE (21)	UK (16)	SI (11)	ES (6)
18	IT (22)	EE (18)	DK (16)	LT (11)	EE (5)
19	BE (20)	FR (17)	FI (15)	IL (11)	LT (5)
20	PL (18)	UK (14)	SE (15)	UK (9)	UK (4)
21	ES (18)	IS (12)	LT (14)	DE (8)	BE (3)
22	FI (16)	BE (9)	NO (14)	BE (7)	DE (2)
23	NL (15)	DE (9)	CH (14)	IS (5)	NL (2)
24	DK (13)	NL (6)	BE (13)	SE (4)	CH (1)
25	CH (11)	SE (5)	EE (13)	CH (4)	DK (1)
26	DE (11)	CH (4)	NL (12)	NL (4)	IS (1)

Ranking	1. Subindex: Prejudice and welfare chauvinism (%)	2. Subindex: Anti-establishment attitudes (%)	3. Subindex: Right-wing value orientation (%)	4. Subindex: Fear, distrust, and pessimism (%)	DEREX (%)
27	NO (8)	FI (3)	PT (11)	DK (3)	SE (1)
28	IS (7)	DK (3)	DE (11)	NO (3)	FI (1)
29	SE (4)	NO (3)	IS (9)	FI (2)	NO (1)

Note: The values for Hungary are indicated in grey. XK, UA, BG, AL, CY, IL, RU, HU, PT, LT, EE, SK, CZ, UK, FR, SI, IE, IT, BE, PL, ES, FI, NL, DK, CH, DE, NO, IS, SE.

In sum, the DEREX index draws our attention to the relevance of two coordinates regarding differences between countries: East-West divide and North-South divide. Moving east, DEREX value tends to increase. In terms of the North-South divide, we found higher values in Mediterranean countries among the fifteen EU countries. All these suggest that psychological demand for extremist right-wing ideology is the highest where nondemocratic regimes (totalitarian, dictatorial, and/or authoritarian) played a major role in shaping the political landscape in the second half of the twentieth century, or in other words where authoritarianism as a "political practice" permeated society.

Special features of Hungary

In the international context, the dramatic fluctuation of data pertaining to Hungary is conspicuous, for the most part illustrated by rapid shifts in antiestablishment attitudes. Based on our analysis, citizens' attitudes to democratic institutions may change fundamentally in just a few years, even up or down. Accordingly, we identify the extraordinary dynamism of attitudes toward political institutions as one of the causes of volatility and impulsiveness frequently observed in demand for the far right. Aside from Hungary, this is also characteristic of the most unstable countries, such as Ukraine. But there can be a national characteristic in this hectic change: excessive and illusory expectations (almost like waiting for a messiah) and unfounded optimism and boosterism (such as before the 2010 elections) tend to turn into a sudden loss of illusion and disappointment, especially when the expectations are not met. Classical characterizations of Hungarians describe it as an inherent Hungarian psychological feature: the "hay fire spirit" of Hungarians (for an overview, see Hunyady, 2000).

Between 2002 and 2009 starting from a relatively low level, the "antiestablishment" value increased steadily in Hungary. The fourth wave of the survey was conducted between February 28 and April 20, 2009. It is worth noting that the resignation of the then prime minister Ferenc Gyurcsány also took place around that time. The extremely dark public mood due to the political and economic crises is mirrored in the DEREX values as well: the number of those opposing the establishment was extremely high (46%) at the time. Since the other three subindices (prejudice, right-wing value orientation, and pessimism) changed less dynamically, the escalation of antiestablishment attitudes raised the total DEREX value to an extremely high level (21%) both in the national and the international contexts. In the ranking of thirty-four countries reviewed, Hungary came in fifth, and it was only preceded by even more unstable countries at the time, such as Bulgaria, Latvia, Turkey, and Ukraine.

The fifth wave of the survey was conducted between October 10 and December 10, 2010, just after Fidesz's landslide victory in the parliamentary and municipal elections. Voter confidence in the new administration and optimism was at its peak then, and this was reflected in the 50 percent drop in the number of respondents opposing the establishment (Figure 3).

**Figure 3:   Public mood and ESSs in Hungary
(source: Medián)**

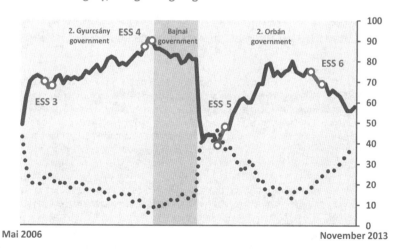

However, by the time of the sixth wave of the survey, conducted between November 10, 2012, and February 17, 2013, the public mood soured again. Based on Medián's figures, at that time 70 percent of the adult population believed that things were heading in the wrong direction in Hungary. This, in turn, was also reflected in data on insti-tutional confidence; that is, the "antiestablishment" subindex value in-creased again. Based on the most recent DEREX data, 25 percent of the respondents were extremely distrustful of political institutions in Hungary. This surpasses the value measured two years earlier and comes close to the 33 percent seen at the end of 2006, in the third wave of ESS.

In other words, DEREX clearly shows the wide fluctuation of confidence in Hungary's political institutions.[5] This volatility, which in most cases turns into extreme distrust, is a source of danger in itself because it can benefit political forces exploiting sudden shifts in public mood. The last two values of "antiestablishment" subindex clearly demonstrate that the government would have had an excellent oppor-tunity to moderate Hungarian public attitudes, consolidate its power, and achieve genuine social peace; however, it squandered this oppor-tunity. This also means that the current political system enjoys but an illusory stability based on its two-thirds parliamentary majority and its relative political dominance thanks to the weakness of the opposition. At the same time, there is no real moderation in the deeper layers of society, and the current level of extreme antiestablishment sentiment

---

[5]   Tarki's *Values 2013* study, published in the fall of 2013 (Tárki, 2013) presenting the findings of the 2013 waves survey, *The social and cultural preconditions of economic* growth, reports similar developments. In the study, researchers examined the development of public opinion in four areas: confidence, norm conformance, assessment of the role of the state, and democracy. In the analysis, they made primarily temporal comparisons, comparing conditions in 2013 to those seen in 2009. On average, in 2013 respondents considered democracy less relevant than in 2009 and, simultaneously, more people described the country as democratic than before. Presumably, this may be attributed to the fact that respondents loyal to the government in office (describing themselves as right wing in 2013) considered the style of governance before 2010 as undemocratic and held the opposite view about the government taking power after 2010. In contrast, those defining themselves as left wing considered the right-wing government as antidemocratic, as opposed to the policies of the government prior to 2010. Tarki's researchers also found that confidence in institutions is highly subject to political identity, i.e., institutional confidence becomes highly relative depending on which side of the political divide is in power. In respect to norms, a situation may develop, where, in addition to commonly accepted values (views about rights and wrongs), people also start to consider who complies and who violates those norms (norms become instrumentalized) (Tárki, 2013).

is considered exceedingly high by international standards, offering scant opportunities for any political system to settle in for the long haul.

The assessment of the DEREX

Of course, DEREX has its limitations. Even with a detailed knowledge of social demand, an analysis of the supply side is still critical for a comprehensive understanding. DEREX measures social demand for far-right ideas, beliefs, and political solutions. Accordingly, it is unable to provide a general explanation for the far right's political role or its position in the political hierarchy of far-right parties and organizations. For social demand is a necessary but far-from-sufficient condition for the consolidation of the far right (Mudde, 2007; Karácsony and Róna, 2011). It is necessary because in a society where the electorate is not susceptible to some aspects of far-right ideology (system criticism, elite criticism, prejudice, ultranationalism, etc.), far-right parties have little chance to command substantial social support. At the same time, it is not sufficient because social demand for right-wing ideas doesn't automatically create far-right political supply. The "volunteerism" of parties also plays a role in shaping demand: while parties' scope for action is limited by social fault lines, to some degree political actors have the opportunity to reshape these fault lines, to widen or to narrow them. In other words, parties do not simply serve the needs of the electorate in all cases but, with some limitations, are able to realign the social and attitudinal foundations of the party system (Enyedi, 2005).

Consequently, while in most cases the correlation is evident, in countries with a high DEREX value we don't necessarily find far-right parties or organizations; meanwhile, such political forces may have a presence even in countries with a low index value. Aside from social demand, this means that far-right political supply is determined by a number of additional factors, such as political traditions, remembrance politics, institutional guarantees, effectiveness of political strategies deployed against the far right, governmental strategies, the structure of the political arena, as well as organizational strength and political effectiveness of the far right itself.

Looking at the relationship between supply and demand, it is also evident that higher demand for right-wing extremism may not simply manifest itself in the emergence of a stronger far-right party, but may also impact other levels of the political and institutional systems. For instance, a low level of public trust may erode the democratic system, undermining its legitimacy and working. Strong anti-established attitudes and demand for economic isolation may compromise the investment climate and encourage those in power to pursue excessively protectionist, paternalistic, and discriminative economic policy. Xenophobia may push all political actors into increasingly extreme positions and incite ethnic conflicts within the society and between nations.

The second limitation is that the date of data collection and the lack of data from some countries strongly determine the overall picture. The measurement of social demand for the far right must rest on the simultaneous analysis of relatively slowly changing attitudes in society (e.g., right-wing orientation to religion and tradition) and other attitudes showing wild swings (e.g., trust in institutions). DEREX meets these criteria, as it is appropriately sensitive to signal changes and, accordingly, the findings must be strictly interpreted with the date of the survey in mind. Therefore, the limitation of the index is that surveys are conducted only biannually (in some countries with less frequency), and data are reported many months later. Thus, DEREX cannot present shifting attitudes toward the far right promptly and in all details, and it does not offer a full picture of all the trends in each country. Furthermore, the index is very hectic, therefore, sensitive to the exact date of the polling.

The third limitation is that the data can only be interpreted with a consideration of the political context. As in all other cases involving the analysis of an opinion-poll survey, for DEREX data it is also indispensable to interpret the trends and corresponding data from various countries in the proper political and social context. Since DEREX is extremely sensitive to the effects of such unique political events as acts of terror, change in government, corruption scandals, and alike, the interpretation of data also requires familiarity with the political climate prevailing at the time of the survey. However, a change should not lead one to automatically assume a shift in the deep layers of so-cial thinking and value system. When comparing specific countries, social and political differences play an equally important role. ESS questions related to xenophobia are phrased in general terms (e.g., "those arriving from other countries to make a living here") without specifying any ethnic group. The exact country of origin of immigrants that the respondent may have in mind or the specific ethnic group they may be the most averse to are questions that must be answered in other studies, keeping the political realities of the given country in mind.

The advantage of DEREX—confirmed by local and international professional feedback as well—is that it helps the complex yet easy-to-understand study of the social and socio psychological background of the far right. It proved to be reliable in terms of psychometric meas-urements (see Appendix for details), and also, it passed the validity tests, as voters of far-right parties regularly show higher DEREX val-ues than voters of the mainstream parties (Political Capital, 2012).

The index provides a reliable indication of the differences be-tween specific countries and regions in Europe with respect to demand for the far right, and appears to provide empirical evidence for theories (involving the nature of a new, "multigenerational" radical right) such as Cas Mudde's theory on the intolerance of the tolerant. It says that the resurgence of the radical right in Northern European countries, considered the bastions of tolerance (e.g., Holland, Sweden, and Den-mark) fundamentally, may be explained not by the spread of general intolerance but the fact that many voters defining themselves as toler-ant opt for radical right-wing parties that oppose Muslim immigrants seen as fundamentally intolerant (Mudde, 2010). In line with the hy-pothesis of the theory, overall prejudice and opposition to immigration is the lowest in these countries (for instance, in Sweden only 3.7%, falling short of the 5.7% showing of the Swedish Democrats in the 2010 election).

DEREX helps to look at changing support for the far right from various angles, and it shows that the rise or decline of the far right may be determined by more complex sociopsychological and political fac-tors. Importantly, it evaluates "demand" at the level of voter attitudes, values, and prejudices; and not at the level of more distant economic figures. Therefore, it considers variables that may have a direct impact on voters' political action (voting, participation at demonstrations or other political action, likelihood of joining a party or organization). The same cannot be said about sociological and economic indicators routinely taken into account by demand-oriented research. For instance, one cannot automatically presume that declining economic growth or unemployment has a direct effect on voters' political choices. This may be the case only if such developments are accompanied by broad-based dissatisfaction, which in turn affects the perception of the political force in power. Finally, the index also has the advantage of being sufficiently sensitive to hectic social changes, a feature with great significance in the case of Hungary.

Who are Jobbik's voters?

After the analysis of the general social demand toward the policies and rhetoric of the Hungarian far right, we aim to give a concise picture on the voters of Jobbik based on the available data, with a bit of outlook to the voters of Fidesz. The two main questions that we aim to respond here are as follows: How big is the political support for the far right in Hungary? Who are Jobbik's core voters?

Jobbik shares the features of successful populist parties and movements in the sense that their electoral breakthrough came quick and as a surprise. In 2007, the Hungarian far right was considered to be the weakest in Europe (Mudde, 2007). Considering this, it is surprising that Jobbik managed to achieve a breakthrough in 2009 and to keep growing ever since, which made it the strongest far-right party of the region.

Becoming a party in 2003, Jobbik ran in the parliament elections for the first time in 2006 as a partner of the Hungarian Justice and Life Party (MIÉP)—an anti-Semitic party with a dominantly urban, conservative intellectual electorate (see, for example, Tóka, 1998). The joint list created under the name of "MIÉP—Jobbik, the Third Way" received 119,007 (2.20%) votes. Subsequently, Jobbik went its own way, and in the 2009 EP election the party already received 427,773 (14.77%) votes, while in the 2010 parliamentary election Jobbik got 855,436 (16.67%) votes. In the 2014 parliamentary election and the EP election held the same year, the number of ballots cast for the party totaled 1,020,476 (20.22%) and 339,501 (14.68%), respectively. Election data show the extraordinary resurgence of the Hungarian far right, by a rate not seen since 1939. Also, Jobbik's performance is atypical in the Central Eastern European far right (for an overview, see, for example, Minkenberg, 2015); the only party coming close to the result of Jobbik in post-transition elections was the Greater Romania Party with 19.5 percent of the votes in 2000. Jobbik's dynamic growth played a key role in the transformation of the Hungarian political scene over the past two years. The party's policies leading to the current situation will be discussed in the second half of the book, while this chapter will discuss the party's achievements at the polls and the major characteristics of its voter base.

Jobbik's performance at the polls: Ups and downs

In the most recent parliamentary election, held on April 6, 2014, support for Jobbik reached an all-time high: with over one million votes received, it seemed to consolidate its place as the third largest political force in Hungary. Furthermore, it achieved the best ever results for a far-right party in post-transitional Hungarian electoral history. With more than 20 percent of the votes and more than one million voters (in a country of eight million voters overall—see Table 4), it could gain twenty-three seats in the 199-seat parliament.

Table 4:   Election results on party lists, 2014

Party	Number of votes obtained[6]	Percentage
Fidesz-KDNP	2,264,780	44.87
Jont opposition list (MSZP-Együtt-DK-PM-MLP)	1,290,806	25.57
Jobbik	1,020,476	20.22
LMP	269,414	5.34
Other	201,887	4.00
Total	5,047,363	100.00

Note: KDNP: *Kereszténydemokrata Néppárt*; MSZP-Együtt-DK-PM-MLP: the joint opposition list, LMP: *Lehet más a politika*;

Looking on the data for more details provided even better news for Jobbik. On the party list Jobbik finished first in 130 municipalities, while the left managed the same only in seventy-four settlements. Jobbik also came in second in 2,165 settlements behind the governing Fidesz-KDNP (*Kereszténydemokrata Néppárt*) coalition, while the left achieved the same result only in 808 settlements. With respect to in-dividual constituencies, Jobbik came in ahead of the left in forty-one electoral districts and in an additional nineteen districts it trailed the left by only a couple thousand votes. The far-right party performed best primarily in rural areas and small towns, while in major cities and in Budapest it definitely performed poorly (compared to the party's overall performance nationwide).

The public was shocked to see that the party exceeded 20 per-cent—previously seen by many, as a clear sign of wishful thinking, as the "ceiling" for its growth (see Figure 4). Surprisingly, for many, Jobbik leaders seemed depressed when commenting the electoral results on the election night. The reason for this was the expectation set too high: despite the fact that Jobbik achieved its best results so far, the leaders

---

[6]   In 2014, for the first time, ethnic Hungarian voters with Hungarian citizenship but without a permanent residency were allowed to vote. Without their votes (given that Jobbik voters were strongly underrepresented among them), considering only the voters with permanent residence in Hungary, Jobbik would have gained 21% of the votes.

of the party expressed even better results: second place on the election, hampering a second two-thirds for Fidesz, and many individual constituencies. "We have to acknowledge that we have not achieved the goal we set in the election campaign," announced Gábor Vona on the election night.

Figure 4:   Votes cast on Jobbik's party lists, 2006–2014

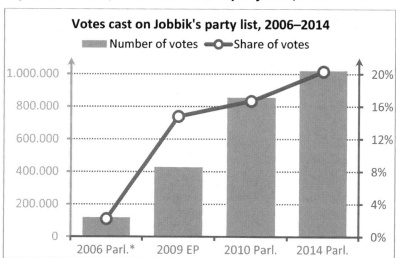

While the differences in support for Jobbik are apparent based on settlement type, with respect to territorial distribution, the ballots cast for the party became more balanced. Even in the past, Jobbik was incorrectly described as a "regional party" of Eastern Hungary. However, the territorial distribution of ballots cast in 2014 shows a considerably more balanced picture. Moreover, the party has made clear gains in the industrialized and more developed Western region of Hungary. In other words, Jobbik's East-West polarization has clearly diminished between 2010 and 2014. In nine counties in the east, the party's average list votes increased from 21.2 percent to 25.4 percent in those four years, while during the same period in the nine western counties they increased from 14.3 percent to 20.8 percent. In other words, the gap narrowed from 6.9 percent to 4.6 percent between 2010 and 2014.[7] Between 2009 and 2014, the support for Jobbik increased above the average in seven out of nine West Hungarian counties. Successes in the west Hungary can be attributed to a conscious strategy, aiming to level the regional support for the party, and also for the party's "softer" communication strategy and shifting toward the center, which makes it more attractive for many voters (see Figure 5).

Figure 5:   Territorial dynamics of Jobbik's electoral success

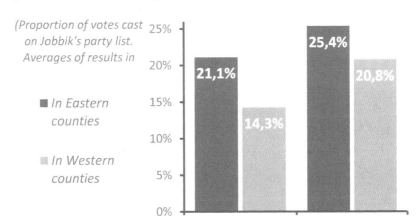

(Proportion of votes cast on Jobbik's party list. Averages of results in

■ _In Eastern counties_

▨ _In Western counties_

With such momentum, one could expect that Jobbik would be able to gain around a quarter of the votes in the EP elections less than two months later. But then, in the EP elections in June 2014, this momentum was broken. For the first time in the far-right party's history, Jobbik's continuous rise in support ended. This result broke the continuous rise of support that we have witnessed since 2006. Jobbik had improved its results on party lists election by election (2006 parliamentary: 2%; 2009 European Parliament: 15%; 2010 parliamentary: 17%; 2014 parliamentary: 21%; 2014 European Parliament: 15%).

This discrepancy perfectly revealed the two most important factors that can determine Jobbik's fate in the future: the shift toward a

---

[7]   These figures do not include data from Pest County, including the capital.

more moderate position, on the one hand, and allegations over the Russian influence in the party on the other.

Jobbik's enthusiasm toward Putin's Russia has been quite obvious for a long time, as Jobbik's politicians did not hide their admiration at all, and there have been regular meetings between Jobbik's politicians and high-level Russian stakeholders. But allegations stepped up to another level one week before the EP elections. The governmental media published an article with a good sense of political rhythm, outlining that the Hungarian prosecutor's office asked the EP to strip Jobbik MEP (member of EP) Béla Kovács's parliamentary immunity, to investigate charges of espionage for Russia. While the public could have not seen enough evidence to decide the validity of such allegations, the well-choreographed political actions against Béla Kovács—including a hearing in the parliamentary committee of national security, followed by huge media attention—definitely had some impact on the party's image. Even if some Jobbik's voters could easily sweep aside the charges and claim them false, saying that the media, the political parties, and the American-Israeli interests have organized a plot against the party, the allegations are harmful as they question the core element of the party's ideology: the commitment to national interests. Jobbik's two-word political self-definition is "national radical"—and the espionage charges questioned the "national" component of this definition, even if it did not prove that harmful on the long run (see more details on the foreign policy of Jobbik in a later chapter).

Furthermore, in the last year, the other component—"radicalism"—was diluted deliberately by the party leaders. As Hungarian voters have become less angry since 2010, this moderate shift helped Jobbik greatly at the 2014 April parliamentary elections (where the turnout was 62%) to target a broader audience—and especially undecided voters. On the other hand, it seems that the "softening" clearly did not help the party to mobilize its core supporters in the EP elections, where the turnout was extremely low: only 29 percent.

Jobbik tried to sell the deteriorating results as a victory—referring to the fact that for the first time in history, they came second place after the governing party Fidesz, performing better than the opposition Hungarian Socialist Party (MSZP). They of course did not explain that the reason was not that they improved their support, but that the left-wing opposition parties who had a joint list in April now ran on three separate lists—that altogether received almost twice as many votes as Jobbik (see Table 5).

In the campaign, Jobbik shifted toward being a soft Euroskeptic party, from a hard Euroskeptic one whose vice president burned an EU flag at a rally only two years ago. Jobbik did everything to avoid being successfully stigmatized as "extreme" in public debates before the EP election. As a consequence, Jobbik was the least successful in bringing the voters who supported them in April to the ballot boxes. Jobbik could bring only one-third of its voters, while the governmental party Fidesz brought 56 percent, and the left-wing opposition 50 percent. What's more, looking at the regional distribution of the votes, it seems that Jobbik failed most notably to mobilize its voters in its core constituencies in Eastern Hungary (see Table 6).

Table 5:   European parliamentary election results in Hungary (2009/2014)

2009				2014	
1,632,309	56.36%	Fidesz-KDNP		1,191,163	51.49%
427,773	14.77%	Jobbik		339,501	14.68%
503,140	17.37%	MSZP		252,494	10.92%
75,522	2.61%	LMP		115,957	5.01%
153,660	5.31%	MDF	DK	225,762	9.76%
62,527	2.16%	SZDSZ	Együtt-PM	167,012	7.22%
41,248	1.42%	Other		21,370	0.92%
2,896,179		Total		2,313,259	

Note: KDNP, Kereszténydemokrata Néppárt; LMP, Lehet más a politika; MDF, Magyar Demokrata Fórum; DK, Demokratikus Koalíció; SZDSZ, Szabad Demokraták Szövetsége.

Table 6:   Mobilization rate: national elections (April 6, 2014), versus EU parliamentary election (without votes cast in foreign missions), May 25, 2014

Hungarian Parliament			European Parliament				Rate of mobilization (May/April)
	Votes	%		Votes		%	
Fidesz-KDNP	2,142,142	43.55%	Fidesz-KDNP		1,191,163	51.49%	55.61%
MSZP-Együtt-DK-PM-MLP	1,289,311	26.21%	MSZP	252,494		10.92%	50.05%
			DK	225,762	645,268	9.76%	27.9%
			Együtt-PM	167,012		7.22%	
Jobbik	1,017,550	20.69%	Jobbik		339,501	14.68%	33.36%
LMP	268,840	5.47%	LMP		115,957	5.01%	43.13%
Other	201,091	4.08%	Other		21,370	0.92%	
	4,918,934				2,313,259		

Note: KDNP, Kereszténydemokrata Néppárt; LMP, Lehet más a politika; MDF, Magyar Demokrata Fórum; DK, Demokratikus Koalíció; SZDSZ, Szabad Demokraták Szövetsége.

This backslide in electoral results did not endure, though. The municipal elections in autumn 2014 brought considerable success for Jobbik. On the previous municipal elections in 2006, and also in 2010, Jobbik performed below the expectations. In 2010, Jobbik only managed to capture mayoral seats in two small villages and one mid-sized town (Tiszavasvári), and later it took over twelve municipalities in part when independent mayors joined Jobbik and in part by winning by-elections.

But they could show up considerable success in 2014. In the municipal election, Jobbik managed to hold on to the majority of its mayoral seats, and gain more: the party occupied fourteen municipalities (compared to the three municipalities in 2006), and in ten municipalities independent candidates who enjoyed the party's support, came in first (see Table 7 and Figure 6). It ended as the second largest party in county general assemblies (where voters choose the candidates via party lists[8]). László Toroczkai, a well-known figure of the Hungarian extremist scene, could keep his mayoral seat. After the closing of the polls, party president Gábor Vona positioned his party as the challenger to the governing party in 2018. The party had made

---

8   Residents of the twenty-three biggest cities with county rank are excluded from voting for the members of county assemblies.

a success to consolidate its position in major urban areas, for in the past its presence was limited primarily to small towns and villages. This time, Jobbik's mayoral candidates won seats in a number of mid-sized towns (not only in Eastern Hungary, the traditional stronghold of the party), such as Tapolca, Tiszavasvári, Ózd, and Törökszentmiklós. In addition, in ten more municipalities, among them Békéscsaba, a big city on county rank, independent candidates supported by Jobbik came in first (see Table 7). As a result of the election, more than 100,000 voters, 1 percent of the population, were residing in cities or villages with a Jobbik mayor. And as a consequence, a policy of strict law and order, discriminating welfare policies, and school segregation gained new momentum in a number of municipalities.

Despite the considerable successes, Jobbik could not achieve all of its goals. Jobbik has failed to take the mayoral seat in Miskolc in Northeastern Hungary, the "rust belt," with a large Roma population. And more importantly, Budapest remained to be the Achilles heel for Jobbik. Despite its efforts to show a more moderate face, Jobbik has failed to make any significant progress in the capital—where two million people, one-fifth of the population, live. While Jobbik had a mayoral candidate in all twenty-three districts of the capital, they got only 40,590 votes altogether—which was only enough to gain a single seat in the Budapest town assembly. This number of votes was far less than what Jobbik received in the April 2014 parliamentary election (111,129), and worse than the result on the EP election in May, when Jobbik got 51,995 votes on the party list. In Budapest, Jobbik's mayoral candidates typically received 4–12 percent, much lower than the national average. With 42,093 votes (1,700 fewer than four years ago!), the party's mayoral candidate for Budapest, Gábor Staudt, received only 7 percent and finished third, far behind its two major rivals. The party's only real success in the capital was that it managed to finish ahead of the green Politics Can Be Different (*Lehet más a politika*, LMP), which was in a stronger position in 2010. The failure of Jobbik to improve its results in Budapest shows the very important, latent dimension behind Jobbik's support: the "center-periphery" conflict—an essentially important dichotomy behind the resurgence of the populist forces all over the world.

Table 7:   Municipality election results: The municipalities of Jobbik, 2010 and 2014

Municipality	Mayor	2014 Municipal election	2014 EP election	2014 Parliament election	2010 Municipal election	2010 Parliament election
Ásotthalom	Toroczkai, László	857 (100%)	109 (18.08%)	432 (27.22%)	-	164 (9.05%)
Bánokszentgyörgy	Baumgartner, László	127 (38.72%)	45 (40.54%)	122 (41.36%)	-	78 (28.36%)
Devecser	Ferenczi, Gábor	1,051 (54.2%)	233 (29.02%)	697 (33.40%)	-	529 (24.93%)
Gasztony	Nagy, Szabolcs	124 (55.36%)	20 (16.53%)	44 (19.73%)	-	26 (10.24%)
Hencida	Szémán, László	333 (58.63%)	51 (28.02%)	154 (39.29%)	285 (59.13%)	174 (42.23%)
Kosd	Kurdi, Ferenc	639 (58.89%)	88 (14.92%)	239 (20.07%)		258 (19.92%)
Mátraballa	Dudás, Róbert	242 (53.54%)	68 (32.08%)	157 (35.84%)	-	148 (33.26%)
Monorierdő	Szente, Béla	838 (55.2%)	212 (27.50%)	574 (30.71%)	163 (11.04%)	522 (26.51%)
Ózd	Janiczak, Dávid	4,214 (38.57%)	1,372 (22.61%)	4,525 (29.62%)	1,323 (13.03%)	5,086 (33.45%)
Recsk	Nagy, Sándor	447 (31.57%)	170 (26.4%)	464 (32.84%)	-	354 (23.58%)
Tapolca	Dobó, Zoltán	1,951 (39.34%)	725 (19.27%)	2,500 (26.50%)	1,098 (22.52%)	1,836 (20.14%)
Tiszavasvári	Dr. Fülöp, Erik Sándor	2,602 (52.1%)	487 (24.29%)	1,686 (32.07%)	2,692 (53.29%)	2,357 (40.09%)
Törökszentmiklós	Markót, Imre	3,761 (47.72%)	1,140 (27.32%)	3,907 (36.12%)	-	2,933 (27.83%)
Tuzsér	Ferkovics, Tibor	1,204 (64.04%)	166 (34.95%)	519 (39.89%)	189 (11.52%)	531 (33.44%)

Figure 6: The map of the municipalities taken by Jobbik, 2014

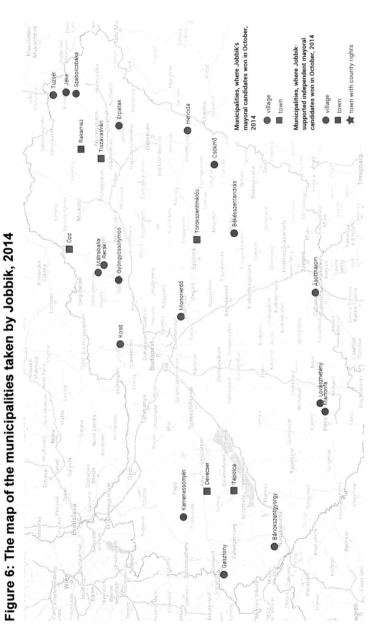

Source: Political Capital Institute; Map data © 2017 Geo-Basis-DE/BKG (© 2009), Google

And then, in a half year's time, fortune was again on Jobbik's side. On April 12, 2015, as a historic breakthrough, the far-right Jobbik candidate won a by-election in the individual constituency of Tapolca (see Figure 7).[9] The results have indicated that the electorate dissatisfied with the performance of the government turned to the political side it considers capable of defeating Fidesz. On February 22, in the Veszprém by-election, the individual candidate supported by left-wing parties, Zoltán Kész, was able to win the mandate—according to the data—with the support of former voters of Jobbik. At the same time, in Tapolca, candidate of Jobbik, Lajos Rig—with the support of some former left-wing voters. This election was the first sign of the "Ukrainization" of the Hungarian domestic politics—a sign of radicalization, in which voters and politicians on the left are increasingly felt that without the radical right, Viktor Orbán's system cannot be challenged (the analogy refers to the 2014 Euromaidan revolution and the following political transformation, in which the far-right Svoboda [*Vseukrayinske obyednannia "Svoboda"*] party, and also the extreme-right Right Sector [*Pravyi Sektor*], played a crucial role).

This victory of Jobbik, following a victory of a left-wing and an individual candidate, was a serious blow for Fidesz. The governing party's "central power field" strategy (Fidesz remains the sole governing force standing at the center of the political stage whose position cannot be challenged by weak and divided opposition forces aligned up at the two ends of the political spectrum) that worked well in 2014 has suffered a setback. So did as the myth that Fidesz can stop the rise of the far right. As the mobilization rates discussed here suggest, in the two interim elections held this year less than half of Fidesz supporters abandoned the party, but the opposition parties made remarkable successes in mobilization. Jobbik could gain a lot of new voters in Tapolca, especially from the small villages. Jobbik could expand its support for three main reasons: (a) their moderate shift; (b) their comfortable position as the only relevant, "clean" political force that has not discredited itself in power; and (c) the lack of strong and united

---

[9]   The election took place due to the death of former Fidesz MP Jenő Lasztovicza in early January 2015.

left-wing opposition. Furthermore, Lajos Rig was a candidate who worked in the local ambulance—which proved to be a strong asset as there have been attempts by the Orbán government to practically shut down the hospital in Tapolca.

The success of Jobbik marked a breaking point: it proved that most of the voters no longer look at the party as extremist and racist, and taboos that have once kept a large number of undecided voters away from Jobbik have fallen to the wayside. That might sound surprising taking a look on the candidate himself, though. First, he has a tattoo similar to the Nazi German SS's infamous motto—which he declined to show to the public during the election campaign. On the other hand, Rig regularly published Facebook posts with a clear anti-Semitic and racist stance. In one of his posts he shared his thoughts about Roma being the biological weapons in the hand of the Jews in order to eliminate the non-Roma and non-Jewish population of Hungary (Horváth, 2015). This victory also proved that there is no ceiling to Jobbik's expansion. Jobbik's attempt to rebrand itself as a moderate party has been largely successful. Simultaneously, the result offered Vona the opportunity to eliminate his opponents inside the party who accused him of being "soft"—and he took the opportunity. The results also proved that fieldwork is important—a factor that contributed to Jobbik's rise as well. Jobbik ran a well-respected local candidate, who was working hard up and down the electoral district and managing to profit even from an antiestablishment sentiment. The policy failures of Fidesz—for example, in the health care sector—contributed to this success.

Interestingly, Fidesz learned a completely different lesson from the election results than Jobbik. While Vona continued his "moderation" strategy, Fidesz shifted in a more radical direction, to create extranormal circumstances and shake the political field and take back political control—their experience from the three consequent losses at by-elections was that if governance becomes business as usual, they can drown in policy problems and corruption scandals.

These elections also made it patently clear that the party has no magic bullet when it comes to mobilization: neither the so-called Kubatov lists (databases used for door-to-door campaigning by party director Gábor Kubatov, a controversial figure with strong links to the football security firms) nor Victor Orbán's personal appeal sufficed to guaranteed victory at the polls. This case also proved that Fidesz has no adequate response for the Jobbik phenomenon. For years having essentially failed to attack its rival to the right on ideological grounds, in the final stretch of the campaign it opted for a tactic of the left that had clearly failed in the past few years: the stigmatization of Jobbik ("Jobbik is a neo-Nazi party"—as leading politicians of Fidesz repeatedly said in the campaign), although it continued to push the message that it represents a guarantee against the far right, both for domestic and international audiences.

The lesson that a few players learned on the left from the Tapolca and Veszprém by-elections—in line with the "Ukrainization" tendency highlighted earlier—is that locally well-established candidates from either the left or the far right have chance to defeat Fidesz in the voting districts—and they should not run against each other.

Figure 7:   The comparison of the results in the Tapolca district, 2014 and 2015

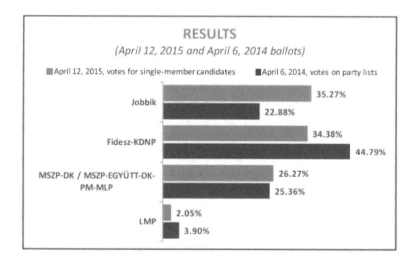

Who are Jobbik's voters?

So far, we mainly dealt with the question that how many voters Jobbik has in different levels of the political system. In this section, we aim to respond the question, Who are Jobbik's voters? Of course, in case of a middle-sized party, we should avoid simplification and stereotypical statements, given that Jobbik has a wide and diverse electorate. Still, especially in the beginning, Jobbik had one of the most characteristic voter bases. Even early researches suggested that Jobbik's electorate does not fit the traditional stereotypes on far-right voters as the "losers" of transition/globalization. The "typical" Jobbik voter, as it seemed in polls in 2009–2011, is economically active, younger, more educated, and better off than the national average. Furthermore, men and inhabitants of smaller towns and villages are overrepresented (Krekó, 2011; Rudas, 2010; Bartlett et al., 2012; Bernát, Krekó, and Juhász, 2013) in Jobbik's support base.

As times change, the outlook of a society develops radically. This process might alter the population's views on immigration, race, and national identity, and these changes affect some people negatively (Ford and Goodwin, 2014). Ford and Goodwin (2014) write that older Britons grew up under different circumstances than the country's youth and, consequently, their views on immigrants and Europe are less favorable. Ford and Goodwin (2014) wrote that the voter base of the populist Euroskeptic right United Kingdom Independence Party (UKIP) (similar to the voters of the far-right British National Party (BNP) beforehand) is mainly made up of older, working-class, uneducated, white men, those who were left behind by the transformation of society. Contrary to this, Jobbik's voter base cannot be described by the "modernization losers" formula adequately. István Grajczjár and András Tóth (2009) say that those who were left behind by the modernization process also play a big part in Jobbik's popularity, because working-class voters from the left change their allegiance to Jobbik. István Grajczjár and András Tóth quote Lipset (2009, p. 13), who said that "because of the bad economic situation of the working-class they are prone to intolerance, which is a result of the race for scarce resources." At the same time, while it is true that there was a shift from the traditional, "proletariat" voter base of left-wing parties toward Jobbik, the party gained the majority of its supporters from the youngest, most educated segment of society (Pytlas, 2015; Bernát et al., 2013), who are definitely not the objective losers of the society. The most important basis of Jobbik's electorate was the middle class (Pirro, 2015). It is especially important to mention that radical right-wing parties employ a dual system of messages, which helps them reach both the winners and losers of society. On the one hand, they have nationalist, illiberal, and Social Darwinist demands, which target the elite, and, on the other hand, they use revolutionary populistic language to gain the support of groups who are financially and socially deprived or feel threatened by deprivation (Grajczjár and Tóth, 2009, p. 23).

It seems though, that the main dividing line between voters of Jobbik and other voters are not sociological, but attitudinal. Pytlas (2015), for example, concluded that anti-Roma attitudes are stronger in Jobbik's electorate than in that of Fidesz, which seems to be the main dividing line between the two groups. Róna (2014) found that Jobbik's voters think that the issue of crime is more important than other voters (while they are not more afraid of crime and have not been affected more by criminal activities than others).

In terms of the age composition of voters, Jobbik seems to be rather the odd one out of radical right parties. According to Róna (2014), only the Freedom Party of Austria and Jobbik can be considered popular among the youth; most other far-right parties in Europe rather build their support on the older generations. Based on Róna's research, it is hard to describe what differentiates the pro-Jobbik and anti-Jobbik groups of youth. The youth is the most liberal layer of society based on their self-evaluation; however, they are also the ones who show the most authoritarian and anti-Roma tendencies. Furthermore, young people supporting the far-right party are more dissatisfied with how democracy works in practice and they distrust its institutions to a higher degree. Based on this, antielite sentiments play the most important role in the far-right orientation of the youth and that the youth supporting Jobbik are more interested in politics and, additionally, that this layer of society needs a community to socialize in more, as this group generally has less experience with relationships and possesses less work experience than the average as well.

In a large representative sample of 3,000 respondents, we aimed to identify the most important characteristics of Jobbik's voters. We found that a majority of Jobbik's supporters (66%) are men, which differs significantly from the support base of the other political parties taken together, where women constitute the majority (56%). Young people are also overrepresented among those who favor Jobbik: every fourth Jobbik supporter is aged below thirty, and every second supporter (52%) is under forty. By and large, Jobbik's supporters have successfully completed secondary education (41% of them have graduated from high school), and the Jobbik camp does not lag behind in terms of the proportion of supporters with higher education degrees. Considering that the share of Jobbik's supporters who have at most eight years of primary education is 50% less than in the two main parties, it becomes clear that Jobbik's voter base is primarily educated young adults, many of whom are men. Furthermore, economic activity is higher among Jobbik's supporters, which means that the poorest and unemployed are underrepresented among them. It supports the thesis (elaborated in the first chapter) that those most receptive to radical ideas are not primarily the poorest but are instead groups that have grown uncertain of their own status yet still have much to lose.

In Hungary, the surge in support for Jobbik in recent years is often attributed to the economic crisis and to deteriorating living standards; however, according to the findings reported earlier, this is not sufficient to explain the demand for either far-right ideologies (Krekó, Juhász and Molnár, 2011) or party preference (Rudas, 2010).

We applied a multivariate statistical tool, logistic regression analysis, to identify the sociodemographic factors that may be considered distinctive features of Jobbik's supporters and raise the chance of voting for Fidesz (Bernát, Krekó and Juhász, 2013. The results showed that gender is one of the most important factors: of those with a party preference, women are not even half as likely (0.39) to support Jobbik as men are. Age is even more significant as a factor, which indicates the "generation-bound" nature of Jobbik: compared to those under thirty years of age, the probability of someone aged sixty or over voting for Jobbik is very low. Level of education is also significant: compared to those with a party preference and with at most eight years of primary education, voters with a higher level of education are 1.5–2.5 times more likely to support Jobbik, and those with a complete secondary education are the most likely to vote for the party. It is in line with the findings of Andrea Szabó (2013, 2015) who found that Jobbik is traditionally very popular among university students—and it became the most popular political force among them by 2015.

Regional distribution seems to play an important role as well—supporting the thesis that the center-periphery divide is extremely important. Northern Hungarian regions differ significantly from the other regions of the country: compared to those living in the central Hungarian region, voters in the northern region are 1.8 times more likely to vote for Jobbik. Income matters as well: compared to the poorest, those in the second and fourth household income per capita quintiles are 2.5 times more likely to vote for Jobbik.

These figures make it crystal clear: most of Jobbik's voters are not from the underprivileged segments of society. On the contrary, most of them have higher-than-average levels of education, though not necessarily highly skilled, earn more than the average, are economically active, and have better living circumstances than the national average. Their receptiveness to far-right and populist political messages may well be due to the fact that they are anxious about losing their present social status—and this sense of fragility on their position provokes hostility toward both the elite above them and the poor below them. This social situation characterizes Jobbik, and more generally, the far-right ideologies.

As for attitudinal features, Jobbik's voters are more pessimistic, more prejudiced, and more mistrustful in the institutions than average Hungarians. And interestingly, they are more willing to leave the country, despite their nationalist sentiments. As we found in the database in 2011, a fifth of Jobbik's supporters plan to go and work abroad for some weeks or months, whereas only 12% of the supporters of other parties have such intentions. Jobbik's supporters are more willing than

the supporters of mainstream parties to go to a foreign country as immigrants, yet they reject the idea of immigrants coming to Hungary to
a much greater degree than other voters with a party preference.

The sometimes covert yet oftentimes open xenophobia contained in Jobbik's messages is also clearer among Jobbik's supporters
than among supporters of other parties. Jobbik's supporters are significantly more likely than the supporters of other parties to find the
idea of a Chinese, African, Roma, or Jewish neighbor unacceptable.
The only exception—in line with the party's positive stance toward
Muslim countries—is their attitude toward a potential Arab neighbor;
statistical analysis yielded no significant difference between Jobbik's
supporters and the supporters of other parties on that issue. What is
important to note is that this result reflected the earlier attitudes of the
voters of Jobbik—when the party followed a strong pro-Muslim stance.

The two most important groups that Jobbik's voters dislike are
the Jews and the Roma—the groups that have been mostly targeted
by Jobbik's rhetoric. About half of Jobbik's voters (49%) would find a
Jewish neighbor unacceptable, compared to "merely" 32 percent
among the supporters of other parties. The most excluded group is
clearly the Roma minority, members of which would not be acceptable
as neighbors for 71 percent of Jobbik followers; supporters of other
parties do not lag far behind in anti-Roma sentiment—61 percent of
them rejected the hypothetical idea of a Roma neighbor.

While anti-Semitism and anti-Gypsyism, and also general xenophobia, are widespread in Hungary, it is alarmingly high among Jobbik's supporters. Still, not every voter of Jobbik is racist: a significant
proportion of the party's supporters said they would have no problem
in having someone who was Jewish, Chinese, or African as a neighbor.

When it came to more specific questions, especially on the
Roma, the difference between Jobbik's voters and the rest of the voters became even more striking. Eighty percent of Jobbik's supporters
agreed (including 43% who agreed strongly) that "a proneness to crim-
inality is in the blood of Gypsies," as opposed to 59% of voters from

other parties (22% of whom agreed strongly).[10] It underlines again the centrality of anti-Roma sentiment in general and the belief of the myth of "Gipsy crime" in particular in the attitudes of Jobbik's voters.

As for anti-Semitism, among those who would not find a Jewish neighbor acceptable, the likelihood of finding a Jobbik voter is 2.6 times higher than among those who have no problems with a Jewish neighbor. Furthermore, the likelihood of becoming a supporter of Jobbik is almost twice as high (1.9) among those who are concerned about a large number of Jewish immigrants settling in the country than it is among those who do not have any such concerns. Mistrust regarding institutions also significantly increases the likelihood of someone voting for Jobbik: on our scale,[11] one unit of decrease in the level of mistrust halved the likelihood of voting for Jobbik among voters with a party preference. In another research, conducted in 2014, we found that Jobbik's voters have stronger authoritarian attitudes and acceptance of violence (Molnar et al., 2015).

All this demonstrates that the ideology of Jobbik, combining nationalism, anti-Semitism, anti-Gypsyism, and antiestablishment attitudes with authoritarian and violent tendencies, is capable of catching a wide range of electorate—but primarily young men with secondary education who fear for their current social status.

These findings may appear self-evident and surprising at the same time. Obviously, Jobbik is a "generational party": its leaders are young; it has strong connections to the "trendy" far-right subcultures; it speaks the language of the youth; it has a rebellious, antiestablishment stance; and it is loud and radical. It also comes as no surprise that respondents who embrace the notion that Gypsies have an innate criminal proclivity and those who distrust the political establishment show greater eagerness for the politics of Jobbik. Given the "macho" image of this "testosterone party," its long history of connection with

---

[10]   The odds ratio in the case of those who "rather disagree" is only 0.43, and it is a mere 0.20 among those who "strongly disagree."

[11]   A principal component containing four questions on trust in institutions. The strength of the impact of institutional trust is demonstrated by the fact that, if omitted, the explained variance of the questions featured in the model is reduced from thirty-three to twenty-eight.

extremist and paramilitary organizations marching on the streets, such as the Hungarian Guard (*Magyar Gárda*), and its language of "force," and often violence, it comes as no big surprise that men are heavily overrepresented among its supporters.

Still, the overall picture may be rather surprising in the light of the still-widespread view of Jobbik's supporters as the losers of socialism: unemployed or low-income, undereducated people living in the villages of northeastern Hungary. In line with the findings of Tamás Rudas (2010), we found that the average Jobbik supporter is a middle-class man with some academic qualification; he may have not suffered any direct negative political or economic consequences after the fall of socialism and thanks to the relatively sound financial background of his family, he may not even have suffered indirectly from the regime change. Such people certainly do not join Jobbik for reasons of presumed or anticipated financial benefit, but rather for symbolic and identity-related reasons. Moreover, it is not indiscriminate, disadvantage-related contempt for minorities in general that inspires such voters. Jobbik's voters mostly target Jews and Gypsies with their hostility.

But if not material factors and existential fears, then what attracts such a wide range of voters toward the Jobbik party? Rudas (2010, p. 512) argues that the ideological bond comes from "their [Jobbik voters'] difficulty in accepting the uncertainty entailed by the pluralism of values." This notion is indeed discernible in the strongly antiliberal stance expressed by Jobbik and its supporters. It is, however, possible that more profound reasons underlie this attitude. First and foremost, it seems that Jobbik voters perceive their status and national identity endangered. The middle-class Jobbik supporters may feel that their social status is simultaneously endangered from "below"—by those who are dragging down the better-off members of the society (i.e., the "parasites" who live off state handouts, which is stereotype for Gypsies), and from "above"—by a tight-knit liberal and cosmopolitan elite group (i.e., Jews), who are taking over positions of leadership in the fields of economy, finance, culture, media, and politics, and excluding those others who want to become part of this elite.

The remedy offered by Jobbik to this threat of national identity is a vision of the nation that is strictly confined and homogeneous both ethnically and in terms of values. Minorities are excluded from this strictly defined national identity, and yet become necessary elements in delineating boundaries of this new constructed identity. In other words, Gypsies offer an object for comparison, allowing right-wing radicals to portray themselves as "better"—more decent, hard-working, and more successful (Dupcsik, 2009). Jews, on the other hand, enable Jobbik to focus more on what is "Hungarian" rather than what is "alien," and serve as scapegoats for the failures and shortcomings of the nation.

Where do Jobbik's voters come from?

As indicated in the opening chapter of this book, defining the far right's social base is often a political-ideological game: where to put the blame? For instance, leftist-Marxist thinking traditionally identifies the lower middle class as the major source of support for the far right, while liberal and conservative schools are more likely to point to the working class as the most susceptible to political extremism.

In Hungary, a related, strongly over-politicized question emerged in public and analyst discourses: from which parties Jobbik's supporters mainly coming from? No doubt, the party's ability to attract supporters from mainstream parties has contributed to its meteoric rise. Hungarian public discourse, including a huge part of the left, appears to accept the fallacy advanced by the right that for the most part of Jobbik's voter base is made up of former MSZP supporters. While none of the studies published in the past few years provide evidence for this claim, this still prevails. While the Jobbik voter base includes some former socialist voters, on the whole the party is definitely not built on a dominantly former leftist base.

Taking the Hungarian Socialist Party's 2006 voter base as our benchmark in analyzing the rise of Jobbik in 2010, we find that some voters did indeed switch to Jobbik, although the majority clearly didn't come from that camp. For the most part, the party's large following that emerged in 2009 and 2010 came from previous nonvoters, young people who didn't even have the right to vote in 2006, and habitual radical voters. This heterogeneous group was joined by previous Fidesz's supporters and former socialist voters.

According to a survey conducted in 2010 within the framework of the Hungarian Election Research Program, in 2006 one-third of Jobbik's voters had voted for MSZP (Hungarian Socialist Party). While this number is far from negligible, even this relatively high ratio means that two-thirds came from somewhere else—mainly from Fidesz and the undecided camp (Grajczjár and Tóth, 2010).

Dis-preferences, measured by Szonda-Ipsos in 2012, point in the same direction. Jobbik's voters are much more averse to MSZP than to Fidesz. The antisocialist attitude was a powerful identity-forming rallying cry in the Jobbik camp, at least at the beginning. Other polls also revealed that more voters came from Fidesz and Jobbik at the time of the emergence of the party (Karácsony and Róna, 2011).

Also, when one compares the 2014 election results to the 2010 results, it would be counterproductive to talk about the capture of left-wing voters by Jobbik: while Jobbik was on the rise, the number of votes cast for the leftist party alliance was also up slightly during the April parliamentary election. Compared to 2010, the left increased its advantage over Jobbik by 100,000 votes. Fidesz and Jobbik's support among the voters with party preferences is usually moving the other way around: Jobbik's rise since 2010 goes hand in hand with Fidesz's decline, and vice versa. And still, it seems that far-right party is in a much better position to attract disappointed Fidesz's voters than the left. Also, traditionally Fidesz is in better position to attract Jobbik's voters than MSZP. In a survey conducted by Századvég Foundation, at the end of 2012, close to one-fifth (18%) of Jobbik's voters said that in 2010 they had voted for Fidesz (Szazadveg.hu, 2012).

Supply side: Far right on the political field

From marginality toward relevance

The regime change and the far right: Return to the limelight

Following World War II and the collapse of the Nazi-allied Arrow Cross government, practically all institutional conditions for the operation of the far right were eradicated. Taking complete control by 1948, the communist dictatorship in part eliminated and in part "absorbed" the membership of former far-right organizations. The system's official antifascist stance suppressed and erased all aspects of far-right ideology—even if former Arrow Cross party members found their way to the Communist party and its oppressive, violent official law enforcement institutions. As a result, far-right ideologies survived only in the Hungarian diaspora and in the Hungarian "underground" far from public view. Because of this invisibility, following regime change society and some opinion makers were shocked to see the reemergence of far-right rhetoric, especially anti-Semitism and xenophobia in Hungarian public discourse. Moreover, the process was helped by the democratization of the country: the extension of civil and political rights—especially free speech—as well as the right of association and assembly. Obviously, these rights were also extended to the extremists, leading to the proliferation of anti-Semitic, anti-Roma chauvinist, and intolerant ideas. But it was far from a Hungary-specific phenomenon; the "democratization of hostility" has rather been a general tendency in the region (Bustikova, 2015).

Simultaneous to the establishment of far-right communication channels, the first extremist, typically anti-Semitic incidents occurred as early as 1989, in relation to the "four-yes" referendum.[12] One of

---

[12]   In 1989, the "four-yes" referendum played a major role in the demolition of socialism; during the referendum "voters had the opportunity to decide four matters: the method of election of the president of the republic, party organizations in places of work, the accountability of the state party and the dissolution of Workers' Guard. The majority of voters opted for yes in all matters,

these involved an anti-Semitic poster war during the referendum campaign and the vandalizing of the statue of the late Swedish diplomat and humanitarian Raoul Wallenberg, known for saving thousands of Hungarian Jews during the Holocaust. But violent and symbolically violent incidents were tied primarily to the skinhead movement considered to be a subcultural phenomenon. The first skinhead groups emerged in Hungary in the middle of the 1980s as fans of a few rock bands, and it reached its peak in the first half of the 1990s. In the years following regime change, a number of atrocities were committed: in Budapest, Eger and Salgótarján skinheads attacked Gypsies, Jews, foreigners, and persons that fit the description, causing fatal injuries in a few cases (Solt, 1992).

The skinhead movement later maintained some relationship with political parties, especially the agrarian-populist Independent Smallholders, Agrarian Workers and Civic Party (*Független Kisgazda, Földmunkás és Polgári Párt*, FKGP), and then the MIÉP, the splinter party from the governmental party Hungarian Democratic Forum (*Magyar Demokrata Fórum,* MDF). Because of their small numbers, the skinheads did not become a serious force shaping politics (Bernath, Miklosi, and Mudde, 2005), but some of their representatives finally found their way to political parties. The most important example is Tamás Sneider, a former leader of the Eger skinhead movement with the nickname Roy, who was convicted for participating in beating up a Roma person. He is currently the vice president of the party, and also the vice speaker of the Hungarian parliament.

The first attempt at establishing a far-right party

Far-right political organizations and players started to emerge around Jurta Theater, a former forum of the democratic opposition, opposed to state socialism (Bernath, Miklosi, and Mudde, 2005). A number of small, short-lived parties and movements held regular meetings at this venue, attempting (unsuccessfully) to unite the fragmented far-right scene. On April 20, 1994 (the birthday of Adolf Hitler), the alliance of

---

while the large number of participants in the referendum provided particular weight to the outcome" (Rytkó, 2008).

three extreme-right organizations led to the birth of the Hungarian Hungarist Movement, which in turn led to the seizure of the organization. While some organizations were even running in elections (e.g. the Hungarian Welfare Alliance (MNSZ), established in 1994 as a Hungarist party, ran candidates in the 1998 parliamentary and municipal elections as well), generally they were unable to cross the threshold needed for broad public recognition and substantial political support, and their impact, apart from some connections to mainstream parties mentioned above, remained rather marginal. In the absence of professional politicians, they were unable to formulate and deliver coherent messages to the electorate and they could not provide genuine answers to the most important (mainly economic) problems of the time. The public essentially ignored the institutional extreme right at this time, and their institutions and media organizations remained feeble and marginal. The effectiveness of these organizations was further undermined by personal squabbles: the majority of far-right organizations formed around prominent and dominant personalities (such as György Ekrem-Kemál, István Győrkös, Izabella Király B., and Albert Szabó) that guaranteed division, for most leaders were loath to enter into compromise with leaders of other organizations. As a result, the small far-right parties emerging after the regime change were destined to fall into irrelevance. By the middle of the 1990s, their members, sympathizers, and functions were absorbed by larger parties, primarily the MIÉP and the populist Independent Smallholders Party—the latter was a significant parliamentary force at the time.

The rise and fall of MIÉP

Even following the regime change, the mainstream right's relationship with the far right had remained unclear. The Hungarian Democratic Forum (MDF), a conservative party made up of a loose coalition of movements and a winner during the 1990 parliamentary election, featured such diverse people as Izabella B. Király, a patron of skinheads, and the popular dramatist, István Csurka, the most notorious practitioner of political anti-Semitism. This far-right strain within the party was one of the reasons behind its relatively quick erosion.

On August 20, 1992, István Csurka published an article entitled "A Few Thoughts" in the weekly *Magyar Fórum*, laying down the fundamental precepts of his rabid anti-Semitism. This left the government, facing major challenges following the regime change, in a difficult position. In addition, the article was also picked up by some of the foreign media and, although Prime Minister József Antall described the piece as part of Csurka's "literary oeuvre," MDF was eventually forced to distance itself from Csurka. This quickly led to an eventual split within the party. First, István Csurka established the Hungarian Path Foundation, describing its political objectives in the following terms: "prepare the nationalist-thinking Christian middle class and position it to be ready to lead the nation." By early 1993, it became clear that with the support of MDF's "folk" "popular" wing, Csurka would attempt to take over the party and, sooner or later, the government itself. But finally he went down in defeat. Expelled from the party in the summer of 1993, Csurka immediately established MIÉP and following 1994 (when it gained only 1.6% of the votes) MIÉP became the flagship of the Hungarian far right. The organization's ideology was determined almost exclusively by István Csurka, whose anti-Semitic, nationalist, Euroskeptic, anti-NATO (North Atlantic Treaty Organization), anti-Israeli, and anti-American rhetorical turns coalesced into a distinctive conspiracy-theory project. Failing to gain a single seat in parliament in 1994, it became vital for the party to remain visible. Therefore, it tried to maintain public visibility through a series of large-scale events, regularly attracting tens of thousands of sympathizers. The main basis of the party was Budapest (contrary to Jobbik later that is the weakest in Budapest), and they performed the best in the elite districts, with well-off higher educated conservative voters overrepresented in their voting camp.

By the 1998 election, the party managed to absorb most of the activists and sympathizers of a very fragmented far right, leaving out such peripheral and insignificant groups as the neo-Nazi, Hungarian Welfare Association led by Albert Szabó, or Hungarian National Front led by István Győrkös. The 1998 elections undoubtedly brought success for MIÉP (Table 8). With close to a quarter million of the votes cast (5.55% of the national list vote), it sent fourteen representatives to the parliament, and it could form a parliamentary faction.[13]

Table 8:   The electoral performance of MIÉP, 1994–2014

Election	Number of votes (first round)	Percentage of votes (first round)	Number of mandates	Percentage of mandates	Passed the parliamentary threshold?
1994	85,623	1.59	0	0	No
1998	248,825	5.55	14	3.63	Yes
2002	245,326	4.37	0	0	No
2006 (with Jobbik)	119,007	2.20	0	0	No
2010	1,286	0.03	0	0	No
2014	2,054	0.04	0	0	No

The following period represented the party's heyday. MIÉP became a force to be reckoned with and the party attempted to build its hinterlands: MIÉP established the Bocskai Free University, the Bocskai Stage, and Pannon Rádió, a nationalist radio station under the control of the party that went on the air in the spring of 2000 promoting nationalist, anti-Semitic ideas. Between 1998 and 2002, when Fidesz governed in coalition with the Christian Democratic People's Party (KDNP) and the agrarian populist Independent Smallholders Party (FKGP), MIÉP criticized the government from the opposition—except the last period after the turbulent political "execution" of József Torgyán's FKGP by Fidesz. As a result of this process, Fidesz practically lost its majority in the parliament, and MIÉP helped to maintain it from outside the government. This semi-oppositional position did not help the survival of the party. Despite the strengthening infrastructure around the party and the fact that in the 2002 parliamentary election the party received more votes than in 1998, due to the high turnout they finished with only 4.36 percent and, to the general dismay of the membership preparing to take over the government, the party dropped out of parliament.

---

[13]   For this the Constitutional Court had to overrule a House regulation requiring minimum fifteen representatives for a faction.

All this accelerated the party's erosion, brought accounting disputes, and led to the failure of party organizing in rural areas to the surface. With the exception of the fast-aging party president, practically all leaders left the party in quick succession. Subsequently, MIÉP gradually sank into oblivion; its supporters and sympathizers abandoned it and in 2006, when it ran on a joint platform with Jobbik (a barely known youth movement just becoming a party at the time), it only received 2.2 percent at the polls. With this, the aging István Csurka reached the end of the rope; he could neither reinvent nor update his extremist message, and the time to pass on the torch had come.

The early history of Jobbik

Jobbik, originally called the Right-Wing Youth Association, was established in 1999 by Dávid Kovács, the president of Eötvös Lóránd University's student union, with the leadership of Gábor Vona and Gábor Szabó, the future president and party director and deputy caucus leader of Jobbik. The name of the organization, "Jobbik," has a double meaning in Hungarian: "Better" or "more right wing." At that time, the university organization essentially operated in the orbit of MIÉP (in 2002, Kovács became a representative for MIÉP) and served as a forum for politically active right-wing university students who organized public events—such as inviting politicians in the universities. Meanwhile, with a membership of 1,000–1,200, in 2002 Jobbik actively assisted Fidesz's campaign by offering the services of its members, such as helping to collect the nomination slips for Fidesz's candidates and distributing leaflets. As in those days Jobbik had the major objective of facilitating the success of right-wing parties, it is understandable that the election results (MIÉP's fallout from the parliament and Fidesz's return to opposition) came as a complete shock—and also, a moment for revising strategy.

For Jobbik it was a defining moment when, due to the close election results, the extremely tense and radical climate of the 2002 campaign lingered on for a relatively long time. Following the lost election, Viktor Orbán established civic circles (*Polgári Körök*) to build up a movement around himself to extend his own power base, and thus guarantee his continued leading position on the right. While these organizations received encouragement from the top, in effect they were self-organized and by forming a national network became an important factor in shaping policies, even as the majority of them represented strongly right-wing radical ideas—more radical than Fidesz. In a speech calling for the establishment of civic circles after the second round of the election in 2002, Viktor Orbán claimed that "the homeland cannot be in opposition" (Index.hu, 2002)—a famous statement of him that describes his ambivalent attitude toward a pluralist system. With this statement, he simultaneously challenged the rival left-liberal coalition's to govern—while this side was the winner of the 2002 election—as well as their patriotic commitment. As Orbán said at the same speech, the civic circles should "stay ready, in case that Fate calls for activity." The new movement, tightly controlled by Orbán and his lieutenants, and symbolizing his personal popularity and mobilization potential on the right, was formed to maintain street pressure on the incoming left-liberal government. While it was officially independent from Fidesz, the activities were coordinated by Orbán's people via the Fidesz media and informal channels, with a key role played by the Fidesz party director Gábor Kubatov.

In the framework of the civic circles, the future leader of Jobbik had the chance to learn about ideology and mobilization techniques from Orbán Viktor himself. Orbán invited Gábor Vona to join the Alliance for the National Civic Circle (Szövetség a Polgári Körökért), a civic circle around the ex–prime minister himself with notable right-wing intellectuals such as the architect Imre Makovecz. Vona participated in the work of the organization until the fall of 2003, and it is clear that the period also offered important lessons for him. The world of civic circles provided groundwork and experiences for the future far-right party on importance of supporting political self-organization and local cells. Also, he could learn the importance of symbolic mobilization. While Jobbik was never as successful in street mass mobilization as Orbán, Vona could definitely learn from Orbán in this regard: how to build up a movement using mobilization techniques similar to the ones used by Silvio Berlusconi—a friend and a political ally of Orbán at that time. But Vona had other links to Fidesz as well at his time: he was the head of the students section of the Alliance of Christian Intellectuals (*Keresztény Értelmiségiek Szövetsége*), an organization close to Fidesz.

While Jobbik definitely received inspiration from Fidesz, when the latter lost the election in 2002, the disillusionment from the party encouraged attempts to organize its alternative (Krekó and Mayer, 2015). While Vona participated in the civic circles, it seems that he already had alternative plans and visions. In May 2002, right after the defeat of Fidesz at the parliamentary elections, three future leaders of Jobbik met in a cheap pub "Arany Korsó" (Golden Pint) on Budapest's Móricz square: Gábor Vona, a history student at Budapest's ELTE university at that time and also a leader of the students' self-government of his alma mater; Dávid Kovács, who had just finished his history studies at ELTE and was also active in the students' self-government; and Gábor Szabó, also a student of history, who was the organizational brain of the radical-right movement—according to the memories of Kovács. Both Kovács and Szabó had been members of István Csurka's anti-Semitic MIÉP. On this meeting, Gábor Vona draw the conclusion: Fidesz never will be able to represent the "national interests" efficiently, whereas MIÉP is an anachronistic and failed organization and never will be capable to do so. This argument convinced Kovács and Szabó that Jobbik must go its own way, because *there was a need for a party that is younger, more dynamic, and more contemporary than MIÉP.* Szabó went on to say that

> the election defeat was a deep shock for all of us. As long as it governed, we judged the FIDESZ more positively, but at the end of 2002, we realized, that this whole government as well as the period of the 'Civic Circles,' which came after the failure, were a big humbug (Varró, 2009, the English translation is from Krekó and Mayer, 2015).

As a result, due to the decline of MIÉP, and the moderation in activity of civic circles, in the fall of 2002 Jobbik's leaders decided to embark on an independent political path. One year later, on October 24, 2003, this vision was materialized in a party. Several well-known public figures, such as Mátyás Usztics, an actor known for his right-wing views, participated at the ceremony. The day of establishment was symbolic, just one day after the celebration of the 1956 revolution against the

Soviet Union. Dávid Kovács became the president and Gábor Vona the vice president of the party. Soon, a number of former MIÉP party members and municipal representatives joined the party, such as Zoltán Balczó and László Grespik.

While Jobbik was far less successful than MIÉP in organizing mass rallies, it managed to attract public attention with a number of spectacular media events. These included the erection of large wooden crosses before Christmas on public squares—as a response to erecting big Chanukah candles at some squares, an obvious expression of Jobbik's religious and political anti-Semitism. Other public demonstrations included the "EU-NO!!!" campaign preceding the referendum on joining the EU (including doing a bit of performance in the parliament), the "Sodom award" for politicians that are supporting the gay marriage, and the "sweep-them-out demonstration" before the headquarters building of the Hungarian Socialist Party. Since its inception, the party made every effort to distinguish itself from Fidesz, although it left open the possibility of partnership with Fidesz—and even referred to the possibility of a coalition with Fidesz before the 2006 elections. In the meantime, while organization building proceeded at a good pace, with the party having local organizations in all counties by mid-2004, Jobbik did not risk running in Hungary's first EP election held in 2004—what they explained with the lack of willingness to legitimize the election with their participation. Starting in October 2005, the once-icy MIÉP-Jobbik relationship also started to thaw, at least temporarily, for practical reasons. As described earlier, the two parties joined forces and ran on a single list in the 2006 parliamentary election. This adventure resulted in a failure (less than 2% popular vote), which has just gave momentum for Jobbik to walk on an even more independent road.

2006: The birth of today's far right in Hungary

The year 2006 is perhaps the most special and important year in Hungarian political history since the regime change, while even the most mysterious one: many events that year still lack full explanation. The parliamentary elections were won confidently by the MSZP led by Ferenc Gyurcsány, the incumbent prime minister since 2004. This meant that the left-liberal coalition held on to power. In other words, the same political force could embark on its second four-year term, a result unprecedented since the regime change, and had been generally rare in post-transitional Central Eastern Europe. However, soon after the election it was revealed that hiding the country's real economic conditions, the government had won with false promises never meant to be fulfilled. As a result of the preelection spending, the public deficit went up to 9.3 percent of GDP (Central Statistics Office, n.d.)[14]—by far the highest among EU member states. While the government promised tax cuts in the campaign, harsh austerity measures followed instead. As a consequence, in a few months, the support for the government shrunk drastically. Moreover, in the fall of 2006, under circumstances unknown to this day, a secret voice recording was leaked. This audiotape played a huge role in shaping the political history of Hungary afterward. This audiotape recorded a speech delivered before the elections, where Ferenc Gyurcsány acknowledges that he had been lying to the public in order to win the elections—especially about the economic conditions of the country. Subsequently—also in a manner no one fully understands to this day but which gave way to conspiracy theories that were proliferating on both sides—street riots broke out in Budapest. The symbolism was very strong domestically as well, given that it was the fiftieth anniversary of the 1956 revolution against the Soviet oppression—when the revolutionaries even occupied the building of the public radio and taking it over. On the eve of the leaked tape in 2006, a mob of far-right supporters and football hooligans went to the parliament and then sieged the public television (MTV). Images of the burning public television building were circulated in the global media. It took the police hours to gain effective control. The situation turned to the other extreme on October 23, 2016 —the official national holiday commemorating the Revolution of 1956. That day, after hooligans clashed with the police, the police brutally attacked even peaceful demonstrators, including

---

[14]   According to the statistics of the Central Statistical Office: Central Statistics Office (n.d.). Az államháztartás hiánya (–) és többlete (+) (2004–2015). [online] Available at: https://www.ksh.hu/docs/hun/eurostat_tablak/tabl/teina200.html [Accessed April 12, 2017].

Fidesz's sympathizers, generating a new wave of political tensions. Eventually, while the government remained in place, it never managed to regain public support. This, in turn, led to a paralysis of the government and radicalization of the opposition. As a result, Fidesz and Viktor Orbán managed to hysterize its own political camp for their own survival following their second defeat in the 2002 national election. But generally, the visible emergence of a far right on the streets, the deepening of the political divisions, and the radicalization of the public discourses helped Jobbik and created good opportunity structures to emerge.

In addition, a tragic murder in Olaszliszka took place in the fall of 2006. On October 15, 2006, a teacher from Tiszavasvári drove his car through the main street of Olaszliszka and accidently side-swept a small Roma girl who, as it turned out later, did not suffer any injuries. The non-Roma driver stopped; the girl's father, along with his relatives, surrounded him, dragged him from his car, and, in the presence of his two daughters, beat him to death. This event greatly contributed to a resurgence of anti-Roma sentiment in the country, and helped Jobbik to introduce the term "Roma crime" in the general political vocabulary. In sum, the reorganization of the far right and the birth of today's Hungarian far right in 2006 took place in this political climate.

The year 2006 represented a historic moment line for the far right, and a moment for building identity. Gábor Vona referred to his movement and supporters frequently as the "2006 generation" (Alfahír, 2012), contrasting it with the "1989 generation"—referring to the transition elite that they regarded to be corrupt and destructive. While in the 1990s the majority of supporters of far-right movements came from the older generation, starting from 2002, and especially after 2006, the presence of younger people among the supporters of the far right became more and more pronounced. Jobbik was mainly run by educated young men with a diploma or still attending a university.

Furthermore, by 2006, the structure of the radical public underwent fundamental change, due primarily to the proliferation of the Internet and subsequently faster, more efficient spread of extremist information (e.g., Bartlett et al., 2012). Specifically, as the Web sites and electronic newsletters replaced printed materials and network connections grew in number, this change perfectly suited the needs of young radicals.

By the middle of the decade, the countercultural role of the far right also became increasingly apparent: an already existing network of rightist publishing companies, book, and souvenir shops continued to expand; pop-music festivals and cultural organizations sprang up; a cottage industry promoting some kind of "national kitsch" emerged, eventually attracting a growing number of supporters and generating much-needed revenues for the political far right.

The pressure from the right to reorganize

The agenda for the first half of 2006 was determined by the election campaign. From the start of the year, MIÉP and Jobbik made repeated efforts to attract public attention and were met with moderate success. From the very beginning, the election coalition was strained; MIÉP's traditional, essentially anti-Semitic policy did not resonate with Jobbik's program, often trying to imitate contemporary Western European models. The first visible conflict surfaced not long before the parliamentary elections. On March 30, 2006, Jobbik announced their intention to invite thousands of protesters to attend a rally on April 4 at Szabadság Square, where the party would demand the removal of a Soviet war memorial. However, when MIÉP boycotted the event, it turned into a genuine Jobbik campaign rally. It was also quite effective when on the same day Jobbik came to the defense of Fidesz politician, István Mikola, who was criticized for his radical statements made during the campaign. Also, on March 31, 2006, István Csurka had said that following the election, he expected Fidesz and the Alliance of Free Democrats (*Szabad Demokraták Szövetsége*, SZDSZ) to form an alliance. He explained this by stating that at the time of the presidential election, SZDSZ essentially helped the Fidesz candidate to win the post. István Csurka also claimed that, in his view, Fidesz only "harmed" the national radicals, a statement clearly alluding to a strategic divide with respect to Jobbik.

Eventually, the election ended in the debacle described earlier. Approximately 120,000 people voted for the Third Path, representing

2 percent of the votes cast, denying the party a seat in the parliament. Between 2002 and 2006, the number of ballots cast for the far right has practically halved, and the party failed to increase the number of votes received in all counties. The dramatic decline was due in part to the fact that the biggest loss was suffered in Budapest (traditionally bringing the largest number of votes), where the number of received votes dropped by almost 60 percent. It is interesting to note that the territorial distribution of votes did not change substantially, although in the east of the country the rate of decline was slightly smaller. On the issue of withdrawing candidates between the two rounds, a debate developed within the cooperation of the Third Path on the night of the first round: MIÉP decided unanimously to deny support to Fidesz in the second round and urged their voters to stay away from the polls. In contrast, Jobbik asked its supporters to go to the polls and support Fidesz candidates.

This story also indicated that internal conflicts within the far right were the most vehement with respect to the parties' relationship to Fidesz. For leaders of the radical right also had to realize that a large percentage of their potential voters were tied down by Fidesz. This had already been suggested on January 23, 2006, by one of the leaders of the Third Path, Zoltán Balczó, who wrote a letter to civic circles asking them to support his party over Fidesz. As he claimed, a number of civic circles signaled their disappointment with the largest opposition party. However, the coordinator of civic circles, Csaba Hende, stated that he saw no signs of attrition from civic circles. This was later confirmed by election results. In other words, the far right could not step out of Fidesz's shadow, and this had not changed even after the parliamentary elections. All these developments had made the restructuring of the far right inevitable.

The aftermath of the election made the need for shaping a new way totally inevitable. Jobbik announced that at the upcoming municipal elections it would support István Tarlós, Fidesz, and KDNP's candidate for mayor of Budapest. At the same time, while the party signed a number of local agreements with Fidesz on joint candidates, Jobbik became embroiled in another debate with MIÉP (fielding its own mayoral candidate) over some financial dispute within the Third Path.

Just before the political crisis in the fall of 2006, the far-right camp saw two parties, both failing at the polls, busy arguing among themselves. All this foreshadowed another defeat in the municipal election. By September 2006, MIÉP all but disappeared from the political landscape, while Jobbik lined up behind Fidesz—watching and building its base at the same time.

The far right taking a leading role

On September 17, 2006, the day the Öszöd speech was exposed, demonstrations started on Kossuth Square. On the first day the demonstration was peaceful, the crowd chanted antigovernment slogans, and the police did not intervene because, under the law, in a campaign period even unannounced rallies are permitted. Groups of demonstrators gathered at the house of prime minister, Ferenc Gyurcsány, and some moved to Alexander Palace (Sándor Palota), housing the presidential office. Among others, István Csurka also showed up at Kossuth Square, but was received by the crowd with shouts of "No need for Csurka!" However, in the next few days, the situation went out of control, riots broke out on the streets of Budapest, there were demonstrations in cities around the country, and a variety of organizations and groups sprang up. In the fall of 2006, the far right undoubtedly made itself visible—in a spectacularly violent way, riding the rising wave of anger.

In the next few months, a number of lengthy articles, commentaries, and essays were written about the extremists. Aside from reporting on the activities of specific organizations, the media also tracked their members' movements and the metamorphosis of far-right groups. However, public attention was primarily preoccupied with specific actions and initiatives—mostly focusing on the Kossuth Square and its surrounding, and representing a bizarre form of direct democracy, calling for a new National Assembly (*Országgyűlés*). After a while, the structures and names of the organizations emerging, such as Conscience 88 (*Lelkiismeret 88*) and Hungarian National Committee 2006 (*Magyar Nemzeti Bizottság 2006*), and the splinter organizations, in quick succession became all too confusing for the general public. As an indication for this, reports often mixed up or misspelled the names of some groups.

In the following months, national media organizations committed to left and right developed strong and characteristic positions regarding the activities of groups behind the demonstrations. Aside from emphasizing the danger posed by the far right, the leftist media tried to banalize the size of the crowd demonstrating against the government, and simply ridiculed some organizations and individuals. In contrast, the media on the right often exaggerated the events and described the antigovernment actions of various extremist groups as a form of civil resistance, or even revolution, glorifying the attempts of the extremist groups.[15]

Only in the last two months of 2006 did the media as a whole return to more factual and objective reporting. In response to the initiatives of radical and extremist organizations covered by the media, the events of the fall were given a public reinterpretation. The media was primarily preoccupied with the siege of the MTV building and the events of October 23. With some hindsight, opinion makers fine-tuned their previous positions. On the right, fewer and fewer commentators referred to the fall riots as a revolution, and on the left there were an increasing number of voices criticizing the excessive force shown by the police on October 23. In connection to the street demonstrations of the fall, opinion makers on both sides of the political divide tended to make a distinction between peaceful demonstrators and troublemakers. With respect to the picture developed of the observed organizations and personalities, the media with the most influence on radical and extremist electoral groups split into two. By December 2006, the "mainstream" right-wing media attributed less relevance to developments in the fall. At the same time, the printed media and Internet sites addressing a more narrowly defined and extremist community continued to focus on organizations emerging during the fall disturbances and provided extensive coverage on their activities.

---

[15]   The reporter of right-wing HírTV described the riot in front of the MTV (public television) building as a "revolution."

In the wake of a steady flow of live coverage of street violence, antigovernment demonstrations took on the air of a permanent and an apparently intractable political crisis, and the public was inundated with a variety of explanations and conclusions. The one extreme was envisioning an impending fascist takeover, while the other extreme was occupied by the advocates of conspiracy theories, attributing every extremist moves to government manipulations. These opinions on the role of the far right in these dramatic and unprecedented events were highly revealing not so much about the far right itself, but about those forming such judgments. In the fall of 2006, before the far right managed to enter the limelight, all political forces and opinion makers had to take a stance regarding their relationship to the extremists. And with everybody talking about them, the far right was also given the opportunity to make a public debut and develop its own policies.

Transforming the agenda

When new topics are introduced to the political discussion, new parties can emerge because they can talk about issues not owned by mainstream parties (Mudde, 2007, p. 238). This is what led to the success of UKIP, when they managed to take ownership of a popular issue—immigration—after the number of people arriving to the UK rose significantly during the Conservative rule between 2010 and 2015 (Dennison and Goodwin, 2015, p. 179). In Hungary, a poll arrived at the conclusion that more voters believe Jobbik to be the most credible expert on the Roma issue than the number of those voting for them (Pytlas, 2015).

Jobbik's rise was facilitated by Hungarian public opinion's shift to the right as well, together with Fidesz's increasingly radical rhetoric, which helped legitimizing Jobbik. The breakthrough of Jobbik in 2009 led people to the realization that they can vote for the party because it is a force to be reckoned with, and offensives directed against the far-right party coming from the left and Fidesz's turn against them also indicated the same thing (Grajczjár and Tóth, 2012). Jobbik was the first party in Hungary to politicize the Roma problem; therefore, they managed to introduce the topic within their own frames (Karácsony and Róna, 2011; Juhász, 2010; Pirro, 2015, p. 79). The Eastern European Roma are often criticized for living on the edge of legality (Pirro, 2015, pp. 42–43), and the second largest ethnic group of the nation is often singled out as a scapegoat for the nation's problems. The process in Hungary started after the Olaszliszka assassination in 2006, after which the Hungarian far-right party demanded a new Roma policy (Pytlas, 2015) and mainstream parties reacted to this quite slowly. Fidesz's counterreaction led to Jobbik being able to introduce a populist argument, namely that there should be a public debate on whether "Gypsy crime" exists (Pytlas, 2015). The debate was instigated by Jobbik and the party successfully framed the issue along racist lines, showcasing Jobbik as the "champion of truth" in the process (Juhász, 2012).

The communication of the reorganizing far right

The political actions of far-right organizations and individuals were contingent for the most part, with no communications strategy developed for the long term. In the midst of all the turmoil of 2006, on the far right Jobbik appeared to be the only organization with an action plan. Following the election of Gábor Vona as party president in the fall of 2006, the party's activism switched to a higher gear—but at the same time, they tried to keep an optimal distance from dangerous organizations. The party leadership did not formally support the rabble-rousers of Szabadság Square and Rákóczi Road, or demonstrators encamped on Kossuth Square—not even the Hungarian National Committee representing Kossuth Square demonstrators, established by Tamás Molnár, a member of Jobbik that time (who later left Jobbik). Following Jobbik's statement, initiated by Vona on canceling a demonstration on Köztársaság Square—where the Hungarian Socialist Party headquarters were located, the reasons for this decision probably being fears over escalation of violence—Jobbik chief organizer and spokesperson Előd Novák resigned, and due to disputes local organizations in Budapest Districts II. and V. were also disbanded. Staying away from the action and the resulting internal conflicts was the price paid by Jobbik for the chance to become a major force at a later date.

By the end of 2006, Jobbik launched planned campaigns generating considerable attention. Exploiting the dispute over the Árpád-
striped flag (a symbol of the Hungarian far right pointing back to pre–
World War II anti-Semitic organizations), Jobbik embarked on a "mission of enlightenment," a year-long national tour featuring street
demonstrations. It chose the red/silver stripes as its official colors, and
it also launched its new Web site. As a gift, it gave the liberal SZDSZ
party an Árpád-striped flag and a coat-of-arms manual, saying that the
SZDSZ should learn about the origins of the flag and stop instigating
the public against it. Also, exploiting the heightened public reaction to
the lynching in Olaszliszka mentioned earlier, Jobbik launched another campaign, stigmatizing the entire Roma population, combating
"Gypsy crime." The party claimed that in various parts of the country
Gypsy criminal gangs terrorize law-abiding citizens, while the government is helpless and the hands of the police are also tied. On the back
of this issue the party received regular public attention; it planned to
submit a petition to the National Roma Self-Government and launched
a subsite dedicated specifically to this issue.[16]

The application of (often sensational, guerilla-style) communication techniques and actions adjusted to the needs of the media became increasingly frequent on the far right. However, these kinds of
actions have a double edge, for they can make the performer appear
frivolous. The first such action took place on January 17, 2006, when,
dressed in a Zorro costume, the then head of Jobbik's Child Protection
Cabinet, Attila Bégány, spray-painted "Jobbik Zorro" on the billboard
of a porno bar. On December 6, 2006, dressed as Santa Claus, three
"Kossuth Square" demonstrators close to Jobbik tried to hand birch
twigs to several leading politicians.[17]

By that time, the use of modern communication techniques became a distinguishing feature of the far right. Given that they were

---

16   This subsite is available at https://jobbik.hu/cimkek/ciganybunozes
17   In this case it was almost charming when a member of the Revolutionary National
       Committee, Batu Bakos, said that "they're going to visit public figures dressed as
       Santa Claus, as private individuals, and on that day their action will enjoy the
       support of any organization."

facing a rather hostile media environment and lacking big media outlets, they had to reach their own audience primarily through the Internet, and paper-based publications played but a secondary role. This
was a big change compared to the MIÉP communication, where party
leader István Csurka preferred the huge, lengthy articles in his weekly
Magyar Fórum. Radical and extremist organizations were characterized by a sophisticated use of the Internet, their Web sites were well
designed and regularly updated, and the majority of their actions were
tied to online campaigns. Extremist Web sites were interactive, their
forums well attended, and, from that point, their sympathizers were
considered highly active.

The success of the communication was also because of the
well-elaborated enemy images. The creation of an enemy (image) and
its linguistic construct is an integral part of far-right political messages.
In all cases, the target always represents a noxious issue, a group, or
a specific person, while the accuser always stands for some good (issue, group, or person), establishing its own identity and objectives in
relation to the enemy. The more extreme the organization, the more
specific the identified enemy. In addition to the abstract enemy images
(e.g., left-liberal media, postcommunists) emerging in 2006, labeling
specific groups and individuals as the enemy steadily increased.[18]

Ferenc Gyurcsány and his government were enemy number
one in the eyes of the far right. For the most part, the extremists voiced
abstract, moral criticisms, and the questioning of other government
measures (austerity and reform policies) took only second place. The
main charge was that, with his lies, the prime minister betrayed the
Hungarian people and plunged the country into a moral and economic
crisis. The most commonly used terms demonizing the prime minister

---

[18]   The Conscience '88 Group usually specifies its enemies. A list posted on its
website in December 2006 specifically incited physical violence against
journalists and public figures by name. The *Red Book* published by the shadowy
National Resistance Movement (*Nemzeti Ellenállási* Mozgalom) had a historical
precedent: The *Black Book* was published on June 21, 1936, by the National
Unity Party (*Egységes* Párt) general secretary Béla Marton. The list, containing
612 names, referred to journalists and parliamentary representatives opposed to
the policies of the Gömbös administration.

were mendacious, postcommunist, neoliberal, treasonous, thief, criminal, antidemocratic, and, last but not least, crazy, that is, mentally unstable. In light of the events of the fall, the other major target was Budapest police chief, Péter Gergényi, and the police itself, because of their role in the violent steps against members of the far right in 2006 autumn.

In general, the far-right discourse is characterized by a preponderance of symbolic issues. In 2006, policy issues came in focus only if they neatly dovetailed into some symbolic topic (e.g., association of the health care reform with the extermination of the Hungarian people). In many cases, the expressed demands were related to some muddled constitutional/ideological idea (replace Stalinist constitution with a historical constitution); a conspiracy theory (instead of the Rózsadomb Pact, genuine regime change); real or imagined historical grievances (instead of Trianon borders, Greater Hungary); symbolic dates, locations, and objects (instead of Soviet memorial, Trianon memorial). In 2006, Kossuth Square became a prominent, symbolic location and topic for some far-right groups. In this context, at extremist forums there was a lot of discussion rehashing the events of the fall and the planned modification of the act of assembly.

In general, extremist rhetoric is built on populist premises, expressing distrust of and opposition to the political elite, and makes the assumption that in their political action people are motivated by their instincts and desires. Thus, the traditional concept of the political party—where society is made up of electoral groups constituted around various interests and values—is replaced by categories of "folk," "nation," or "people" that can essentially cover the entire body politic. This is not accidental that Jobbik defined itself as a movement instead of a party. In turn, depending on the context, these concepts can be interpreted at will: it can stand for the "people," as the personification of genuine sovereignty, for the national community, or for the general population (Canovan, 2004). It follows logically that, in most cases, extremist organizations and individuals tend to talk for the people and, as opposed to politicians holding power, identify themselves as "suppressed" civilians. As a result, increasingly various extremist political organizations appropriated and monopolized such expressions gaining currency in Hungarian public discourse as "civil society" and "civil initiative."[19] In another typical expression of a populist attitude, in most cases, extremist demands go hand in hand with a rejection of indirect, representational democratic institutions and promote various instruments of direct democracy (typically, referendum initiatives). As mentioned earlier, after the fall of 2006, on the far right it became fashionable to talk about "genuine democracy." The Kossuth Square demonstrators considered themselves the trustees of "true democracy and the rule of law," and their objectives included "genuine regime change" and the convening of a Constituent National Assembly. However, this was nothing other than a polite expression of the far right's antiestablishment attitude, that is, an attempt at its disguise. In their case, the demand of "genuine" regime change and democracy, and the drafting of a new constitution meant nothing more than the rejection of parliamentary democracy and an attempt at establishing a new political order. Finally, it must be noted that talk on the far right about "citizenship," "democracy," and "citizen action" were tied primarily to street demonstrations. After the fall of 2006, antigovernment demonstrations and protests became regular. For the protester it had the advantage that the media was eager to magnify the smallest street action, although it also carried the danger that with demonstrations becoming a part of daily routine, their relevance gradually decreased, and the media and the public lost interest by the end of the year.

The structural consequences of events in the fall of 2006

In addition to the emergence of new far-right players introducing new communication techniques and becoming nationally known, the fall of 2006 also brought substantial structural changes for the far right. Regular demonstrations on Kossuth Square and turmoil on the streets of

---

[19]   In Hungary, the frequent use of "civil society"–"political society" dichotomy is already an expression of an antiestablishment attitude. As pointed out several times by Miklós Gáspár Tamás in the past few years, the use of the term "civil society" in this sense is incorrect, because political parties (originally opposed to the crown or the government) are the most authentic incarnations of civil society.

downtown Budapest presented part of the Hungarian right as an un-controllable, marginal minority between the ages of 17 and 35, ready to take to the streets and clash with the police for purely symbolic objectives.

While earlier the most relevant organizations tried to reach their goals within the confines of established political institutions, the groups emerging and mobilizing in the fall of 2006 rejected the political system in its entirety, and vaguely expressed a desire to establish some kind of new "national" state order. The Kossuth Square demonstrations quickly lost steam, ran out of ideas, and without a specific action plan, failed to mobilize the entire society. However, the organizational structures of the far right underwent fundamental change. Earlier organizations were mainly characterized by closed, authoritarian, and hierarchical structure, while the reorganized far right started to function within a looser and more flexible framework—like a movement. Instead of attempting to organize and manage the movement subordinated to the needs of the leader or the president, influencing the entire society became the primary objective. There was no longer the need to integrate activists into some kind of organization or movement, thanks to open and regularly updated communication channels, organizational integration was no longer conditioned on a steady flow of information. With this, the networking of the far right got under way.

Crisis of crises: Consolidation of the far right

Following 2006, the political climate underwent fundamental change, greatly contributing to the resurgence of the far right. Of course, the social, political, and cultural constellation and ideological predispositions generating demand for extremist policies did not emerge overnight. On the contrary, events in the years after 2006 brought to the surface and combined latent features that fueled a longing for radical (law and order, prejudicial, and authoritarian) responses in society. Below we shall analyze the crisis of the economy, the government (governance), Roma and non-Roma coexistence and policies countering the far right, as well as media strategies, and finally, the special features of the Orbán system evolving after 2010, although only in the context of a political climate contributing to the consolidation of the far right. A constellation of crisis events combined to deepen society's susceptibility to far-right ideas and messages. "Appropriating" the crisis, radicals successfully build their support base that led to successful electoral results from 2009.

Economic crisis

While the economic crisis definitely did not play a leading role in the emergence of the far right, it helped the process. In Hungary, the economic crisis started as early as 2006, the start of a period characterized by painful austerity measures. The business mood declined sharply already that year. According to the government's original plan and promises, a period of "thaw" was to follow all austerity measures, and from 2008, they hoped to start a new preelection spending cycle— but the economic crisis totally thwarted all these plans. The global economic crisis "spilled over" Hungary later and the electorate was convinced that the wrong economic policies of the previous years were the major contributing factors for the slowdown in 2008–2009. In 2008, the growth of the economy was only 1 percent, and in 2009, the economy contracted by 6 percent. The crisis aggravated society's already existing antigovernment sentiments.

However, the economic crisis expanded far right's scope for action in a number of other ways as well. Crises tend to deepen already existing social differences. Existential fears and the actual loss of social status for many increase dissatisfaction with the entire system (based on general experience, *a sudden rise in unemployment* is one of the best indicators for the resurgence of extremist movements), widening the social base from where radicals may recruit more supporters.

As demonstrated by general and empirical evidence, external threat and related fear in most cases reinforce society's predisposition for authoritarianism and prejudice (Jost, Glaser, Kruglanski, and Sulloway, 2003). As a rule, crises make the policy of "firm hand" more attractive and reinforce the electorate's yearning for "conclusive" solutions devoid of "democratic dithering," something offered by radicals.

At one and the same time, crises confront the electorate with the co-ercive forces of facts and dramatically undermine society's sense of reality. Simultaneously, they make negative utopias (globalization as a form of a final stage) projected by extremists more credible for the general public, reinforce faith in miracles, and rekindle a desire for "positive" utopias' extremists promise to deliver once elected to power. In times of crisis, extremists can often address a broader range of the electorate with "more from less" unfeasible populist promises, which are perceived to have more credibility in their camp because these ideas are never put to the test in a position of power.

Failed crisis management considered as inadequate offers ex-tremist forces an opportunity to consolidate their support and makes society more susceptible to their arguments. Moreover, as a rule, cri-ses restructure the political arena, loosen, shift, or deepen established fault lines, opening the way for new schools of thought, and political players to identify and consolidate their place in the political/ideologi-cal playing field with relative ease. Crises help scapegoating (Glick, 2002): in frustrating situations, the preexisting stereotypes can be eas-ily exploited on an ideological ground, making the "usual suspects"—in Hungary, mainly the Roma and the Jews—responsible for every problem.

Crisis of government—and governance

As demonstrated in the previous chapter, the events of the fall of 2006 (restrictive measures conflicting with campaign promises, the revela-tion of the Őszöd speech,[20] street demonstrations, and the reconstruc-tion of the far right) accelerated the electorate's loss of confidence not

---

[20]   The memory of the Balatonőszöd speech and its widely accepted interpretation in the past few years became a powerful political symbol, part of political discourse. In this sense, as a symbol of lying, the Balatonőszöd speech remained part of public discourse even after Ferenc Gyurcsány's resignation. At the same time, it is a common misunderstanding that support for the coalition established in 2006 and MSZP collapsed due to the leaking of the speech. A rapid loss in popularity occurred already in the summer of 2006 because soon after the elections it became evident that the government was preparing to implement measures contradicting its campaign promises. The Balatonőszöd speech was

only in the government but also in the political elite and its symbol, the democratic institutional system.

The Gyurcsány cabinet's inability to govern efficiently and its crisis management consistently, resulting in bad compromises, only reinforced this trend. All this has made apparent the operational failures and anomalies of state organs (not only of parliament and the government but also those of law enforcement agencies), leaving the population with the impression that a rickety political and state apparatus, often unable to perform even the most elementary functions, is powerless in facing the challenges created by the economic crisis. From the fall of 2006, the voters could see a chronically unstable government. In the following eighteen months, this was clearly demonstrated by the breakup of the coalition of the socialist MSZP and liberal SZDSZ in the spring of 2008, the creation of a minority socialist government, and a change of prime minister in the spring of 2009—for the first time since the regime change.[21] Following a no-confidence motion, Ferenc Gyurcsány was replaced by Gordon Bajnai.

The frequency of personal changes became the most visible sign of the government's instability. In the three years under review, a total of twenty-four ministers were replaced and only three portfolios (national defense, agriculture and rural development, and education and culture) were spared, indicating the weakness of the government in itself. A constant shift in the composition of the government led to structural and organizational changes as well. In the case of some portfolios, it actually prevented the implementation of policy programs and even the drafting of political decisions underlying these programs.

Starting in the spring of 2009, the Bajnai cabinet focused on closing the previous era and the opening of a new political phase, as did the second Gyurcsány cabinet after the 2006 election. The term of

---

leaked only afterward and it came to serve as a permanent point of reference against the prime minister. Eventually, Ferenc Gyurcsány was unable to rebuild his own, his government's, or his party's credibility. There is reason to assume that with better governance and a more effective political agenda from MSZP, the relevance of the Balatonőszöd speech would not have been blown out of all proportion.

[21]   Not calculating with the replacement of József Antall by Péter Boros due to the death of Antall in the first post-transitional parliamentary cycle.

the minority government is also considered to be a failure that cannot be explained with incompetence alone. The minority government enjoyed a parliamentary majority all along, yet it failed when it could not manage to make a clear break with the practices of the previous administration. In other words, the government consistently failed to define its own political agenda, the logic of its decisions, or its political framework, and it was unable to explain its objectives even to its own voters. Consequently, any government measure came to be presented to the public in the context of its potential effect on government stability. The global economic crisis with severe effects on Hungary from the fall of 2008 did not bring a fundamental change—either in a positive or a negative sense—in the government's stability, and, following a temporary period of consolidation, it created a political climate where the issues weakening the government already in the previous years had come to full force.

In this respect, the position of the Bajnai cabinet was hardly better than that of the second Gyurcsány cabinet because, to guarantee a parliamentary majority, the new government continued to be held hostage by the previous era regarding the government's personal composition, structure, and, most importantly, political environment.

The crisis of Roma integration

After 2006, the Roma and non-Roma conflict definitely developed into an urgent social problem, a problem for which the political elite had not found a solution since the regime change and, in fact, had never made a serious attempt to find one.

Following the regime change, the majority of the Roma with steady jobs have lost their employment—mainly as a consequence of the crumbling heavy industry. It was not unique—the same thing happened in other countries of the region as well. While the Roma have already been the most unpopular minority before the transition, their social status has rather declined after the transition. The strong segregation (e.g., in schools) contributed to the concomitant educational deficits of the Roma population. In sectors requiring low-skilled labor (e.g., the heavy and processing industry), economic restructuring resulted in large-scale job losses. Since then, the extremely high rate of unemployment keeps the majority of the Roma in abject poverty (Bernát, n.d.). In addition, relentless social stigmatization and segregation have left the Roma in a pariah status, severely limiting their chances for advancement, increasing the incidence of deviance, and developing strong aversion to the majority population in their ranks. Integration policies, unfortunately, so far failed in practically all countries of the region, and it has also become evident that a welfare policy based on direct assistance cannot be sustained, for it perpetuates the Roma population's dependence on the state, reduces their chances of adapting to the market economy, and reinforces the majority population's bias, viewing the Roma as "parasites." But most importantly, the political will for integrating the Roma has been rather lacking in the political elite. One reason might be that the political elites were afraid this issue can alienate the anti-Roma voters in the majority, while the Roma have never been regarded as an independent voter group that needs to be targeted: they do not go to vote, or if they vote, their votes can be bought up and manipulated (Atlatszo.hu et al., 2015).

There has been pent-up tension for years. While the population's hostility to the Roma remained consistently high and the conflict has been viewed as an important social problem, and the exclusion of the Roma continued to get worse, this issue has been put on the margins in political discourse. Then the ticking bomb exploded as serious social conflict broke to the surface and became a political issue through specific incidents (the 2006 lynching in Olaszliszka, a murder case in Veszprém, and the Miskolc police chief's statistics on crime committed by Roma) in a public climate where the majority of the electorate was in no mood to listen to other than racist and ethnicity-based arguments.

These incidents brought the problem to the limelight in a dramatic manner that provoked a moral panic and prevented any discussion of this complex issue. Instead, it turned the plight of Roma simply into a criminal case. The social conflict on the verge of explosion has been exacerbated mainly due to events unrelated to the economic crisis.

At the same time, the crisis obviously deepened already existing conflicts by reinforcing the general public's predisposition for anti-

Roma messages. The increasing relevance of redistribution issues and rising unemployment intensified social competition, as well as discrimination and citizen chauvinism, assigning the Roma, "barely getting by on assistance" (due to an increasing labor market discrimination), the role of victim and the scapegoat simultaneously. Often, existential fear renders more convincing extremist political rhetoric, blaming the minority for all social problems. Distribution disputes intensifying due to the crisis often take on an ethnic character and find their target in a Roma population in need of state assistance. In the wake of the crisis the cultural divide also deepens, and the majority population's tolerance level declines. With all this, crisis hits especially hard sectors, where at least some of the mostly unskilled Roma population could still find employment (e.g., construction and processing industries). As a consequence, a presumably already high Roma unemployment rate (around 70% in some regions of Hungary) continued to increase, entrenching the Roma's social deprivation and exclusion, further increasing the odds of friction with the majority population.

The Jobbik-Fidesz relationship

Fidesz: Transformation from liberalism to national populism

The history of the Hungarian far right cannot be understood without understanding the main player of the right, Fidesz, since 1997 (Krekó, Juhasz, and Szabados, 2015). Fidesz, defining itself at the time as a radical-liberal alternative youth movement (Bozóki, 2010), emerged at the time of the transition. Whereas at the time the party wished to rise above the right-left/urban-populist/east-west divide, later it takes a diametrically opposite position.

History of the party
The party's right-wing turn to the right began around 1992, but became more spectacular after the dismal performance at the 1994 general election. Essentially, it filled the vacuum left by the Hungarian Democratic Forum, a conservative party that practically collapsed by bearing

the political responsibility of heading the first postcommunist govern-ment between 1990 and 1994. In 1998, Fidesz already returned as a member of a right-wing governing coalition.

While displaying authoritarian and chauvinistic tendencies al-ready in the second half of its term, the first Orbán cabinet pursued conservative policies in an effort to consolidate the position of the mid-dle class and developed a solid social base as a result. With all that, the 2002 general election resulted in the defeat of Fidesz by a narrow margin, and in the subsequent eight years spent in opposition the party increasingly became more radical and populist. As a spectacular move of personalized populism mentioned earlier, after 2002, Orbán (partially following the model of Silvio Berlusconi) started to build a movement called "civic circles"—a movement that is loyal towards him personally and not toward Fidesz (Gyulai et al., 2006; Juhász and Sza-bados, 2006).

Fidesz (Alliance of Young Democrats was the name in the be-ginning) started as a generational party that mainly attracted young urban intellectuals. But after 1994, the party was quite successful in gradually building itself up as a classical popular party in the sense that they were able to gain voters from every segment of the society. Especially after 2006, when several former socialist voters started to gravitate to Fidesz, the party's voter base almost lost its sociological characteristics. But as for the core electorate of the party, they are the middle-aged (thirty to fifty), mainly better-off people from the country-side. As we can traditionally observe in the case of right-wing parties in Hungary, Fidesz is stronger in the small villages than in big cities, and they are stronger in the western part of the country than on the east.

Party leadership
From the very beginning, Fidesz has been under the control of its char-ismatic leader, Viktor Orbán, who, after eliminating the party's liberal wing in 1993, became the undisputed leader of Fidesz. The election defeats in 2002 and 2006 notwithstanding, Orbán never lost his lead-ing position and continued to make key decisions even when formally the position of party president was filled by someone else. Since the

party's 2003 highly centralized structural reform, his dominant position has been essentially unchallenged. Fidesz was highly successful in keeping and broadening its voter base and changing their attitudes, as well as deliberately reshaping the political cleavages in Hungary to their own benefit (Enyedi, 2005).

Place within the party system

The Fidesz core voter base, estimated to consist of around 1.2–1.5 million people, is also held together by the political affiliation to Orbán personally. The majority of these voters are middle aged and belong to the middle class with right-wing values. At the same time, to some extent due to a surge in the number of supporters, the Fidesz camp is becoming "older" and the party became more popular among less educated and poorer segments of the population (Enyedi, Fábián, and Tardos, 2014), even as the party continues to embrace the strengthening of the middle class, and its policies deliberately hurt those at the bottom of the social ladder.

Fidesz's current position in the party system is the result of the "central political power field" proclaimed by Viktor Orbán. In essence, Fidesz has a vested interest in maintaining a relatively strong Jobbik on one side, and an equally large, but fragmented left on the other side, where, standing in the middle, Fidesz may set itself up against its rivals as the only force capable of governing, while protest votes are split between the far right and the left—"the extremes on both sides," as Orbán is calling them.

At the same time, a relatively strong Jobbik is also important for Fidesz because it allows it to present itself domestically and abroad as the only guarantee for democracy, preventing the far right from capturing executive power. And finally, there's a third reason for this peculiar Fidesz-Jobbik relationship, namely that Fidesz uses Jobbik as a shield. Its ideas, barely different from those of Jobbik, have been usually expressed in more brutal language by Jobbik, allowing the governing party to present itself as the champion of moderation in comparison.

After the left suffered a catastrophic defeat in the 2010 election and essentially imploded, and transition parties disappeared into the wastebasket of history for good, the Orbán system, based on Fidesz's two-thirds parliamentary majority, could embark on its program unhindered. Among others, the second Orbán cabinet tried to distinguish itself from its predecessors by abandoning the so-called neoliberal economic and social policies of previous years (characterized by austerity measures and the International Monetary Fund conditions) and, instead, moved to consolidate the role of the state.

Moreover, to prepare the ground for the most efficient realization of its central-power objectives, it systematically curtailed the rule of law that, incidentally, has never taken deep roots in Hungary. The policy has never been unpopular among the majority of the electorate; since the regime change a number of Hungarian and international comparative studies found a strong demand for paternalism on the part of the Hungarian public (Molnár and Krekó, 2010). The majority of Hungarians are disappointed with the market economy and the political system established following the transition and have no confidence in state institutions, while demanding a strong state. Taking a cue from these social attitudes and perceptions, Viktor Orbán built his policy on the foundations of an ideology whose component parts are an almost perfect fit of Fareed Zakaria's (2014) description of Putinism, that is, nationalism, religion, social conservatism, state capitalism, and a media controlled by government. Following the Putin model, "Orbanism," steeped in Hungarian national ideology, defines the nation, the people, the governing side, and the state as a single concept, while for all problems it blames liberalism and liberal democracy, whose institutions never worked properly in Hungary.

Regarding the position of the EU and its values, Fidesz has a contradictory position: while Fidesz's politicians, especially on the domestic level, are frequently using Euroskeptic rhetoric that are making their position more similar to that of the parties in the Euroskeptic European Conservative and Reformist group (or sometimes even more radical like Nigel Farage's European Freedom and Direct Democracy or Marine Le Pen's ENF) in the EP, Fidesz's MEPs are sitting in the European People's Party [EPP]. The European politicians of Fidesz are obviously playing a "moderating" role in Fidesz's policies, eminently following the mainstream line of the group in most of the cases.[22] While Fidesz is a valuable partner of the EPP because of its considerable size (they delegated eleven MEPs to the EP in 2014), and leaders of EPP are officially supporting Fidesz in every sense, Fidesz is facing—sometimes harsh—criticism on the European level from conservative political players as well because of the "illiberal" transformation of the Hungarian political system, ignoring political norms and strong ties between Orbán and Putin.

Ideology and international models: EU and the East
Conceivably, Viktor Orbán and Fidesz embarked on this path purely for pragmatic reasons, but by now they appear to have been entrapped by their own ideology. In its thinking the current Hungarian right stands firmly on an antiliberal foundation: it promotes national collectivism and maintains the primacy of the national community over the individual, and it advocates strong government intervention in economic, social, and cultural affairs. Viktor Orbán's 2014 speech at Baile Tusnád, generating a great deal of attention, reflected the same ideas when he talked about building an "illiberal state" in positive terms (Tóth, 2014). All this can be taken as an anti-West stance if one assumes that the West stands for a comprehensive system of civilizing values and ideas giving preference to individualism instead of collectivism, liberal democracy instead of unlimited state powers, and freedom instead of bureaucratic order. Orbán received the intellectual inspiration from the work of Gyula Tellér, an ideologue around Orbán famous for his radical, nationalistic, anti-individualistic thoughts, who has elaborated his theory before the 2014 elections (Tellér, 2014).

Incidentally, Fidesz's prominent opinion makers and ideologists do not represent a unified front on all issues, they cannot be put in neat categories, and their thinking affects the entire right, including Jobbik. In addition to specific antiliberal traditions of Hungarian national ideology, the theorists themselves are beholden to international antiliberal and antimodernization tendencies.

With respect to its relationship to the EU, Fidesz believes it can continue to build its illiberal state pursuing a shuttlecock policy within a framework provided by Western civilization and the EU. At the same

---

[22]   See, for example, Votewatch's statistics in this regard.

time, far-right Jobbik harbors even more misgivings about Hungary's ties to the West than Fidesz. It would keep the country in the EU only if the integration of Europe followed its own script.

Apologists of the Orbán system also attempt to justify the alleged corruption cases as simply a means of redistributing positions of economic and political power, openly defined—often by the prime minister himself—as giving preference to "national big business" at the expanse of "global/foreign big business" (see also Tellér [2014] for a nice example of the ideological justification of corruption). While earlier governments were in the habit of intervening in the economy to satisfy the Hungarian public's penchant for state dependence and paternalism, the second Orbán cabinet is primarily motivated by the desire to redistribute assets (to the clientelist structures) and consolidate its own economic and political positions. Accordingly, government decisions are typically the result of weighing power and political interests, while policy considerations are given short shrift. This also means that in the longer term the Orbán system will be unable to resolve or manage economic and social problems. Since 2010, social inequality has grown at an unprecedented rate since the regime change (Kopasz et al., 2013), with poverty becoming deeper and more prevalent. In the social sense, only some Fidesz's supporters can be considered winners of the system, which means that rising political discontent can only be held in check by steering losers in the direction of political apathy. In the past years, Fidesz's policies were successful in this, while the party (if not completely) managed to hold on to a large part of its support base. True, it was also helped by the weakness of the opposition that, preoccupied with its internal conflicts and the struggle to rebuild the left, has failed to substantially improve its position.

As Fidesz's leaders were always perceiving a hostile media environment that surrounds the party, Fidesz was always very conscious in building up its media background, both in opposition (between 1994 and 1998, and 2002 and 2010) and on government (1998–2002 and 2010). The strong media background definitely helped Fidesz's election in 2010 and reelection in 2014. While this media background of Fidesz seemed to be extremely stable and strong, after the 2014 elections Fidesz seems to lose a lot of its former media due to the harsh conflicts between Prime Minister Viktor Orbán and the most important former oligarch behind Fidesz, Lajos Simicska, who directly or indirectly owns a lot of the media on the right. The outcome of this conflict is hard to predict, but it definitely undermines Orbán's media positions and image.

Dismantling of liberal democracy and the central field of force

After the left was roundly defeated and essentially collapsed following the 2010 parliamentary election, and the successor parties active around the regime change were consigned to the dustbin of history for good, with Fidesz's two-thirds parliamentary majority the Orbán system went to work unhindered. Among others, the new government tried to distinguish itself from its predecessors, for years describing their economic and social policies as "neoliberal," by consolidating state powers and curtailing the rule of law (never deeply ingrained in Hungarian society) in order to guarantee the most effective enforcement of the central will. The wish to create a "strong state" in the sense advocated in Jobbik's program was also a response by the new government to an electoral demand for law and order expressed with elemental force. Simultaneously, by necessity such a policy raised a lot of conflict (with students, trade unions, teachers, health care workers, among the many). But Fidesz managed to handle the problem rather effectively using a variety of power tactics and political instruments: mainly turning the public opinion against the group that is protesting.

The government followed a "protectionist neoliberal" economic policy line, simultaneously cutting taxes (and introducing a flat tax) and welfare costs (offering public work instead of benefits). At the same time, Orbán reduced the utility-cost cuts in a highly interventionist, populist, but very popular move. Concurrently, it tried to secure continued state revenues and balance the budget without directly taxing the population by imposing higher contributions on some sectors of the economy where the "extra profit" is created, such as the retail chain sector (or its parts owned by multinational companies), the banking pharmaceutical sector, the energy sector, and the telecommunications sector. While state intervention in the economy has never been negligible in Hungary, in this context, there was a qualitative jump after

2010. Thanks to Fidesz's two-thirds parliamentary majority, the entire state apparatus came under the control of interest groups lined up behind the governing party and, for all practical purposes, practical all control mechanisms over the government have been eliminated from the political system. In other words, the phenomenon defined by Transparency International as "state capture" cannot be described simply in terms of corruption, but rather as a new form of intervention in the business sector.[23] But the solutions the government used to favor "people" against the big business, inspired by Jobbik, proved to be really popular.

The Orbán cabinet used nationalist rhetoric in an effort to justify the redistribution of economic and political assets in a number of areas, openly describing its policy (often by the prime minister himself) as giving preference to "national big business" at the expense of "global and foreign-owned big business." This rhetoric, practically justifying endemic corruption, is extremely popular among right-wing voters, which also explains Fidesz's continued popularity in the face of all the scandals following the redistribution of specific sectors of the economy. By all appearances, the rhetoric also worked even as many of the measures do not neatly fit the clash between "national and foreign capital" narrative.

Whereas earlier governments' redistribution policies intervening in the economy were motivated by a desire to satisfy Hungarian society's state dependence and the electorate's longing for paternalism, the second Orbán administration was mainly motivated by redistribution aimed at consolidating its own economic and political power base. Accordingly, government decisions are typically based on power and political interests, while relevant policy considerations are pushed to the background.

The Orbán administrations' main goal is not to manage single long-term economic or social problems. Following 2010, social inequality increased by a rate unprecedented since the regime change

---

[23] The phenomenon is defined by Bálint Magyar as "mafia state." See Magyar, B. (2016). *Hungarian Octopus—Post-communist Mafia State*. 1st ed. Budapest: Noran.

(Kopasz et al., 2013),[24] while poverty increased and deepened. The health care sector is in a catastrophic state, and the results on the Programme for International Student Assessment (PISA) test have reached an all-time low by 2016. At the national level, only a part of Fidesz's supporters can be considered to be among the winners (practically the higher middle-class families), which means that a rising disappointment in politics can be avoided only if the "losers" of the regime are steered toward political apathy. In the past few years, Fidesz conducted a successful policy on this front, which was also indicated by declining turnout rates in elections. Of course, Orbán's regime was helped by the weakness of the opposition that, preoccupied with its internal conflicts and the struggle to rebuild the left, has failed to substantially improve its position.

But the main reason for the success of Orbán is not the change in the constitutional order, but its ability to maintain the underlying balance of political power. In this context, the "central political force" strategy plays a crucial role. In essence, Fidesz has a vested interest in maintaining a relatively strong Jobbik on one side and an equally large, but fragmented left on the other side, where, standing in the middle, Fidesz may set itself up against its rivals as the only force capable of governing, while protest votes are split between the far right and the left. Given that in 2014 parliamentary elections, Fidesz could make a two-thirds parliamentary majority again while receiving less than half of the votes, it is easy to see that this tripolar political field is very helpful in the mixed Hungarian electoral system to keep the power.

At the same time, a relatively strong Jobbik is also important for Fidesz because it allows it to sell itself abroad as the only guarantee preventing the far right from capturing executive power. And finally, there's a third reason for this peculiar Fidesz-Jobbik relationship, namely that Fidesz uses Jobbik as a shield. Its ideas, barely different from those of Jobbik, are expressed in more brutal language by Jobbik, allowing the governing party to present itself as the champion of

---

24   GINI: Growing Inequalities' Impact http://www.tarki.hu/en/research/gini/, http://gin i-research.org/articles/political_and_cultural_impacts_analysis. Country report: http://gini-research.org/system/uploads/448/original/Hungary.pdf?1370090544

moderation in comparison. In other words, while Fidesz adopts and implements parts of Jobbik's program, it confronts with the party increasingly, labelling it as extreme. At the same time, especially since the refugee crisis, Fidesz moved towards more radical policy positions (making the fence at the Southern border of Hungary, erected by the Orbán-government in 2015–2016, the main symbol of their governance), and also, is using a more militant language against its enemy images, such as the refugees, George Soros, or Brussels. For example, the Hungarian police formed a "border hunter" group of volunteers in 2015 with the goal to "defend" the border from refugees. The government launched a billboard campaign against George Soros in summer 2017. And the main message against Brussels was given when in September 2017 the government stated in reaction to the European Court of Justice, the EU's top court, dismissal of the refugee complaint of Hungary and Slovakia that "the fight has just began" (see Figure 8). At the same time, Jobbik tries to resign from the use of militant language.

Figure 8:   **An advertisement for police and a Facebook meme of Fidelitas (Fidesz's youth branch)**
Upper: "Be a Border Hunter—Duty, Service, Career".
(Source: police.hu, 2016)
Lower (from 2014): "Betrayal of Brussels—the real fight has just begun!" (Fidelitas, 2017)

Jobbik's strategic shift:
From extreme to mainstream ("cute campaign")

As we mentioned earlier, the self-definition of Jobbik traditionally was the "national radical." As an interesting, but internationally not unprecedented effort, Jobbik gradually started to dilute the second part of its self-definition: Radicalism. International models for such campaign were FN, the French far-right party, and the Serbian Progressive Party (*Srpska napredna stranka*), a splinter of the Radical Party (*Srpska radikalna stranka*) of Vojislav Seselj that is currently governing Serbia. Lot of far-right parties in Europe made moderate shifts with political success.

This change became the most spectacular on the 2014 parliamentary election campaign. While Jobbik's campaigns in 2010 were characterized by a dark tone and sharp messages on "Gipsy crime," "politician crime," and "parasites," by the second half 2012, Jobbik started to reposition itself from a "bad" party to a "good" party. The 2014 parliamentary campaign, in stark contrast with the 2010 campaign (see Figure 9 for illustration), was characterized by positive messages such as "The future cannot be stopped," colorful billboards looking like Benetton advertisements, and pictures of the party leader Gábor Vona with heart-shaped messages, dogs, and pets. The tone of the party's messages has been softened as well, with a shift from the racist, anti-Gipsy, and anti-Semitic statements to the more mainstream messages of improving living standards, creating jobs, and improving education.

Figure 9:   Official campaign billboards of Jobbik.
             (Source: Jobbik.hu)
             Upper (from 2010): "People's verdict: 20 years for 20
             years. Impeachment! Jobbik—with clean power
             Lower (from 2014): "The future cannot be stopped!
             Jobbik—already the most popular among youngsters

As Hungarian voters have become less angry since 2010, this moderate shift helped Jobbik greatly at the 2014 April parliamentary elections (where the turnout was 62%) to target a broader audience—and
especially undecided voters. Also, it helped them in 2015 to gain their
first individual constituency in Tapolca, with the ex-neo-Nazi candidate
presenting himself as a serious politician, dealing with mainstream
problems. On the other hand, it seems that the "softening" clearly did
not help the party to mobilize its core supporters in the EP elections,
where the turnout was extremely low, only 29 percent.

In the EP campaign in June 2014, Jobbik shifted toward being a soft Euroskeptic party, from a hard Euroskeptic one whose vice president burned an EU flag at a rally only two years ago. Jobbik did everything to avoid being successfully stigmatized as "extreme" in public debates before the EP election. As a consequence, Jobbik was the least successful in bringing the voters who supported to the ballot boxes. What's more, looking at the regional distribution of the votes, it seems that Jobbik failed most notably to mobilize its voters in its core constituencies in Eastern Hungary. Also, this moderation strategy seems to rather be an obstacle for growth in the political climate after the refugee crisis, when the Fidesz-led government could exploit the rising antirefugee sentiments.

While Jobbik has softened its public position in several issues (using less anti-Gipsy and anti-Semitic rhetoric, following the EU-mainstream, etc.), part of this (highly ambivalent and contradictory) moderation strategy was to sideline political opponents. The most important step in this effort was the party congress in 2016 that was both characterized by the moderation strategy, both by the denial of softening.

Do you think I am behaving cute, when I am visiting the houses of the gypsies during the night? Have we become too soft? Not even in the bed! (Magyar, 2015). It was a sentence from the speech of the reelected vice president of Jobbik, Tamás Sneider, the ultranationalist party in Hungary on this party congress in 2016 May. Tamás Sneider, nicknamed "Roy" beforehand, is well known for his ex-skinhead past. He beat up a Roma with his mates back in 1992, for which he was found guilty and received a suspended sentence in jail (Hetek.hu, 2014). Now, besides his party obligations, he serves an important public office as well: he is the vice speaker of the parliament. His remark about "softness" is about rejecting the widespread criticism from the rank and files of the party that the leaders, especially President Gábor Vona, are betraying the original principles of Jobbik by shifting it to the center for mere political opportunism.

What is quite atypical, though, is that the very person that represented the extremist line of a party wants to push it in the moderate direction. Gábor Vona, who is posing with children, cats, and dogs to improve his image (see Figure 10), has been the president of Jobbik since 2006. He headed Jobbik when it was an unquestionably anti-Gipsy, anti-Semitic, racist party. He invented the Hungarian Guard, a paramilitary wing of Jobbik back in 2007, which is aimed at recruiting supporters with marches on the countryside to "defend the majority from the Gipsy crime." The organization has been banned by the Hungarian courts.

Figure 10: **Pictures from Gábor Vona's Facebook page, expressing the new image of the party**

The changes in the leadership revealed well the contradictions. Occupying the center looks a wise move when the Hungarian government is shifting more and more to the right, becoming a genuine radical-right party. But it is a difficult exercise for a party with such an extremist past and membership. Beside Tamás Sneider, László Toroczkai, a very well-known figure of the Hungarian extreme right, was also elected as vice president with almost 80 percent of the votes. He led the siege of the building of the public television back in 2006, still serving as the honorary leader of violent extremist movements, and since then, announced a ban of entrance for gay and Muslims in the village he is leading as a mayor: Ásotthalom. While Vona sidelined one of his important challengers within the party, Előd Novák, expelling him from the chair of the vice president parliamentary group as well, this was much at least as much about punishment for the lack of loyalty then breaking with extremism.

But at the same time, Jobbik keeps its extremism to some municipal-level policies, that were formerly mentioned as "laboratoires of governance". In some Jobbik-held municipalities such as Ózd and Tiszavasvári, there is a tendency for "scapegoat-based policy-making", mainly targeting the Roma, such as denying social benefits from households that are not keeping their environment tidy and surveillance of public workers with cameras. For a while, Jobbik supported Orosz Mihály Zoltán, a prominent extremist figure and mayor of Érpatak who drew attention when he symbolically hanged the effigies of Simon Peres and Benjamin Netanyahu in protest of the Gaza War. Orosz Mihály Zoltán is an admirer of arrowcross leader Ferenc Szálasi and introduced municipality policies based on the dichotomy between the "builders" and "destroyers". László Toroczkai, the mayor of Ásotthalom and vice president of Jobbik, formed a "migrant-hunter" militia and introduced a plan to ban Muslims and gay people from his village in 2016. These phenomena are difficult to fit into the image of the party shifting towards a more moderate position—and sharpen the conflict between the center and the periphery (Kovarek- Róna-Hunyadi-Krekó, in press).

Generally, in his political moves, Vona learned a lot from an important political master in Hungary—even if his current moves point to another direction. Last year, he told in an interview:

> In Hungarian politics, the only person you can learn from is Orbán. I do not demonize him as the left does, I am watching what he is doing and see what I can implement in my policies instead (Panyi, 2015).

Vona, as it was mentioned, before establishing Jobbik in 2003, was a member of Viktor Orbán's so-called Civic circle, the network of loyal groups to his policies that later became the recruitment basis of the radical right as well. The quick ideological shift, the centralization of the party, the way of demonstratively sidelining challengers, and alienating party members with questionable loyalty—these are all moves from Orbán's cookbook. With these tools, back to the 1990s, Orbán turned Fidesz from a radical-liberal party to a conservative popular party. Vona now wants to turn Jobbik to a conservative popular party as well—from a radical ultranationalist party. And he has been doing it with unquestionable success. Jobbik is not the same extremist party in the eyes of the voters than it was. Partially because of it, Jobbik could gain more than 20 percent of the votes on the 2014 national election, has almost twenty municipalities, and gained an individual constituency on an interim election in 2015. Jobbik became the most popular opposition party, enjoying the support of about one-fourth of the active electorate. These successes made Vona self-confident, and he practically revealed his strategy in a surprisingly sincere text on his Facebook page in 2016 August (Vona, 2016a), where he said that "I gave the spirit for Jobbik, and I take it away now," in order to make the party a ripe, mature adult party from an adolescent, and to make it "spiriting for the whole national community."

But strangely, unlike its European counterparts, the refugee crisis broke Jobbik's political momentum. In most European countries, including Germany, Austria, France, Sweden, and Slovakia, the far right has been able to capitalize on the refugee crisis, while popularity of mainstream parties has been shrinking. In Hungary, it was just the opposite. As a consequence of Orbán's successful antirefugee campaign and measures (including erecting the fence that reduced the number of refugees from thousands a day to practically zero), Orbán could occupy the "savior of the nation" role, leaving no air for Jobbik. The irony is that currently Jobbik, unlike, for example, Alternative for Germany (*Alternative für Deutschland*) or FPÖ in Austria, is much more interested in a more moderate political environment, to be able to challenge the government in policy and corruption issues.

The interaction between the two parties

As Figure 11[25] on the first parliamentary term of Jobbik indicates, Jobbik and Fidesz have a rather inverse support: when the popularity of Fidesz is on the rise, Jobbik starts to decline, and vice versa. It also suggests that traditionally, Jobbik and Fidesz target the same, or very overlapping, voter base.

Figure 11:   Support for Fidesz and Jobbik

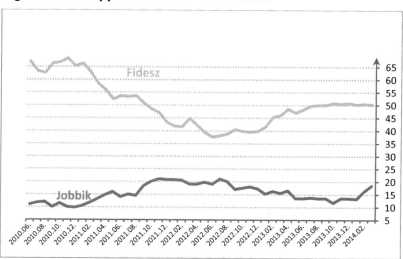

Experts do not usually mention corruption as a driving force behind Jobbik's rise, and nationalism is another factor that cannot be considered as such. In terms of nationalism, in certain cases, Fidesz even

---

[25]   This figure indicates the percentages as a percentage of committed voters with party preferences. Average of data from Ipsos, Medián, Századvég, and Tárki.

managed to go further than the far-right party. As a result of nationalist feelings being suppressed under communism (Pirro, 2015, p. 37), some form of ultranationalism is present in the policies of mainstream Central Eastern European parties, which restricts the political space available to far-right parties. After the conservative turn of Fidesz, MIÉP steadfastly lost its support as a result of the party taking over the topics of MIÉP and despite the fact that the same strategy did not work against Jobbik, Fidesz was still identified as the party "most dedicated to strengthening national identity" by voters (Pytlas, 2015, p. 168). Euroskepticism is also a factor that does not carry a strong influence on Jobbik's success, as this is generally a trait of the far right not shared by the population they claim to represent (von Beyne cited in Minkenberg, 2015, p. 22). The basic assumption is that populist radical-right parties may be able to change the "normative boundaries of the system; challenge the ideological and symbolic aspects of the system or the rules of the game; or even introduce new patterns of political competition" (Pirro, 2015, p. 119). The radical right has an influence on the agenda-setting and policy-making of their respective countries (Minkenberg, 2015). Mudde (2007) examined the far right's policies in local government and found that they emphasize symbolism, meaning that they rename public spaces and roads; they display national symbols wherever possible; and, in the case of Hungary, they might set up street name plates with runic writing.

At the national level, Jobbik unquestionably had an effect on Fidesz's policies. The governing party has moved toward an antiminority stance since 2010 (Pirro, 2015, p. 131). This is reflected in, for example, their welfare policies, as they realized Jobbik's 2010 election manifesto in this area by tying the acquisition of welfare benefits to participation in the public work program. The nationalization of private pension funds and the financial pressure exerted on multinational companies were also introduced as a result of pressure coming from Jobbik (Pirro, 2015, p. 141), and June 4 became a public holiday because of the influence of the far right as well.

Jobbik's worldview

While the social, institutional, and political environment laying the foundation for the resurgence of the far right is important, the most important factor has possibly been Jobbik's policy serving as an effective tool in channeling and articulating tendencies outlined earlier to its own advantage. Jobbik was very conscious in the way it builds up its politics, voter base, and messages (Bíró and Róna, 2011). Considering Jobbik's political agenda, three factors are considered particularly relevant: (1) The symbolic power of the party's ideology and rhetoric, (2) the successful exploitation of the far-right camp's "civic" self-organization as opposed to party politics, and (3) the appropriation of the Roma issue. Aside from integrating the entire far-right support base, all this allowed Jobbik to address voters either disappointed in or always having kept a distance from parliamentary parties.

Intellectual background: Conspiracies everywhere

The intellectual background of today's Hungarian far right (and essentially that of the mainstream right) is fundamentally based on European modernism-criticism of the 1920s and 1930s, as well as its rehashed and updated interpretation. As the period's dominant intellectual current, this criticism runs the gamut from Marxism through *Mein Kampf's* radical racism. One of the earliest and definitely the most effective works adopted by the right is Oswald Spengler's *The Decline of the West*, whose main argument is that the development of cultures emerging throughout history is not linear, but rather a succession of birth, development, decline, and fall. The two other significant authors, René Guénon and Julius Evola, agree with Spangler when it comes to the criticism of modernism and the decline of the West. They also describe the history of cultures, including that of the West, as a form of cyclical evolution moving, through a process of degeneration, from an original or early natural or normal state toward chaos, alienation, abject materialism, and spiritual impoverishment.

The two were strongly attracted to esotericism and mythology, to a contrast between East and West, and holding up the East as an example, where, and in as much as, the social organizing power and tradition of spiritualism are preserved. In their view, Western civilization driven by the rationalism of Enlightenment pursues the delusion of "progress." However, the path followed by the West represents the renunciation of the intellect, spiritualism, and the community.

While we cannot say that Jobbik in general is a fascist party, some theoreticians of the fascist criticism of modernity definitely found their way to Jobbik's ideology. The major theoretician of Italian neofascism, Julius Evola, is all the more relevant because Gábor Vona wrote the preface to the Hungarian edition of his work, *A Manual for Nationalist Youth*. In the preface, Vona writes:

> The true right should not emerge as a weaker and increasingly contaminated backlash to the left, but as an autonomous action (...) The goal is a pure right build on the foundation of universal Tradition. This requires a deep intellectual immersion. Genuine right-wing action is not spontaneous and uncontrolled, and its true strategy must be preceded by a thorough philosophical and spiritual quest (Evola, 2012, p. 8).

He goes on to write:

> The general understanding of modern political philosophy notwithstanding, intellectual openness and an entrepreneurial spirit are definitely not leftist, but rightist attitudes, and therefore we can comfortably call it proto-right because, if an appropriate open-mindedness is accompanied with proper intellect, a rightists spirit can be the only result (Evola, 2012, p. 10).

In other words, Jobbik's president associates values, openness, turning to the future, activism, and will power to rightist ideology—especially compared to the left showing signs of exhaustion—that may hold attraction for politically active youth.

In today's Hungary, László Bogár is the most prominent representative of the school of thought opposed to modernism. He, along with Gyula Tellér (one of Viktor Orbán's advisers), is considered an important opinion leader and theoretician in Jobbik and Fidesz circles. Between 1998 and 2002, Bogár was political state secretary in the Prime Minister's Office, and Tellér's colleague advisor. Later, he slightly distanced himself from Fidesz, although after 2010 he was offered a position of lecturer at the National University of Public Service (*Nemzeti Közszolgálati Egyetem*) and, as a public figure, he is regularly present in Hungarian political discourse. Bogár believes that globalization is not simply a dead end of civilization, but a plot executed along the principles of a globalizing ideology, and he recommends the development of a counterforce offering national protection. This would be based on some kind of sacral national "mode of being" in opposition to the tenets of Enlightenment, which, however, he has never spelled out in detail. The alternatives he offers have few contacts to reality, and instead they represent some kind of theoretical construct attempting to offer a different narrative of the world. Bogár believes that those responsible for regime change delivered Hungary to pro-globalization forces in the West, and subsequently the local political representatives of a comprador-bourgeoisie serving these powers came mostly from the ranks of the liberals, that is, SZDSZ, the party that had lost all its parliamentary seats in 2010 and was later dissolved. Bogár's paranoid antiliberalism is well illustrated by his belief that the disappearance of SZDSZ is just a ruse, because the "background power," which lately he has come to refer to as "global SZDSZ," or "ancient SZDSZ," is bent on bleeding Hungary dry. By now, Bogár's thinking is dominated by all but incomprehensible conspiracy theories. Today, he interprets Hungary's history going back 150 years in terms of the machinations of a 'global SZDSZ'.

Bogár's conspiracy theories return in the most vulgar and sensational form in János Drábik's ideas (see, for example, Drábik, 2005). He emigrated from Hungary in the era of state socialism and, after failing to make a career in the United States, he returned to Hungary as a journalist following the regime change and has essentially become a full-time U.S. hater and hawker of conspiracy theories. His books and Internet postings have ardent followers, primarily on the far right. According to Drábik, Jews created Freemasonry that, in turn, created the United States. He believes that the world is governed by secret plots. In a political sense, Drábik no longer has anything in common with Hungary's governing party, and even Jobbik's ideology relies on him less and less. However, his relevance lies in the fact that he is popular, that his ideas influence more people than either Bogár's or Tellér's. Both Bogár and Drábik were frequent guests at Jobbik's campaign rallies in the last few years, while they seem to be supportive toward Fidesz as well.

Finally, one has to mention the Russian theoretician Aleksandr Dugin receiving increasing attention in Hungarian far-right intellectual circles, whose thinking is characterized by strong anti-West and antiliberal ideas. One knows from Gábor Vona himself that Dugin's theories have great influence on his thinking. In 2013, the Jobbik president gave a lecture at Moscow's Lomonosov University at the conference, *Russia and Europe—Geopolitics in the 21st Century*, organized by Dugin. At the conference, he gave a strong criticism of the United States and stated: "The future of Europe is tied to Russia, Turkey and Germany, and thus he believes good relationships must be developed with these countries." "You must save Europe" was his message to the Russians, and he expressed a desire to join a future Eurasian Union. One year later, Vona had the following to say on the same subject: *For me Euroasianism means that Hungary could act as some kind of mediator between Europe and Asia* (Kocsis, 2014). Vona Gábor mentions Dugin's Fourth Theory as one of the most important books (Vona, 2013).

Jobbik's ideology

As illustrated by the diversity of the intellectual background of the political agenda of today's Hungarian far right, it would be a mistake to think that Jobbik simply stands for a neo-Nazi ideology, even if the party is often superficially labeled as such. The situation is more complex than that, and it was so even before the party's moderate shift. In reality, in a descriptive sense, Jobbik can barely be described in national-socialist terms for it comes from a different tradition: from the European tradition of modernism-criticism and, with respect to local precedents, mainly from an indigenous Hungarian nationalist and racist tradition. Looking at its ideology, Jobbik has increasingly become a new type of far-right party gradually moving to the center, which has its variations all over Europe, all characterized by antiestablishment attitudes, Euroskepticism, ethnocentrism, and the appropriation of locally popular topics (the Roma issue in Hungary). In addition, anti-Semitism, serving as some kind of world explanation in the party's ideology, is another specific, East European feature characterizing Jobbik. Jobbik, from the very beginning, is much more a neopopulist political organization than a neofascist one (Tamás, 2007).

The ideology of the Hungarian far right is traditionally the antithesis of liberalism, and Jobbik followed this line from the very beginning. In the words of Gábor Vona who said a few years ago, *When the time comes, we have to air the rotten smell of liberalism* (Origo.hu, 2013), at *European liberalism is the grave-digger of Europe* (jobbik.hu, 2015). The Hungarian far right has a nationalist collectivist worldview, where the individual is pushed to the background, and individualism is the incarnation and fulfillment of man's inherent fallibility. Also, "aliens" and social groups failing to live up to the expectations of an idealized community must endure disadvantages. As a result, far-right thinking embraces ethnic exclusion, to a certain extent social Darwinism, chauvinism, and xenophobia, often expressed in paranoia against minorities (especially the Jews) and welfare chauvinism. At the same time, it has an essentially universal antiglobalism, as globalization is connected to openness and diversity to be important values. The contrast between the liberal ideology and the ideology of the Hungarian far right (sharing the general features of the European populist radical right) is summarized in Table 9.

Table 9:　A comparison of liberal and far-right value systems

Main components	Liberal ideology	The ideology of the Hungarian far right (collective nationalism)
What stands in the center?	The individual	The nation
What is your concept of man?	Man is good by nature	Man is evil by nature
What is the highest value?	Freedom	Order
What is the ideal society like?	Inclusive	Exclusive
What is the ideal state like?	Minimal	Strong/Total
What makes a community better?	Competition	Unity

The pessimistic anthropological premise in the Hungarian far right's political thinking represents an extreme version of classical conservatism's concept of man—the one that we can read in several works, from Hobbes until Evola. Accordingly, individual man is fallible, weak, selfish, in fact, immoral and wicked. He has no rational understanding of his own interests, and on his own he is frail and unable to survive. And fallible man needs a context that provides security and the prospect for meaningful life, the family at the micro level and, in most cases, a presumably organic national community at the macro level. In other words, the individual is saved from his weaknesses and errors by the family offering security and stability, a microenvironment representing society's smallest and most fundamental unit. On the other hand, the national community provides the broadest context for human life, a concept that most far-right thinking believes with quasi-religious fervor and places it in the center of its worldview.

In the constitutional sense, the existing form of the national community is the nation-state, which on the far right is held in opposition to "globalism," conceived of as some sort of secret plot. A fetishized nation-state creates a secure environment and stability through the maintenance of order, postulated as the highest value. Also, the nation-state is the best tool in the eyes of the Hungarian far right to save the Hungarian community from its enemies. Márton Gyöngyösi, the foreign policy leader of Jobbik, summarized it in an interview the following way:

> The socialist governments (…) are clearly and obviously go against the national idea, and for them it almost does not matter if it is the bolshevist internationalism or the American neoliberal globalism that is pushing down the national ideology. The main thing for them is that the nation-state has to die or at least become a subordinate to a power above the nations (Alfahir.hu, 2014).

According to this worldview, under ideal conditions the state wields strong power over economic, social, and political developments, something essential for the maintenance of order, and this always enjoys primacy over individual freedoms, for these, in this mind frame, may lead to chaos, to uncontrolled consumption, and eventually to the destruction of all human values. To avoid all these pitfalls, a functioning community needs unity. Competition, or simply pluralism, destabilizes politics, the economy, culture, and society, and breaks down order. The constant reference to "unity" as the only indicator of the strength of a community, though, is a typical feature not only in Jobbik's communications but in Viktor Orbán's statements as well.

The Hungarian far right, like most of its European counterparts, holds strong anticapitalist views and is often hostile to market economy and economic competition. This is also deeply connected to the Hungarian anti-Semitic tradition. One of the reasons is that the emergence of modern-day anti-Semitism in Hungary in the last third of the nineteenth century was closely tied to a rejection of capitalism, scapegoating triggered by economic and social changes, and conspiratorial thinking. The Jews—who played an exceptionally important role in the development of the middle class in Hungary—were considered to be the main advocates of capitalism blamed for destructive social developments. The Hungarian far right gathering strength between the two world wars was characterized by the same kind of thinking, and later— unlike in other, mainly Western European countries—the far right reemerging following the regime change in Hungary was seized by the same ideas. As suggested by the research data introduced in previous chapters, a belief in anti-Semitism and in a Jewish world conspiracy plays a central role in the thinking of the Hungarian far right. Obviously, this may also be attributed to the fact that a narrative blaming the Jews for all the ills of modernization and capitalism has been regularly reinforced from the supply side as well.

At the same time, the Hungarian far right's anticapitalism is inherent not only in anti-Semitism raised to a complex explanation of the world but also in its economic and social policy concepts. Radical ideas for social reform also appear in their theories and written political programs with a yearning for a strong state capable of intervening, a desire for a centralized planned economy and the implementation of a collectivist philosophy as perceived by the right. In its purest form, all this characterizes the Hungarian far right between the two world wars, and the policies of today's far right include some of the same ideas, albeit in a more couched language. In the 2010 program of Jobbik, "rethinking" the role of the multinational companies in the Hungarian economy received a subchapter, with the idea of putting extra taxes and burdens on them (Jobbik.hu, 2010b). Even before that, back in 2006, the party was calling for chasing away all the multinational retail chains from Hungary. The party has softened its position in this issue as well, and right now just calling for the reduction of role of multinational companies in Hungarian economy (Zágráb, 2006).

It must be noted that there are some theories, coming especially from the system critical left, that, using a capitalism concept fundamentally different from the one presented in this book and in contrast to earlier interpretations, talk about the role of far-right ideas serving the interests of global capitalism: "Neoliberal" far-right parties. Accordingly, fascism and Nazism promoted some sort of "preventive counterrevolution" as opposed to revolutions led by leftist (communist and socialist) mass parties. Moreover, later and current far-right movements, it is claimed, pose no challenge to the capitalist system or the power of the middle class; on the contrary, they are serving the interest of the current system.[26] We think that this approach is far fetched, and the anticapitalist elements of the far right in Hungary—even if they are different from the far left, as put the ethnicity, and not the class in the center of our redistribution-based policies—are serious. In fact, Fidesz

---

[26] See on the subject: Tamás Gáspár, M. (1999). On Post-Fascism: How citizenship is becoming an exclusive privilege. *Boston Review*, [online] (1999 summer). Available at: http://new.bostonreview.net/archives/BR25.3/tamas.html [Accessed April 13, 2017].

implemented several such measures on power, partially inspired by Jobbik (Krekó and Mayer, 2015).

Jobbik's symbolic policy

Traditionally, but especially since the transition, the political right is much stronger in symbolic politics than the left. The far right was extremely successful in exploiting this tendency, with the appropriation and popularization of a series of events, topics, traditions, and symbols—such as the Árpád stripes or the Greater Hungary motif. It is all too evident that in a symbolic political arena the rational/pragmatist political language—partially part of the technocratic traditions in Europe, but partially a heritage of the socialization in the communist regime, still important in the Socialist Party—used by the left has been ineffective against the right for quite some time (Szilágyi, 2009). However, in this context, even the mainstream right is a bit lagging behind the far right: instead of taking up the challenge, the traditional right adopts and reinterprets the symbolic political arsenal of the far right. Below we take a look at the main features of Hungarian far-right policies from the point of their symbolic content.

Self-definition

Jobbik defined itself as a *national radical* movement almost from the beginning, serving the interests of "Hungarians" and the "people" with its policies. The 2007 program of Jobbik, the Bethlen Gábor Program (2007), firmly describes the party as a "new force" representing a "new radicalism." With the exception of nationalism and radicalism, as a general rule Jobbik rejects definitions referring to any kind of political ideology, saying that what they represent is beyond ideologies. Furthermore, they have been consistently refused to be labeled with the pejorative words "extremist" or "far rightist." Party politicians regularly describe neoliberalism and liberalism as extremist and "inhumane." In their eyes, the government, the mainstream Hungarian parties, and the EU are all representing certain forms of liberalism and neoliberalism. While Jobbik's policies obviously have strongly exclusionist elements, they define their politics as clearly inclusive, pointing to an idealized vision where different peoples coexisted peacefully within a greater Hungarian national body (see, for example, Vona, 2016b). Of course, this game is not typical of Jobbik alone: with the exception of some clearly antiestablishment groups identifying with the Arrow Cross, all organizations on the political far right reject the "extremist" label—especially the ones that want to have a mass support. Jobbik even went to court in 2012 after a left-leaning commercial channel, ATV, labeled the party "far right" in a news program. After highly inconsequential decisions from the Hungarian judiciary, finally the Constitutional Court verdict claimed that the term "far right" reflects an opinion and not a fact—and therefore should not be part of news coverage (Kovács, 2016). The moderate shift of Jobbik in the last few years had an impact on the self-definition of the party as well, and the party is more reluctant to call itself "radical"—Vona labels the party as a "people's party" instead.

Jobbik's concept of "nation"

Jobbik used the slogan "Hungary is for the Hungarians" extensively, although based on its programs and messages it is unclear who qualify as "Hungarian" in the eyes of the party's politicians. For the most part, in their mind the concepts of "nation" and "Hungarian" represent some kind of cultural/historical community, which is not to be defined on an ethnic basis, but on the basis of the slogan "a Hungarian is who defines himself as a Hungarian" (Jobbik.hu, 2010a), although they also use arguments that raise additional criteria for being a member of the nation. However, the concept of "Hungarian" is essentially left undefined in Jobbik's rhetoric and thus the option of excluding "non-Hungarians" is implicit in the concept itself. And the paradox of such chauvinistic exclusionary definitions of "Hungarian" is that they can reduce the number of the "real Hungarians" substantially—to a much lower level than the citizens of the country. This is well illustrated by an interview with Gábor Vona from back to 2009, from the most extreme period (Gábor, 2009):

\<Dialogue\>

Q: Do you consider Gypsies to be Hungarian?
A Yes, the ones who believe that this is their home and don't see it as a country that should be bled dry, robbed and murdered. The homeland means that one is ready to make sacrifices for one's country.

What are these sacrifices?
That one works, for instance.

In other words, those living in impoverished regions, have little schooling and no work, have a lot of children, and live on welfare—they are not Hungarians?
Of course, you can play around with who does and who doesn't belong. I told you what I have to tell on the subject, and I believe this is an inclusionary slogan.

\</Dialogue\>

National traditions and values also constitute the core of Jobbik's nation concept. For the far right to successfully put itself in the position of "the savior of values," it must depict current conditions as deficient and decadent, use an apocalyptic language, and present itself as the indisputable and exclusive protector of the nation. Accordingly, the nation—similar to the West as a whole—is in a state of decline, on the way to degeneration, losing its values and traditions and, concurrently, becoming the object of social reengineering and manipulation, a hoard of ignorant slaves, and a compliant tool in the hands of big business and multinational companies with no national entity. The crisis of values undermines the fundamental institutions of society: the population is declining, the institution of the family is disintegrating, Hungarians become secondary citizens in their own country, the environment is degraded, and, in the absence of strict rules and moral standards, order breaks down and is replaced by anarchy and a sense of insecurity. Jobbik considers the prevention of these trends to be one of its most important missions through the preservation of traditions, moral education, "national reawakening," and, of course, the exclusion of various groups defined as alien and blamed for all the decay described earlier. On the ideological horizon of radicals, the defense of the nation often comes with protection of the environment: the connecting link is the "Hungarian land," that is, the protection of nature as a shared ancestral value. The image of such a nation, which by now can be protected only by radical means, is already outlined in the Program "Bethlen Gábor," and in a more detailed and less virulent version in Jobbik's 2009 political agenda developed for the EP election campaign (Jobbik.hu, 2009). The constant reference to 'values' and 'traditions' remains an important point in Jobbik's ideology despite the moderate shift, and despite the fact that the younger voter base of Jobbik is, in fact, less traditionalist and conformist than most of the society (Krekó and Kovács, 2016).

Jobbik's concepts of enemy

The main feature of the far right is the existence of enemies, and the identification and analysis of construed enemies themselves can be helpful in the typology and characterization of far-right movements (Mudde, 2007). Jobbik's and, more broadly, the far right's enemy concept is frequently vague and generalized. There is a whole system of enemies, connected by a conspiracy aimed against the nation and based on global connections. Globalization serves the interests of lobby groups financed by international capital that, through their local lackeys, execute their plot of destroying nations and indigenous values. The immediate enemy is the political elite and, in part, intellectuals representing foreign interests, whose major crime is their antinational bent (Jobbik.hu, 2010a). The main archenemy, the "axiomatic enemy," for the Hungarian far right is traditionally the international liberal elite and Jewry, who, conspiring with the pseudo-national elites, are ruining the country. So, in Cas Mudde's typology, this is a grand conspiracy involving players who are "within the state, within the nation," *with others who are* "outside the state, and outside the nation."

It is worth noting that the Roma, regularly referred to in Jobbik's communication in a negative context, is not the real enemy, or the archenemy, but only a tool or symptom in a conspiracy against the Hungarian nation. While the following lines are from an ex-politician of Jobbik, this line of thought appeared several times in statements or communication of other Jobbik-related actors (such as on the Facebook page of Lajos Rig, currently the MP of the party elected in the Tapolca by-election in 2015):

> [...]Why is it that no political force in position of power has anything to say about Gypsy crime? How come they don't see that an ethnic-bomb is ticking in Hungary? Don't they see that the local gypsy population is led by people under police investigation and those already condemned in court? Of course they do! However, presumably they have a vested interest in seeing the plan presented by Israeli president, Simon Peres, implemented where Hungary comes under total Jewish control. So, what is exactly Gypsy crime? Let's not fool ourselves: it's a biological weapon in the hands of Zionism. [...]. (Juhász, 2010) Tibor József Bíber, former Jobbik vice president, April 13, 2008

While Jobbik's politicians reject the "charge" of anti-Semitism and consider it unfounded, the party's communication relies heavily on contemporary and symbolic anti-Semitic arguments. The Jews constitute the ideal enemy for the far right: the usual stereotype on them is that they are both malevolent and powerful—therefore, capable of organizing conspiracies (Krekó, 2011).

The often-denied anti-Semitism was clearly demonstrated in "Napkelte" aired on August 10, 2009, where to the question of television host János Betlen, whether he would recommend Jobbik followers to attend an event of an organization wishing to commemorate Rudolf Hess, Gábor Vona responded as follows: *If you're so interested and preoccupied with the Jewish issue, you should move to Israel. And there you can deal with this all day long.*[27]

While Gábor Vona, especially since 2015, is trying to actively oppress the anti-Semitic statements of the party, anti-Semitism and anti-Zionism are still an important, however, rather silenced topic in Jobbik's policies and rhetoric. Gábor Vona himself, though, was an emblematic member of the party, echoing the usual anti-Semitic and anti-Zionist, Holocaust-relativizing topics. In his writing in 2009, he

---

[27]   Vona Gábor Izraelbe küldte a méltatlan kérdéseket feltevő Betlent. https://ww w.youtube.com/watch?v=ZSuBrX5Xckk [Accessed April 12, 2017].

again, mentions Simon Peresz's statement as the "proof" of an ongo-
ing conspiracy:

> For those crying for legal prohibition, instead of the Holocaust denial, actually
> wish to ban all talk about Israel's buyout plans. Their goal is to compromise all
> those who dare to speak up against Simon Peres' statement, and especially the
> reality underlying that speech. If Jobbik were to question what all this Israeli
> capital is doing in Hungary, what's this appetite for construction all about, why
> do we have more Israeli than Hungarian security companies, all these questions
> could be settled with a sloppy response: "well, we told you so, all these are anti-
> Semites." Alfahír.hu, 2009a)

To give a name to the main enemy, the party often refers to "Jewish
big business" and "Holocaust-business," and Israel's colonizing ambitions in overt or covert language (couched in antiglobalist rhetoric)
that, translated into specific political terms, in their view is manifested
primarily in liberal ideology and its representatives (Alfahír.hu, 2011).
Accordingly, while the antinational charge is extended to all parliamentary parties, Jobbik's radical rhetoric attaches the greatest importance
to SZDSZ, the liberal party, although the party had all but disappeared
by 2009. In Gábor Vona's words:

> In this case, SZDSZ operates as a parent party. Of all the parties organized
> following the regime change from the top down, MSZP, Fidesz, MDF and
> SZDSZ (allowed to stay in the Hungarian Parliament not by accident) SZDSZ is
> the top gun. It executes the political program of the so-called regime change,
> i.e., throwing Hungary to the wolves, in the most aggressive, most discrimina-
> tory and anti-Hungarian manner. Through its tentacles it has a presence in all
> parties. Through crypto-SZDSZ politicians they control the entire current parlia-
> mentary gang. With Bokros they took over MDF, with Gyurcsány and Bajnai
> they have a hold on MSZP, and with the help of Deutsch, Pokorni, Szájer and
> Mária Schmidt, they also hold the cards in the Fidesz leadership. Even if SZDSZ
> fails to win a single seat in Parliament, they still wouldn't lose control of the
> country. (Alfahír.hu, 2009a)

In the far-right ideologemes, liberalism, globalism, and international
Jewry are interconnected and hardly separable, forming the main enemy. Their activity can be tracked anywhere, even in the operation of
the government, be it privatization, reforms, or a neoliberal economic
policy seen as destroying the nation. While the enemy is strong, it can
be defeated easily. In short, the enemy is, as suggested by Umberto
Eco (1998, p. 42), "simultaneously extremely strong and extremely

weak." Former prime minister Ferenc Gyurcsány was painted in the same colors. For a long time, he embodied everything representing the enemy in the eyes of the far right. At the same time, while acknowledging his symbolic importance, they did not see him as an outstanding politician and, in fact, many times they referred to him as a "clown," a "knucklehead," or a "lunatic."

All things considered, at the foundation of Jobbik's ideology and rhetoric is a bipolar explanation of society standing above political parties: in their judgment the country is divided into national and antinational forces. Jobbik also tried to eliminate Fidesz from the "national side"; according to a 2009 definition by Gábor Vona, the Hungarian political spectrum is made up of an "antinational" MSZP, SZDSZ, and MDF, a "bourgeois liberal" Fidesz, and the "national side" represented by Jobbik. However, so far its strategy has been unsuccessful with respect to Fidesz. In this context, Fidesz has a strong position because, as mentioned earlier, Viktor Orbán's policies may have served as an inspiration for Jobbik. For, following its election defeat in 2002, Fidesz resorted to a new legitimizing strategy: Fidesz, as the natural representative of the "national" side, is the genuine representative of the nation, whether they win majority in parliamentary elections or not.

As demonstrated earlier, the main dichotomy is that radicals define themselves as nationalist, while the "them" group is labeled uniformly and categorically as antinational. In this perspective, by definition, the "we" group represents the oppressed national "people," while the antinational entity stands for various, cosmopolitan elite groups (Szabó, 2005). The umbrella term for labeling the enemies of the nation is—referring to the words "anti-Semitism" and "anti-Tziganism"—"anti-Hungarianism," a term that the extremist Web site kuruc.info.connected to Előd Novák has a section on.[28]

While it is quite paradoxical when a party or political movement uses arguments attacking political parties or politics in general, this is a typical phenomenon for Jobbik. An antipolitical, antielitist populist attitude is an inherent feature of Hungarian far-right rhetoric: between

---

[28]   See https://kuruc.info/t/26/ [Accessed April 16, 2016].

the two world wars, Hungarian racist movements built their entire argument on this logic (Gyurgyák, 2007), and—while not on a nationalist
basis—the one-party system of the communist dictatorship was built
on the same political concept. Following the regime change, social
discontent and dissatisfaction related to democratic transition provided fertile ground for the survival of an antiparty and antipolitical populism. It has been observed that for short-term political gains, parliamentary parties are keen to resort to this tool, and fail to realize that in
the long term they undermine their own credibility and only strengthen
the radical right (Juhász and Szabados, 2006).

Jobbik's concept of "state"

Jobbik's 2007 program states:

> With Hungary's 1944 occupation by Germany, the country was [knocked] off the
> course of legal continuity, and neither the communists nor the regime-changing
> elite had an interest in resolving the constitutional crisis, i.e., we have yet to
> close a long 20th century (Jobbik.hu, 2007).

The party believes that the legitimacy of the state can be reestablished
with the restoration of the "historic constitution" built on the doctrine of
the Holy Crown. But this section is talkative in one more aspect as
well: officially, Jobbik does not have—at last on an official level—admiration toward the Arrow Cross Movement, the Hungarian fascist
(Hungarist) movement that was the Third Reich's ally when Germany
occupied Hungary. They admire Mikós Horthy, a controversial historical figure, an autocrat, conservative governor of Hungary, who led the
country into World War II on the side of the Nazis but did not support
the fascist and Nazi movements himself.

In the early approach of Jobbik, the party had three objectives
about reestablishing the statehood of Hungary: as a first step, the government must be replaced, followed by a "genuine regime change"
(not like the "stolen transition" that happened in 1989–1990), and the
final goal is the "full restoration" of Hungarian legal continuity, which is
based on merging the concepts of state and nation. This line of thinking, obviously, breaks with the idea of parliamentary democracy and,
instead, envisions a self-reliant state removed from the global system

and based on some kind of "national democracy," or authoritarianism. As we have indicated earlier, in this logic the state is not posited as part of an institutional order but as a national symbol set against globalization. And in this context, the "historic constitution" of the Holy Crown, a mystical element that occasionally appears in Fidesz's rhetoric as well, expresses a desire for a radical range, that is, a drastic regime change, a will to fuse nation and state that, incidentally, would incorporate ethnic Hungarians living in neighboring countries into the Hungarian body politic. (Fidesz did it partially, giving right to vote to ethnic Hungarians.)

At this point we have to mention the strong ambivalence of Jobbik toward liberal democracy, which is essential for understanding the Jobbik phenomenon. While Jobbik is procedurally supportive toward the main institutions of liberal democracy (e.g., participates in elections, accepts results, and—with a few exceptions from the past—does not envision a violent takeover of power), the party leaders, including Vona, have been frequently expressed their antipathy with liberalism. As Vona summarized back in 2012,

> We are not communists, we are not fascists, we are not national socialists—but we are not even democrats—in the sense that it is used today, as we do not put money and profit in the centre of our ideology" (Jobbik.hu, 2012).

In the weekly of Jobbik, *Barikád*, an article was published afterward, explaining and interpreting this speech, with the title "Considerations on the ideological foundations of Jobbik" (Alfahír.hu, 2012), which claimed that Jobbik's ideology should be put on four main pillars: Traditionalism, Monarchism, Turanism (a rather mystical ideology expresses the Eastern origin and fate of Hungary), and Hungarism (the ideology of the Arrow Cross Movement, the Hungarian version of fascism). Needless to say, that these four ideological foundations would define a politics and a system that is essentially antidemocratic in every sense is a bizarre form of traditionalist-totalitarian monarchy. In the more recent interviews of Vona, he tries to dissolve every doubt about the democratic nature of Jobbik. In 2014, he said that Jobbik believes in democracy, but does not believe in liberal democracy, as it ruined the country, but a so-called value-based democracy (Bálint,

2014). This definition between democracy and liberal democracy is a thought that frequently appears on the European populist right—and one of the central elements of Orbán's illiberalism.

Concept of history and the most important historical symbols

The ideology of the radical right is heavily historicized, as advocates of the far right usually define their political project as a program to reestablish an ill-defined, construed "golden age" from the past. For the Hungarian far right, the areas that are exemplary and idealized are the ones that are characterized by a strong-handed leader and "unity" (from Atilla's empire and the Árpád Age through powerful feudal kingdoms) or, in the absence of sovereignty, a struggle and fight for freedom to overcome oppression and fragmentation (Rákóczi-freedom fight, the 1848–1849 War of Independence, and the 1956 Revolution). These historic models provide a recipe for resolving the country's current problems. Hungarian prehistory holds a special interest for the far right, because groups radicalized by Hungary's tragic twentieth-century history (primarily the Trianon Peace Treaty) find the most inspiration keeping the struggle against historic injustices alive in those early times. For instance, Jobbik's 2007 program called for the foundation of an institute of Hungarian prehistory with a mission to promote research based on an assumed Hun-Avar-Hungarian continuity (Jobbik.hu, 2007).

The far-right parties are clearly aware of history's political usefulness and apply it very consciously and more effectively than other parties in Hungary. It intends to create some kind of "alternative history," challenging the academic mainstream history narratives. This is not unique though, since 2010, the Fidesz government expressed similar intentions with awards (e.g., for Kornél Bakay, an alternative historian with strong anti-Semitic views [Kuruc.info, 2015] and a positive opinion on Ferenc Szálasi, Arrow Cross leader).[29]

The increasing popularity of a mystical view of the past offers the far right a double political advantage: on the one hand, it creates

---

[29]   For more on him, see: http://hungarianspectrum.org/tag/kornel-bakay/ [Accessed April 12, 2017].

a community reaching beyond the potential supporters offers the far right the chance to invest put its policies on a strong symbolic ground. For instance, mystifying the Hun Empire of Hungary in the ancient times symbolizes the strength of Hungarians, a proud self-image set against a sense of submission, as well as physical/spiritual and intellectual power. In fact, such imagery can also express the radicals' independence from the establishment. The radical right has appropriated the Scythian-Hun origin story in opposition to the official prehistory based on the Finno-Ugric theory, and used it to build a complex set of symbols to serve its own ends.[30] For groups of people preoccupied with ancient Hungarian history and ideals, this also creates a point of reference for daily life: rediscover ancient religion, learn to write runic script, shoot an arrow, ride a horse, play music, and do crafts. Today, so many people are engaged in these pursuits that entire cottage industries have sprung up around these pursuits. And also, these alternative narratives provide a strong, conspiracy-theory-based counter-identity against the mainstream: Our real history is denied, oppressed, and silenced.

The far right also puts a big emphasis on sacral symbols as it tries to fuse ancient Hungarian beliefs with Christianity. In this context, the "Turul" Bird and the Scythian cross are key ciphers, believed to be the symbols of "early Christianity in Hungary" and Scythian myths. In this syncretic belief system, ancient Hungarians were not pagans but Christians, and in the age of St. Stephen Hungarian Christians—including "Taltos" priests—joined the Catholic Church. "Taltos" priests believed that God was first symbolized by the sun (Turul) and, following the birth of Christ, by Jesus. They simultaneously believed in the force of natural elements and the Holy Trinity. The kings of the House of Árpád were healers, resurrected the dead, and moved mountains (St. Ladislaus) and, among other things, in the eyes of the radicals the age is exemplary due to its sacral charge. In part, the Holy Crown fits in the order of sacred symbols, where its superhuman qualities and

---

[30]   The far right's penchant for prehistory is nothing new; the recent trend grew out of Turanism flourishing of the interwar year. See: Paksa, R. (2009). Far-right movements in the 1930s. In: I. Romsics, ed., *Hungarian Rightist Tradition, 1900–1948*, 1st ed. Budapest: Osiris, pp. 275–304.

sacred force are key aspects: under this doctrine, the crown symbolizes the divine origin of the law that cannot be changed by man. Moreover, today's radical right goes back to the political Catholicism of the interwar years, making the link between popular culture and a Christian nation concept. These symbols show up in Jobbik's politics as well; for years, to attract attention before Christmas the party erected a large wooden cross in a public square; it has some active supporters in the clergy and in its program it calls for a statue to commemorate Ottokár Prohászka, an emblemic priest, a figure of political anti-Semitism. At the same time, it is also evident that due to a mostly nonreligious support base and its confused pagan-Christian spiritual background, Jobbik is careful not to overplay the religious card: Religion only helps to draw the boundaries of "normality" in everyday behavior and to define conservative views.

Certainly, the flag has a central role in the symbolism. Jobbik's Gábor Bethlen program traditionally calls for giving the "Árpád-striped" flag an official status as a national symbol. The Árpád stripes, strongly and traditionally associated with the Hungarian far right's symbolism, also serve the tool for provocation, as the flag was widely debated because of its extremist and anti-Semitic connotations. For many people, the "Árpád-striped" flag (and the Turul) used by the far right has come to represent the Arrow Cross Movement. Accordingly, the "Árpád-striped" motif is featured on a variety of platforms, including on the Web site logos of the radical right's extensive Internet network and stickers with the map of a Greater Hungary seen on an increasing number of cars. (According to a poll, there is a Greater Hungary flag on 5% of the cars [Median.hu, 2007], and even Viktor Orbán, the prime minister of Hungary, had such a symbol on his car.) In the past few years, the side criticizing "Árpád-striped" organizations in public discourse has clearly been on the defensive, and the symbol is not only widely accepted but has also become an integrative force on the far right.

SUPPLY SIDE: FAR RIGHT ON THE POLITICAL FIELD   155

Symbols with a similar weight as the "Árpád stripe" are Trianon[31] and Greater Hungary—an issue that incorporates almost all content relevant for radicals. In the Trianon treaty after World War I, Hungary lost two-thirds of its territory—a national trauma that shaped and fueled Hungarian nationalism and chauvinism greatly in the last 100 years. First of all, in the spirit of "a Hungarian is he who is hurt by Trianon" (a bon mot by Gyula Illyés), identification with the national tragedy and solidarity with ethnic Hungarians living in neighboring countries are a measure of Hungarian identity. Second, Trianon is a cornerstone of the enemy concept construed by the far right, conclusive evidence of the conspiracy, injustice, and double standards of the West against Hungary. Furthermore, it provides justification for prejudice against neighboring peoples and countries (most importantly, against Slovaks, Romanians, and Serbs) for arguments based on historical grievances and a revisionist foreign policy because, in their view, ethnic groups living in historical Hungary usurped the country, while, under the aegis of the Holy Crown, they had once lived freely and in peace. In other words, Trianon is the most direct symbol of the deliberate destruction of a historical Hungary: the expression "Greater Hungary" has been in use since the 1920 Treaty of Trianon. And finally, Trianon is a constitutive part of the far right's political and state concept. In the logic of the radical right, Trianon cannot be resolved within the current constitutional framework: the state must encompass the entire nation, that is, including the ethnic Hungarian populations of all neighboring countries. The Trianon nostalgia is an inherent part of the Hungarian right's worldview and Fidesz made several steps on government to express it—introducing the Trianon commemoration day and giving voting rights to ethnic Hungarians—both aimed to express that the Hungarian community goes beyond the administrative borders of Hungary; for Jobbik, this issue has really central importance. The "policies" of Jobbik and its allied organizations (such as the Sixty-Four Counties movement) in this issue have been ranging from calling for greater autonomy to calling for open revisionism. This

---

[31] About the historical, political and social interpretation and misinterpretation of the Trianon Peace Treaty, see Ablonczy, B. (2007). Trianon-problems. *Kommentár*, 2007(4), pp. 57–67.

is well expressed by the words of Csanád Szegedi, Jobbik's ex-MEP, who said, on the Trianon commemoration of the openly revisionist Sixty-Four Counties youth movement ceremony on June 13, 2009:

> We are not going to Brussels to make friends, to make backroom deals or to be liked in the European Parliament, but to fulfill our mission and to place the issue of Trianon borders before everything else (Bumm.sk, 2009).

Jobbik's foreign policy

Jobbik's foreign policy fits well to the general patterns of the populist foreign policy (European Policy Center, 2016), with a tendency to prefer the "bad guys" in international politics (politicians who are generally considered as authoritarian, cruel, and enemies of the West) from Ahmadinejad through Assad until Vladimir Putin. It serves a double goal: (1) provocation of the domestic and international community, to raise attention and be able to form an alternative policy platform as a denial of the mainstream foreign policy doctrines and (2) building of alternative alliances that especially forces of the far right are in desperate need, because they are often rather excluded from the traditional foreign policy networks.

The 2014 policy program of Jobbik provides a relatively concise summary of the main foreign policy goals of the party. In the opinion of Jobbik, a foreign policy trying to satisfy "foreign expectations" has failed, a policy that since March 1944 has been consistently acquiescent, first meeting the expectations of Moscow, then Brussels and Washington—pushing the representation of Hungarian minorities in neighboring countries to the back burner. The party continues to stress the importance of "Eastern opening," a closer cooperation with countries in inner Asia with close cultural and ancestral ties to the Hungarian people. Thanks to its geographic location between Europe and Asia, Hungary could play a mediating role. Beside the West, Russia, China, and Turkey regained their large power status, which means that Jobbik's foreign policy focuses on three countries: Germany, Russia, and Turkey. For, in the course of our history, these countries have always influenced our region, and due to their size, proximity, and economic and political weight, they carry strategic importance. Jobbik plans to abandon a unilateral Euro-Atlanticism as part of a foreign pol-icy paradigm shift based on global changes and recognition of "natural allies." To this end, the party plans to review treaties and commitments related to Hungary's membership in the EU, the International Mone-tary Fund, and NATO. Facing up to political taboos is equally important for Jobbik, including the EU's "colonial policies," the "unjust wars" of the United States, and a Zionist Israel's "global- and country-conquer-ing" attempts. The program pays special attention to the importance of Russia, acknowledging its superpower status, its geopolitical sway, the secure and reliable natural gas and oil supplies it provides, and as a potential market for Hungarian agricultural goods. Referring to an-cestral ties to ancient Turkic peoples living in inner Asia, Jobbik plans to develop closer economic ties to Turkey.

Aside from an anti-Israeli stance, in foreign policy matters this is demonstrated primarily in an anti-American and anti-West attitude expressed in Jobbik's turn to some Eastern countries or its expressly pro-Russian, and before the refugee crisis, the pro-Muslim, pro-Ira-nian policies. In this context, all governments prior to 2010 and in some cases the current Orbán administration are presented as sub-servient "pawns" that backed by global business and the international "liberal," "Zionist," "Atlanticist" order.

In the following section, without the need for giving a complete overview, we will focus on two aspects of Jobbik's foreign policy: its relations with Iran and Russia, as we think these are indicative gener-ally about the foreign policy of the party, and its development.

Jobbik's relations with Iran[32]

One of the main features of Jobbik's alternative foreign policy has been its general pro-Muslim, pro-Palestinian stance in general (an an-tithesis of "Zionism") and strong model role of Iran in particular. The history of the relationship between Jobbik and Iran goes all the way

---

[32]   This chapter originally appeared in English as part of a study titled "Mutual Benefits" on March 31, 2015. Accessible at: http://www.riskandforecast.com/use ruploads/files/pc_flash_report_20140331_mutual_benefits.pdf.

back to the party's foundation. Relations with Iran are not directly related to an announced policy of "Eastern opening" and instead can be
traced to other factors, such as a personal network of some prominent
individuals, the general foreign policy goals of the party, and the strong
anti-Semitism. These are verifiable causes, as opposed to allegations
and unsubstantiated rumors that the party is financed by Iran, a charge
that has not been verified yet.

Gábor Vona had already visited Yemen in February 2003, before Jobbik was established as a party. He delivered a speech at an
Arab conference, accepting the invitation of a staff member of the Palestinian Embassy in Budapest. He was representing Jobbik as a right-
wing youth association. In Yemen, he spoke up for the establishment
of an independent Palestinian state at an event organized by a pro-
Saddam, Yemen-based Ba'ath Party. But he first outlined his major
foreign policy position only in a 2007 article published in *Barikád*. At
that time he described Iran as the leader of the Muslim world:

> (...) Hopefully, the world monopolized by the United States is in its last throes.
> The US will be unable to fight on several fronts facing China, Russia, a Muslim
> world led by Iran and Latin America. While we have little in common with the
> latter region, we definitely have to find a road to the first three" (Krekó and
> Juhász, 2014).

In other words, components that later came to define Jobbik's foreign
policy had already emerged at the very start of Vona's presidency. In
his mind the policy of "Eastern opening" is not simply based on the
"Eastern origin" of Hungarians, or cultural and pragmatic economic arguments, but also on a more profound and complex conspiracy theory,
as well as an ideology based on the expected collapse of the West.
Hungary's interest in breaking with the West and forming alliances with
Eastern powers can only be explained by taking into consideration the
decline of the West and its "colonizing ambitions."

An increasing and open commitment to Iran was demonstrated
by Gábor Vona's speech on October 23, 2008, where the chairman of
the party asked Iranian president Mahmoud Ahmadinejad to send observers to the 2009 EP election, including assistance from the Iranian
Revolutionary Guard (*Pāsdārān-e Enqelāb-e Eslāmi*, Sepāh). In a

2008 interview, Vona justified this by referring to a statement made by the president of Israel, Simon Peres:

> Right now Hungary is a country that Israel wishes to occupy or has already occupied. I'm thinking of the statement made by Simon Peres, and if there is a need to monitor the fairness of the elections, we cannot rely on Western Europe or the European Union[33] (Krekó and Juhász, 2014).

The interesting point is that Jobbik's foreign policy and agenda related to Iran—and to "Eastern opening" in general—is perplexing and, in fact, barely tolerable even to its supporters, who have similarly strong prejudices against Muslims than the majority of the Hungarian population. It means that the interests motivating the party's foreign policy have little to do with domestic party politics. The sensitivity of the Muslim issue is demonstrated by Gábor Vona's trip to Turkey in the fall of 2013, where, to the shock of some people in his party, he described Islam "as humanity's last hope in the darkness of globalism and liberalism" and said that compared to Christianity Islam represents more communal and cohesive power (ATV.hu, 2013).

Therefore, Jobbik regularly operates with anti-Semitic arguments best understood by its followers. For instance, on December 2, 2011, it organized an "antiwar peace march" protesting sanctions imposed on Iran and the enforcement of Western Zionist interests. Along with a number of other Jobbik representatives, Márton Gyöngyösi also addressed the crowd as president of parliament's Hungarian/Iranian Friendship Society.

Pro-Iranian and anti-Israeli, anti-Semitic positions are closely interconnected in Jobbik's ideology. In turn, the relationship is obviously a valuable contact for Iran because it would find few (and increasingly fewer) major parties supporting its anti-Israeli and anti-Semitic policies in the EU; the majority of anti-Muslim West European far-right parties such as Geert Wilders's Freedom Party or the Sweden Democrats

---

[33]   At a banquet given by Tel Aviv-based Chambers of Commerce in October 2007, the president of Israel Simon Peres jokingly remarked that Israelis are ready to buy up Manhattan, Hungary, Romania, and Poland. According to a statement issued by the president's spokesperson after the event, Mr. Peres did not intend to insult anyone and didn't call on businessman to "take over a country or two," although he admitted that the remark had been inappropriate.

(*Sverigedemokraterna*) are usually strong supporters of Israel at the same time.

An anti-EU policy is another important component of "Eastern opening": prior to the 2009 EP election, Jobbik explained its "Eastern opening" policy aimed at China, Russia, India, Japan, Iran, and Arab countries with a need to find markets in the East and reduce Hungary's dependence on the EU.

At that time the Iranian connection visible to the public involved but a few persons, including Gábor Vona, restaurant owner and businessman, Dr. H. Jahromi M. Afi, Márton Gyöngyösi, who later became the head of Jobbik's foreign affairs cabinet, and Iran's incumbent ambassador.

According to media reports, it was Gyöngyösi's idea to make the rapprochement with Iran the centerpiece of Jobbik's foreign policy. Iranian-born dentist, Dr. H. Jahromi M. Afi arrived in Hungary in 1992 as a student and has lived in Hungary ever since (he has a family and a Hungarian wife). Aside from his private practice, as the owner of Shiraz restaurant and the president of the Friendship Society of Hungarian and Iranian Businessman, Jahromi Afi is a prominent member of the Iranian community in Hungary, and his central role as a contact person has been bolstered by the fact that for some time he had been on the payroll of the Iranian Embassy.

Following Gábor Vona's 2003 visit to Yemen (Hetek, 2014), these individuals may have played an important role in arranging a series of official meetings with top party officials reported by the media. In 2007, Gábor Vona had a meeting with Iranian ambassador Ali Irvash Reza at an Iranian exhibition held in Pilisvörösvár meant to celebrate common Iranian/Hungarian cultural roots. The party's then recently elected representative in the EP, Krisztina Morvai, also visited Iran in 2009 to attend a "human rights conference" (Political Radical, 2014).

With Jobbik entering parliament in 2010, its relation with Iran rose to a new level. Moving beyond some casual statements and the building of personal ties, views on Iran became an integral part of the party's foreign-policy agenda: the party embarked on the establish-ment of institutional ties at the parliamentary and municipal levels alike.

In April 2011, Gábor Vona introduced the "Béla IV plan," a ref-erence to the business potential offered by Russia, China, Turkey, Central Asia, the Arab world, and Iran, described as an economic tool helping to end Hungary's dependence (threatening national interests) on the EU and multinational companies (Krekó and Juhász, 2014).

What have been the most important elements of this alliance in terms of content? First of all, an open support of Iran's foreign policy ambitions and nuclear program. As a parliamentary party, Jobbik has made a number of gestures and statements defending Iran's geopolit-ical interests, rejecting international sanctions aimed at the country. In January 2012, Jobbik's deputy faction head, Tamás Hegedűs, ob-jected to the EU's and the US' latest sanctions, describing these measures both as serious threats to peace and "warmongering" aimed at a peaceful Iran, which "has never attacked anyone before" (Political Radical, 2014). The deputy faction head also reminded that while there is no evidence for Iran's military nuclear potential, "Israel has close to 200 nuclear weapons"—a totally unfounded statement. Jobbik is also a loud supporter of the Syrian regime, the beneficiary of Iran's support through a number of channels. Aside from the demonstrations and meetings mentioned in the section Chronology of meetings be-tween Jobbik and Iranian representatives, the forms of open support include a demonstration in the end of 2011 against the banning of the Iranian foreign minister's plane from Hungarian airspace. Most re-cently, Jobbik welcomed the Geneva agreement easing international sanctions on Iran's nuclear enrichment program. Also, they welcomed the Iran deal in 2015 (Mandiner.hu, 2015). The second feature of po-litical ties is official political networking. After the party entered parlia-ment, with the help of parliament's new Hungarian/Iranian Friendship Society, with members belonging only to Jobbik and Fidesz and led by Jobbik's Márton Gyöngyösi, Iranian networking and lobbying efforts have gained an institutional forum.

Chronology of meetings between Jobbik and Iranian representatives

November 2010. The King Attila Folk College (*Attila Király Népfőiskola*) held a reception for representatives of Syrian, Lebanese, Iranian, Malaysian, and Indonesian embassies accredited to Hungary in the Church of Homecoming (*Hazatérés Temploma*) led by Lóránt Hegedűs Jr. At the event, among others, Gábor Vona and Krisztina Morvai briefed diplomats on the details of the party's "Eastern opening" policy. Márton Gyöngyösi talked about Simon Peres's "take-over plans" and Israel's "real estate crimes" in Hungary, and speaker of the parliament, Zoltán Balczó, presented Jobbik's position on the partnership agreement between the EU and a "genocidal" Israel. With English subtitles, a film of Gábor Vona's parliamentary speech delivered on the day of passing the partnership agreement was presented. The discussion ended with a reception at Shiraz restaurant.

January 2011. Márton Gyöngyösi attended and gave a speech at a Quran-promotion event organized by the Hanif Islam Cultural Foundation, where the chief imam of Istanbul's Fatih Djami Hafiz Osman Sahin read passages from the Quran. In addition to Jobbik's representatives, the event was attended by Qatari, Moroccan, Palestinian, Malaysian, and Iraqi ambassadors and diplomats.

October 2011. A large business delegation arrived to attend a five-day conference series with the aim of assessing commercial and investment opportunities between Hungary and Iran. During their visit, participants visited Tiszavasvári, Gyöngyös, and Gyöngyöspata, municipalities led by Jobbik mayors. The Iranian delegation was also received by Budapest mayor, István Tarlós, who delegated Jobbik representative Gábor Staudt to work out potential forms of cooperation between Budapest and Iran. At the conference, Gábor Vona said: *For Iran Hungary represents the West, and for Hungary Iran is the gateway to the East.* Documents expressing a desire for cooperation were signed and the visit was closed in the Church of Homecoming where, among others, speeches were made by Gábor Vona, Márton Gyöngyösi, pastor Lóránt Hegedűs Jr., Iranian ambassador Dr. Saeed

Seyed Agha Banihashemi, and the president of the Friendship Society of Hungarian and Iranian businessmen Dr. H. Jahromi M. Afi. *September 2012.* Four members of Jobbik's Székesfehérvár party chapter paid a visit to Iran's embassy in Budapest. At the meeting, Jobbik politicians emphasized the party's solidarity with the people and the government of Iran in its fight against the superpowers, and condemned Israel as an aggressor. *April 2013.* A meeting on expanding commercial ties between Iran and Hungary took place in Shiraz restaurant in the presence of a delegation from the Teheran-based Chamber of Commerce, Industry and Agriculture and the Iranian ambassador. Aside from Gábor Vona, the meeting was attended by a number of Hungarian businessmen and leaders of County Chambers of Commerce, as well as Dr. Jahromi H. Afi.

Finally, a third feature of political ties has been "sister city" relations. Nothing demonstrates the increased clout of Jobbik than the fact that a number of municipalities led by Jobbik mayors established sister city links with cities in Iran. In 2011, Tiszavasvári, considered as the capital of Jobbik, twinned with Ardabil in Iran, and in 2012 Gyöngyöspata developed similar ties with the city of Qum, with a population of one million. It is also interesting to note that by now Iranian politicians were the ones looking for opportunities to establish contact, and as a result there were one or two major meetings each year.

By all signs, contacts between Jobbik and Iran helped both sides to improve their political capital. In the case of Iran, it was obvious that any relationship established with an EP party helped to ease the country's international isolation in the Ahmadinejad era and offered an opportunity to influence European politics—even when the sanctions against Iran were easing. And for Jobbik, friendship with Iran was convenient not only for expressing its opposition to the West and Israel but also for presenting itself, well beyond its actual political weight, as an international "player" and an ally of a geopolitically prominent Iran. With its friendship with Russia and Iran, the party sent a domestic political message as well: it cannot be easily sidelined in the domestic political arena.

The economic dimension of these relations should not be over-estimated, though. While some Jobbik and Iranian politicians and businessmen often present Iran as a potential market for the Hungarian economy, and especially for its agricultural sector, in reality Hungarian farming is not in a competitive position either in terms of output or geographic location. Under the burden of sanctions, commercial ties with Europe have been obviously important for Iran but real economic partners could come primarily from major Western countries. Therefore, it's not surprising that aside from some symbolic twin-city ties Hungary has not seen a single major investment project coming from Iran, and even in the Jobbik cities, the source of growth was EU funds—as everywhere else. So, in practice, this alternative foreign policy did not bring substantial results. For the Persian state, the Hungarian connection was not relevant in and of itself, but only as an entry point to the political and economic markets of the EU, which is also the case for other Eastern countries.

When it comes to the party's widely rumored financing, all but impossible to analyze it based on publicly available data, still it is known that Iran is not loath to provide financial assistance to foreign radical organizations it considers important,[34] and Jobbik also has lobbying capabilities within the Hungarian political system that could benefit Iranian entrepreneurs with business interests in Hungary. Mutual advantages are apparent when one notices that back in 2011 Jobbik signed an HUF 3.2 million service agreement with Shiraz Kft., the operator of Shiraz restaurant and owned by Dr. Jahromi H. Afi, a prominent member of the Iranian community in Hungary, under the title of "managing organizational responsibilities and professional programs connected to the Iranian connection" (sic). But in this case, Jobbik paid for a businessman close to the Iranian embassy and not the other way around. Maybe it was part of a bigger financing scheme, but no direct

---

[34] Based on an analysis of the Washington Institute, Iran supports the Lebanon-based Shiite Hezbollah terrorist organization to the tune of USD 100–200 million a year, and Hezbollah and Iran both finance the Al Qaeda terrorist network. In the Syrian Civil War, Iran provides military and financial support to the Assad regime, and describes Syria as its "thirty-fifth province." In addition, in the name of "Islamic awakening" Iran provides general support to other revolutionary groups promoting the cause of the "Arab spring."

evidence has been found yet, and of course, Jobbik's politicians have denied any kind of financial support. What we do know, though (but this is not atypical in the Hungarian political scene), is that Jobbik's expenditures and financial position are not in line with the official reports—and, what is at least as much talkative, we do not have official information. Jobbik's murky financial position before it entered parliament raises the issue of illegal party financing. Between 2003, the year of its foundation, and 2010 the party never published mandatory annual financial statements, and in January 2010 the chief prosecutor's office launched an investigation into the case. The financial statement published in January 2010 prompted by the investigation shows that between 2004 and 2009 the organization's annual cash flow fluctuated between a mere HUF 1–3 million that, in the estimation of hvg.hu, equals the turnover of a "small family business" and doesn't even come close to accounting for the estimated tens or even hundreds of millions spent on the 2009 EP election campaign of the party. In the past, a number of organizations have looked into the party's finances and, according to media reports, a former member of the parliament's National Security Committee, József Gulyás, stated that before 2010, the committee suspected that the party received financial aid from Russian and Iranian sources, although no concrete evidence has turned up. The media also reported that the CIA looked into Jobbik's finances in 2009.

Nonetheless, the party's financing from abroad has never been proven conclusively. Moreover, as a current parliamentary party, Jobbik's financial options have become incomparably stronger, which means that its improving ties with Iran are more difficult than ever before to be explained only on the basis of hypothetical financial dependence. The most one can assume is that external financing, if there was any, helped the party's emergence in the beginning, and may have also determined the balance of power within the party. Financial support provided to the party may have played an important role in the development of some political careers within the party. However, from the perspective of Iran single individuals may be less relevant, and the real benefits may lie in the information brought by the relationship and a chance to enter European politics. And on the European level, Job-bik is—and it had been even more at that time—an isolated player.

But even so, until 2014 the relationship between Jobbik and Iran has spawned an increasingly comprehensive institutional framework cementing personal and political ties between Iran and Hungary. Ide-ologically, when it comes to its relations with Iran, Jobbik found itself on a slippery slope. On the one hand, by promising simple economic and foreign policy benefits, Jobbik could easily sell its attraction to an authoritarian, anti-Western, and anti-Israeli Iranian regime to a small percentage of its supporters. On the other hand, Islam and an orien-tation to the East in general are hard to reconcile with Jobbik's de-clared Christian identity, not to mention the universal xenophobia (Ber-nát et al., 2013) of the party and its followers. This also explains why it needed a comprehensive worldview that justifies contacts with the East by making references to the decline of the West, a global Jewish conspiracy and prehistoric Hungarian myths, and the Turanist ideol-ogy, about the common origins with Iran.

This challenging contradiction seems to disappear from the problem map of the party, though. Since 2013, the takeover of the Iranian presidency by Rohani, the relationship between Jobbik and Iran has been gradually losing importance. While in April 2013, there was a big, demonstrative meeting between the leaders of Jobbik, Ira-nian businessmen, and diplomats in the Shiraz restaurant (Jobbik.hu, 2013), the 2014 parliamentary election program of Jobbik mentions explicitly the need for boosting economic and diplomatic relations with Iran (Jobbik.hu, 2014). In 2015, Jobbik welcomed the deal with Iran. We cannot see any indication of the perseverance of ties between Jobbik and Iran. It would be easy to assume that the Iranian regime, breaking out from the isolation and having access to mainstream, gov-ernmental political players throughout the world, is downplaying ties with extremist movements—as they do not need them anymore.

On the other hand, the ideological connection has weakened from the side of Jobbik as well. Since the beginning of the refugee crisis in 2015, Jobbik has rather shifted to the ideological direction of the mainstream Western European far-right parties, and the pro-Mus-lim position of the party has turned into political islamophobia almost overnight. In the domestic political approach of Jobbik, there is no stark differentiation between the different Muslim countries; therefore, from 2015 on, we can see more and more Muslim-critical statements, with the beginning of the refugee crisis. Jobbik spokesman Ádám Mirkóczki called for some Arab states to make more sacrifice in accepting refugees—mentioning, in specific, Oman, the United Arab Emirates, Qatar, Saudi Arabia, Kuwait, and Iran (Jobbik.hu, 2015).

During the deepest conflicts of the refugee crisis, the Facebook site of Jobbik promoted the same islamophobic material than we can see in Western Europe (see Figure 12). And as an even more bizarre expression of the anti-Muslim stance, the mayor of Ásotthalom, and the vice president of Jobbik, László Toroczkai banned the burka, the Muslim religion, and mosques in his village (Hvg.hu, 2016). This move has also revealed the deep divisions within the party in this issue: another (extremist) mayor supported by Jobbik, Zoltán Mihály Orosz, infamous for his homophobic, anti-Semitic statements and fascistoid municipality policies, openly criticized Toroczkai for his decision and, according to Toroczkai, sent a complaint to his Muslim friends in this issue (Vs.hu, 2016) (Ásotthalom Nagyközségi Önkormányzat Képviselő-testülete, 2016).

As a consequence of Jobbik's anti-Muslim turn, it became rather an enemy in the eye of the (very small) Hungarian Muslim community. A leader of the Hungarian Muslim community criticized Jobbik in a Facebook post in August 2015, claiming that the party, which was supported by the Muslim community with votes beforehand, turned from a friend of Muslims to a party that sees its archenemy in the Muslims (Ablonczy, 2015).

Figure 12:   Meme from Jobbik's Facebook site, showing the dangers of "Islamization"

BALATON 2015   BALATON 2030?

www.facebook.com/JobbikMagyarorszagertMozgalom

The Eurasia concept and Jobbik's connections to Russia[35]

While Jobbik's politicians are keen on calling out other parties for serving "foreign interests," this accusation was the most applicable to the far-right party itself: first in relation to Iran, and then even more evidently with Russia. The increasingly apparent ideological link between some European far-right parties—including Jobbik—and the current Russian leadership can be understood within the framework of a Russian geopolitical strategy also inspired by Aleksandr Dugin, mentioned earlier, a strategy that since the start of the Putin era has left the socioeconomic weaknesses and the resulting international bargains behind and aspired to restore Russia as a world power. Underlying the strategy is Russia's view of itself as an imperial power conducting a unique modernization experiment backed by energy-industry resources (Stent, 2008).

Russia's foreign-policy activism has been given a new impetus in Vladimir Putin's third presidential term. Prior to taking this path, Putin presented his foreign-policy aspirations in what he termed, "Eurasian Union," in a 2011 article published by the daily *Izvest*. Subsequently, the president's ideas were elaborated by the journalist and

---

[35]   Parts of this chapter originally appeared in English as part of a study titled "I am Eurasian" on March 2015. Accessible at: http://www.politicalcapital.hu/wp-content/uploads/PC_SDI_Boll_study_IamEurasian.pdf.

political strategist Modest Kolerov, the head of a presidential institution responsible for foreign relations. The doctrine promised post-Soviet states national development and "genuine sovereignty," without the EU's "gratuitous restrictions." These points are well complemented by Putin's reformulated ideology built on authoritarianism, law-and-order policies, nationalism and statism, and the proclamation of a kind of—using a term coined by János Ladányi and Iván Szelényi—"postcommunist neoconservatism" against Western values perceived to be on the decline.

The downright anti-EU attitudes of the far-right forces are ideologically compatible with the "Great Russia" concept and Russia's hostility toward the European Union, inspired by the neo-Eurasian ideology. This joint platform makes these far-right forces natural allies of Putin's Russia.

European network of pro-Russian parties[36]

We could observe a general strengthening of the links between far right and Russia after 2014. The present 2014 Ukraine on the verge of civil war and the Syrian geopolitical gambit are representative of the Russian-Georgian conflict in 2008. In these conflicts, some parties on the European far right supported pro-Russian Ukrainian Viktor Yanukovych and Syrian Bashar al-Assad. Aside from Russia's global and regional interests, the shared interests with respect to energy industry, issues of primary importance to Russia are also striking.

In most postcommunist East European countries, Russia with its Soviet past has been regarded as the external enemy number one for a long time. However, in recent years this enemy concept seems to have changed. A rather dramatic case would be the East European far-right parties whose pro-Russian stance became stronger even as, under Putin's watch, the promotion of nostalgia for Russia's imperial past went hand in hand with the positive "reinterpretation" of the country's communist past.

---

[36]   This chapter originally appeared in English as part of a study titled "The Russian Connection" on March 14, 2015. Accessible at: http://www.riskandforecast.com/u seruploads/files/pc_flash_report_russian_connection.pdf

According to the explanation widely shared by the media, Russia provides material support for some European far-right parties. However, just a bit of evidence has surfaced to prove the account conclusive—such as the support of the FN by Russia. Simultaneously, the ideological and political affinity of far-right parties to Russia is apparent for the following reasons. Russia's authoritarian political system, its heavy-handed leader, its great-power rhetoric, the suppression of basic freedoms, state control over strategic sectors, the constant reference to "national interests" overriding market mechanisms, and a controlled economy keeping "big capital" in check offer a state organization model for some European far-right parties. Paradoxically, even though some extreme-right parties proclaim national self-reliance and isolation and wish to demonstrate their criticism of the EU, they meanwhile advocate for the breakup of the Euro-Atlantic community by moving closer to Russia. Russia's new geopolitical strategy coincides with the European far right's antiestablishment platform and policy interests. Moreover, through what Putin terms as the "active means" (*aktivnye meropriyatiya*) of his "Eurasian Doctrine," Russia provides political support to "friendly" parties and organizations.

In his summary report, Sinikukka Saari mentions three major components: (1) proactive political initiative taking, which involves the contacting of foreign political actors, the establishment and coordination of pro-Russian parties, and the export of political know-how and expertise; (2) "NGO diplomacy," which essentially means the establishment of nongovernmental organizations such as youth, minority, separatist civil organizations, and think tanks for the promotion of Russian interests; (3) support for friendly media enterprises. The "media" component is aimed at influencing domestic and foreign public opinion through existing media channels or media yet to be established. For instance, pseudo-civic organizations have cropped up in Estonia, Trans-Istria, and Southern Ossetia. The Russians have provided financial and political support to Moldavian and Georgian separatists. In Latvia, a formerly insignificant Harmony Center party (*Saskaņas Centrs*) won the elections with strong Russian backing (Saari, 2011, pp. 3–5).

In other words, the gains from the trade-off for far-right parties are not necessarily and solely financial, as commonly assumed. (While there is a general assumption that it plays an important role in the case of Jobbik with Béla Kovács, the MEP of the party serves as a mediator.) They receive more valuable professional, organizational, and media assistance; that is, access to networks and political know-how. The effective use of such political know-how by Russia represents a risk for an emerging European pro-Russian party network. Russia is clearly present on all fronts. Russia is simultaneously trying to assert its interests in the political mainstream and extremist parties alike, as well as venturing into a number of alternative scenarios. Telltale signs in Italy, Greece, and Hungary show parallels between each country's far-right parties and Russian support. Meanwhile, Russia continues to maintain its regular intergovernmental contacts.

Russian influence may be effective not only because of its direct relations with specific parties but also because these parties as of late, thanks to their resurgence, have become influential in their respective party families within the EU. In short, there is reason to believe that Russian diplomacy seeks to build party families in Europe. This is suggested by Russia's policy for encouraging far-right parties to hold conferences with Russian assistance and to form alliances with European parties such as the Alliance of European National Movements and European Alliance of Freedom but also with parties such as the French FN, the Austrian FPÖ, the Italian Northern League (*Lega Nord*), the Greek Golden Dawn, and the Belgian Flemish Interest (*Vlaams Belang*).[37]

Jobbik and Golden Dawn were both invited to the Russian National Forum organized by the Intelligent Design Bureau (close connections to Putin) on October 4 and 5, 2014, in St. Petersburg. The significance of the forum is attributable to the large number of invited guests (1,500) to a conference with the following agenda: the joint development of a new national doctrine for Russia and Europe, and the creation of a permanent coordination committee for the implementation of national policies adopted by the conference. This event was

---

[37]   For more information, see Anton Shekhovtsov (2017).

important because it evidently showed (together with the alliance between the United Russia party [*Yedinaya Rossiya*] and the Austrian
FPÖ) that some of these links, contrary to the statements of the skep-
tics, are official in nature.

Historical context of Russian-Hungarian relations[38]

Due to historical reasons, generally Russia's image is not favorable in
the Hungarian public and political elite. Russia's role in smashing Hungarian freedom fights (1849, 1956) and installing (the Hungarian Soviet Republic, Rákosi and Kádár regimes) and maintaining decades of
Russian military occupation has obviously not helped to strengthen
friendly views on Russia. After regime change, for the most part it was
the political left—within that the MSZP as the successor to the former
Hungarian Socialist Workers' Party (*Magyar Szocialista Munkáspárt*),
along with the marginal far-left Workers' Party (*Munkáspárt*)—that
maintained some contacts with Russia, while Russia had no established channels with the Hungarian right.

In fact, in most cases, parties on the right watched with suspicion and criticized the left for its Russian diplomatic contacts. Typically, before 2009, Fidesz, in opposition at the time, and Viktor Orbán
himself strongly criticized the Gyurcsány government for the South
Stream gas pipeline agreement signed by Hungary and Russia in
2008 and for the potentially growing influence of Russia due to the
Paks extension project. However, once in power, Orbán became one
of the main supporters of these projects. In other words, until quite
recently, Prime Minister Orbán, today considered as "Putin's man" and
the political identity of the Hungarian right, was characterized by the
rejection of close connections to the topical Russian regime. Accordingly, the first Orbán government between 1998 and 2002 was keen
on keeping Russia at arm's length. Even though connections to Russia
endured in the left-wing camp and consequently Russian politicians

---

[38]   This chapter originally appeared in English as part of a study titled "I am Eurasian"
on March 2015. Accessible at: http://www.politicalcapital.hu/wp-content/uploads/
PC_SDI_Boll_study_IamEurasian.pdf.

often placed more confidence in left-wing political actors, nevertheless the left then in power considered Euro-Atlantic integration as key goal.

From a historical point of view, by looking at the far right one cannot find any apparent signs of intense Russian contacts. Compared to the mainstream right, however, one sees a difference, namely that Turanism (i.e., the idea of kinship with Eastern people) has always played an important role for adherents of far-right ideology. Moreover, for national socialist organizations (Hungarian Welfare Association [*Magyar Népjóléti Szövetség*] and the Hungarian National Front [*Magyar Nemzeti Front*] that reject the parliamentary system) emerging after the regime change, Russian national socialist organizations have served as a model since the mid-1990s. It must also be noted that ultra-right media organizations, describing themselves as the spiritual leaders of the Hungarian far right, were the first to introduce Alexander Dugin and his ideology to Hungary (Boross, 2014). In short, the pro-Russian stance of the Hungarian far right is based in part on contacts established between Russian and Hungarian paramilitary forces following the regime change, the spiritual tradition of Turanism and the ultra-right ideology's uncritical attitude toward Russia. Jobbik, established in 2003, and to a lesser extent some members of circles close to Fidesz, returning to power in 2010, continue to rely on these sources.

Current relations between Jobbik and Russia[39]

Kremlin finds the Hungarian far right extremely valuable for at least three reasons. First, Russian stakeholders can channel more direct influence on Jobbik than on Fidesz. Jobbik's foreign policy standpoint can be almost totally derived from Russian interests, so as their energy policy relying totally on Russian gas and nuclear energy. Second, Jobbik is gaining popularity, and after an electoral success on a by-election in Hungary when they came first in an individual constituency,

---

[39]   This section is based on the summary of our researches on connections betwen the Hungarian far right and Russia, published on the Stratfor website: https://www.stratfor.com/the-hub/kremlin-connections-hungarian-far-right.   The references of the information contained in the section can be found in this summary, and the "I am Eurasian" study of Political Capital's colleagues.

they have a strong chance to become a governmental force in the future. Third, Russia has a vested interest in exacerbating public discontent with the West and indirectly destabilizing the EU from inside, and Jobbik proves to be a useful tool for these attempts. All these points remain valid despite the fact that the stronger ties between Viktor Orbán and Vladimir Putin diminish the importance of Jobbik-Russia ties: as long as Russia can receive what it wants from the mainstream, why go to the extreme?

Jobbik advocates not only the Russian position uninhibitedly but seems to be a tool of the information warfare and secret service machinery of the Kremlin, with MEP Béla Kovács, who is charged with espionage with Moscow, and his wife having strong connections to Russian secret services. Along with several other far-right forces in EU such as FN in France, Golden Dawn in Greece, or the Freedom Party in Austria, Jobbik helps not only in the division, destabilization, and delegitimization of the EU and its member states but also in the legitimization of the Russian regime, for example, with election observers at Kremlin-organized elections. Similar to other European far-right parties, Jobbik also legitimizes the Russian regime by sharing a set of conservative ideological values with Russia's current official state ideology. By them, the EU is seen as a declining institution and a puppet of the United States, while the Eurasian Union envisioned by Russia is a realistic, value-based alternative. At the EU-Russian Interparliamentary Work Group's 2013 meeting in Kaliningrad, MEP Béla Kovács asked a representative of the Russian Federation Council: *What is the future possibility of an EU member state initiating accession talks with the Eurasian Union?* Jobbik would certainly "reassess" Hungarian membership in NATO, calling for a referendum, and would rather favor "neutrality" of the country in the conflict between West and Russia. In order to help spread pro-Russian views regarding the Ukrainian conflict, the party launched a series of public discussions in Hungary in 2014—while the Hungarian public showed minimal interest in the topic. Also, Jobbik consecutively tries to put pressure on the Hungarian government in order not to fulfill its EU and NATO duties, which in this case involves stepping up against Russia.

Jobbik's election program described the development and maintenance of good relations with a "Russia wielding increasing influence" as vitally important. The party took a similarly unequivocal position regarding the country's energy policy; it puts its support behind the South Stream project and the new Paks II nuclear facility financed and built by Russia. In April 2014, under the supervision of Béla Kovács the first off-site meeting of the EU and the Russian Federation Energy Parliamentary Work Group was held in Hungary, where Gábor Vona announced that Europe must break out of the dominance of the United States and finally has to stand on its own feet and develop its independent Russian policy.

Surprisingly, this blatantly pro-Russian standpoint cannot be explained at all with the demands of the voters, which just show in the opposite direction. Pro-Russian attitudes have not and still do not characterize the majority of the population, and not even the far-right voter base that has expanded significantly in recent years. According to a Medián survey conducted at the end of 2014, 48 percent of Jobbik's voters would side with the United States, and only 27 percent would side Russia.

Furthermore, Jobbik was at the beginning a strongly anticommunist and anti-Russian political force. The party's and its media's turnaround began following 2005 when Béla Kovács with a strong Russian background (his party members called him KG Béla) joined the party. The first loud public declaration of support for Russia came in 2008, at the Georgian-Russian war. Kovács soon became the head of the party's Foreign Affairs Cabinet and M EP after the 2009 European elections. Through Kovács, the president of Jobbik Gábor Vona could establish contact with high-level Russian stakeholders and made a series of official trips to Moscow since then, when he always welcomed at a high diplomatic level.

Besides the advantage of being supported by a superpower (a rare luxury for far-right forces), we have a reason to assume that Jobbik had other advantages of this relation as well. Jobbik's murky financial background prior to 2010, the surprising pro-Russia turnaround of them and their media, as well as the funds provided to the party by

Béla Kovács in the early days of Jobbik all together raise the suspicion regarding this party's Russian financial support.

Russia might see Jobbik and the more extreme organizations connected to it as a useful tool to destabilize not only the Hungarian and European political landscape but the region as well. Jobbik legitimized Russian military intervention in Eastern Ukraine and propagated Transcarpathian territorial autonomy for Hungarian and Rusyn minorities living in Western Ukraine with rallies, statements, and organization-building attempts among ethnic Hungarians. In the early stages of the Ukrainian-Russian crisis, MEP Béla Kovács acted as an "independent" European observer in the March 2014 Crimean referendum. Márton Gyöngyösi, the secretary of the party's Foreign Affairs Cabinet and vice chairman of the parliament's Foreign Affairs Committee, monitored the presidential election of the Donetsk Republic in November 2014. President Gábor Vona asked the governing United Russia party to support the establishment of Hungarian-Rusyn autonomy in the Transcarpathian region during his official visit to Lower House of the Duma in June and reiterated his claim again in Moscow in November 2014.

Russian influence also visibly extends to paramilitary organizations to the right of Jobbik, especially when it comes to the destabilization of the region. The more an organization and its infrastructure are beyond mainstream politics, the easier it is for the Russian state to exert its direct influence in its purest form. In the hands of a Russia bent on destabilizing the region, these organizations and their organs may become dangerous instruments and may present political and national security risks, even though the support for such efforts is marginal. While there is no official information on Hungarian citizens joining the rebels in Eastern Ukraine, the extremist organizational scenery around Jobbik sees a historical opportunity in the Ukrainian crisis to reclaim the Transcarpathian region of Greater Hungary lost after World War I. Russia-supportive far-right blogs, Web sites, and Facebook sites try to fuel secessionist sentiments amplifying voices calling for taking back Transcarpathia and Transylvania, and have also been spreading recruitment propaganda of the Russian-backed rebels in Eastern Ukraine. In a shocking case, a pro-Russian extremist with links to the Russian military intelligence service GRU (Main Intelligence Agency) shot a policeman in Hungary in September 2016 (Krekó and Győri, 2016).

In the meantime, whether intentionally or by accident, the Hungarian government is more likely to promote rather than hinder Russian propaganda efforts through its policy measures and political discourse. Jobbik's role has been evident in this context as well; the far-right party regularly tries to steer the government in the direction of pro-Russian policies, especially when it comes to the Ukrainian crisis. Moreover, as the largest opposition party, Jobbik poses a political risk to Fidesz, with the far-right party continuing its "de-demonization" (a la Front National in France) strategy to rebrand itself as moderate alternative to the governing party.

Generally, the danger for Jobbik in the foreign policy field—as elsewhere as well—is that their policies are more and more becoming equivalent to Fidesz's. Fidesz practically implemented the Eastern Opening program that Jobbik had been repeatedly calling for. While Jobbik claims that Hungary's main foreign policy partners should be Germany, Russia, and Turkey, the Hungarian government is talking about the "Berlin-Moscow-Ankara Triangle," which draws the boundaries of Hungarian foreign policy (24.hu, 2016a). Criticism of the EU and the United states has become standard governmental sound byte. While there are a lot of differences in detail, the only main division between Jobbik and Fidesz is the relation toward Israel: while Orbán is in very good relationship with Benjamin Netanyahu, and the bilateral ties are flourishing, Jobbik is still hostile toward Israel—even if much less loudly than a few years ago.

Jobbik's public policy programs

Jobbik's most recent manifesto (*We say it. We do it. Jobbik's parliamentary election program*, 2014) consists of three main parts. The "seven chieftains plan" deals with the special areas of job creation and, aside from that, the "60 steps program" identifies six fundamental cri-

sis areas: (1) land protection, (2) currency crisis, (3) population decline, (4) sustainable utility-cost cuts, (5) "Hungarian-Roma coexistence," and (6) the settlement of public debt. The third part of the program summarizes special policy and sectoral subprograms, recommendations, and promises.

The main function of policy programs for Jobbik is twofold: (1)
to show to the domestic public that Jobbik is a serious political force,
with policy measures, and not only the "party of Anger"; (2) to show
the international public that Jobbik is not that extreme that it seems to
be. The highly redundant program as a whole is reflecting the general
ideological features of Jobbik's politics, namely populism, antiestablishment and antiglobalization positions, xenophobia, and anti-Roma
sentiment in particular, as well as opposition to mainstream political
parties and the EU. A number of program points are based on some
form of antinational conspiracy theory. As a relatively new party, Jobbik distinguishes itself from Fidesz and MSZP by the dual concepts of
"purity" and "colonial mindset," and distances itself from the past
twenty-four years, that is, the entire period following the regime
change. Jobbik maintains that Fidesz and MSZP consent to the
"homeland and nation's" subjugation economically and, as a consequence, politically and culturally as well. An assessment of the current
state of culture, receiving but a few pages in the program, calls for a
new "culture war" to be waged against "left-liberal cultural circles" put
in position by the former socialist regime. Jobbik intends to replace a
"business-minded, globalized approach" threatening Hungarian culture and the very existence of Hungarians, with "the spiritual-cultural
foundations of Hungarian Euroasianism," building simultaneously on
Eastern and European roots, on the dual "Hungarian tradition" of Tu-
ran-ancient Hungarian and Christian-new Hungarian tradition.

According to Jobbik, Hungary's abject status is expressed in re-
pression by the EU, using Hungarians as cheap "slave" labor and simultaneously as consumers of Western products. Due to the exploitation, "indigenous slaves cannot run successful business operations,
have assets sufficient for self-preservation, own land or unmortgaged
real property, etc." In this context, Jobbik also attacks the government,

charging it with manipulating employment statistics, which not only distorts reality but also fails to offer genuine solutions for problems related to public works programs and multinational "slave labor."

On the whole, the program's ideological frame presents Hungary and Hungarians in the familiar role of victims of historical suppression, pointing to Western states and the EU as the enemy. As an antidote, the party envisions and promises a "new Hungarian conquest."

The "seven chieftains plan"

With respect to job creation, Jobbik identifies three major areas and problems threatened by foreigners. "Dependence on the union" results in "third-world wages" and the vulnerability of Hungarian industry and agriculture and, as a solution, Jobbik proposes the renegotiation of Union agreements or withdrawal from the EU, with the simultaneous establishment of an East-Central European cooperation alternative. The other problem is the indebtedness of the state and households blocking economic development, necessitating the rescheduling or the waving of the debt. The third issue is the "the vulnerability of Hungarian land and water resources" in danger of being acquired by foreigners. This is also tied to the EU and fundamental economic freedoms guaranteed by the Union, which Jobbik would like to curtail.

To create new jobs, there is a need for "autonomy in the food industry," the creation of water management and energy security, the reopening of mines, state-financed home construction, and the development of wellness tourism.

In the food industry, the party announces an "economic freedom fight" against foreign-owned producers, retailers, and products. The production and sale of Hungarian products using Hungarian raw materials would end the country's "colonial status," and as part of the program Hungary would export raw materials and import finished goods. To protect markets, the party calls for a restructuring of relations and regulations developed with the EU and multinational companies—as a result of which 80 percent of the goods on supermarket shelves would be of Hungarian origin—closed factories would be reopened, and new markets, primarily in the East, would be acquired for Hungarian agriculture. As a result, 200,000–250,000 new jobs would be created in agriculture, with an additional 100,000 jobs in the processing industry. As part of water management, dams and water reservoirs would be built to prevent drought and produce environmental-friendly energy. These would create an additional 100,000 jobs over the project's ten-year run.

Energy security, according to the party program, would come from the expansion of the Paks nuclear plant with Russian technology, simultaneously bringing energy independence and lower energy costs for households. The utilization of mineral wealth is essentially based on the reopening of coal mines, which would create 30,000 jobs directly and an additional 120,000 jobs in related services.

According to Jobbik, the construction of rental housing would not only boost the construction industry but would also slow the migration of young people by offering young families affordable housing. With the help of the program, by 2020 the housing problems of "citizens ready for social integration and willing to become useful members of society" would be resolved, where "integration" is an indirect reference to the Roma minority and its housing problems. The program would also generate tens of thousands of jobs in the construction industry.

The development of the IT sector would be extended to education, as well as to small- and medium-sized enterprises and, in fact, the party would provide free mobile Internet services for all Hungarian citizens. Job creation would come from a doubling of employees working in the IT sector.

According to Jobbik, the road to becoming a superpower in health tourism is through subsidies to health care providers and independent or hospital-affiliated "medihotels" serving foreign health tourists. The program also criticizes the Fidesz government for giving preferential treatment to dental tourism, which is in no need of special assistance. Here again, the program is expected to generate tens of thousands of new jobs.

The job creation program demonstrates, to put it simply, that Jobbik has no idea of what to do with modern capitalism's cooperative pressures and opportunities. It argues for a closed and protectionist agricultural policy, while simultaneously calling for the need to enter foreign markets. Also, it proposes to provide energy security—with Russian technology. Which is ironic, as Jobbik's policies would that tie the Hungarian energy industry to an unpredictable authoritarian state that has proved several times that it can withdraw the energy supply for political purposes (e.g., in the case of conflicts with Ukraine). Its plan for developing the IT sector is also a paradox for, while in theory Jobbik plans to increase reliance on technological advances offered by the West and, in fact, the United States, it plans to wage an "economic freedom fight" against the same actors.

The 60-step program

The six crisis areas and, with two exceptions, all related policy proposals in the 60 steps program are reflected well-known clichés of the nationalist, xenophobic, populist discourses. "Protection of the land," as a main symbolic goal of the program, aims to introduce a ban on foreign land acquisition in the Basic Law (constitution), in direct violation of EU regulations. Land is not only a guarantee of Hungarian sovereignty but also the symbol of opposition to the Union, to "defeatist Union negotiators" and to all previous governments. A proposed constitutional provision banning large landed estates is a message to the governing party (surrounded by suspicion of nepotistic corruption in the redistribution of the lands) and the local business establishment at the same time.

When it comes to foreign currency loans burdening the population and businesses and foreign-owned financial institutions, former leftist prime minister Ferenc Gyurcsány and his government, according to Jobbik, are taken to task for letting Austrian, Italian, and German banks to colonize Hungary. Jobbik claims to have proposals to resolve the problem: the Forint conversion of loans at the exchange rate prevailing at the time of borrowing and an introduction of an eviction moratorium and the institution of private bankruptcy. In addition, debtors "paying unreasonably high installments" should be entitled to compensation, and the operating licenses of responsible banks shall be suspended.

The issue of utility-cost cuts or rising housing costs is also tied to the "luxurious profits" of foreign companies controlling strategic sectors, as well as the reckless privatization policies of social-liberal governments. Jobbik does not agree with Fidesz's current utility-cost-cutting policy, because, according to them, it essentially subsidizes loss-making service providers with taxpayer money. Jobbik would resolve this problem with a program of insulating the housing stock and improving energy efficiency, although again it has no solutions for turning a loss-making sector profitable. As the next phase of utility-cost cuts, the party essentially repeats the Orbán cabinet's proposal for the buy-out of service providers and forcing utility companies to run as not-for-profit operations.

The party considers Hungarian public debt "unmanageable," saying that its current level stands in the way of further economic progress. Therefore, it calls for talks with foreign creditors with the aim of rescheduling and waiving debts and proposes to follow the Argentinean model (!)—which is a direct reference and euphemism of controlled state bankruptcy.

Jobbik would turn around the negative trend in population growth by lowering the value-added tax on items needed for child care, by introducing a welfare card, family planning, fetal protection, and parental annuity. Overtly and covertly, the welfare card and family planning program are also aimed against the Roma minority, for the card would guarantee the targeted allocation of family support, and a reform of the family allowance would prevent "childbearing for a living." It would only be provided to parents over the age of eighteen (also implicitly targeting the Roma) and after the third child in the form of a tax allowance. Parental annuity would allow adult children to transfer a percentage of their income tax to supplement parents' pension benefits.

The Hungarian-Roma coexistence program praises earlier Jobbik and Hungarian Guard efforts in addressing the "Gypsy problem," swept under the rug by previous governments and a "politically correct" discourse. The policy proposal package calls for a constructive debate of the problem, the elimination of "race-based positive discrimination" (dividing the population into "builders" and "destroyers" along the "Érpatak model," introduced by an extremist mayor supported by Jobbik) and helping the development of local leaders considering Hungary as their homeland. To guarantee public safety, the party calls for the establishment of a gendarmerie and legally licensed self-defense organizations (e.g., legalization of the Hungarian Guard). The welfare card mentioned earlier, according to Jobbik, provides solutions for resolving the social problems of the Roma population, although Jobbik would deny social assistance to "people capable of but refusing to work." While in this section of the program the party does not take a position on segregation, for Roma students "with problems to adjust to the school environment" it already proposes the establishment of a network of boarding schools.

Further sectorial programs

Since the programs broken down to specific sectors repeat in part statements already made under the main program headings, we shall mention only a few sectors and problem areas.

Jobbik considers the flat tax introduced by Fidesz to have failed, because the policy has resulted in lower income for 85 percent of those employed. Therefore, the party would restore progressive taxation with the lowest rate set at 12 percent. At the same time, Jobbik would hold on to sectoral special taxes and, in fact, it would extend it to achieve a more proportional public contribution by large companies. Moreover, the party would rescue small and medium enterprises (SMEs) from foreign exchange (FX) loans through forint conversion, and to facilitate lending it would set up an SME bank. SMEs, in the approach of the Hungarian right, are the antidotes to the multinational companies, the strongholds of evil globalization.

With respect to employment and welfare policy, Jobbik, similar to the governmental party Fidesz, supports public works programs, although it would introduce a system with a "public works wage scale" where people would be differentiated based on education. With respect to employment policy, they promise to take steps against multinational companies if they profit from labor fluctuation, or if employees lose their jobs due to their business decisions. Unemployment benefits would be extended for a period of 180–360 days, and the minimum wage would be adjusted to the prevailing poverty line. To provide basic services for small pensioners and low-income people earning under HUF 200,000 a month, the party would establish welfare bank accounts. In the pension system, it would restore retirement benefits paid by the employer; under certain conditions it would permit the retirement of men, and introduce an individual pension account for everyone. The program stresses that one of the intractable components of social problems is the Gypsy population, "childbearing for a living," fraud involving family assistance, and the spate of crimes committed by Gypsies. Jobbik maintains that the government and the National Roma Self-Government signed an empty agreement in the spring of 2011, where the two parties agreed to bring 100,000 unemployed people to the labor market and sponsor 10,000 Roma youth through high-school graduation and 5,000 through university. Moreover, the program challenges the government's "manipulation" of employment statistics, doctoring the figures with public works programs, while ignoring hidden unemployment and people working abroad.

The party's assessment of public security problems focuses on highlighting the responsibility of previous governments, on the steady worsening of crime statistics, and on the deterioration of the population's personal sense of security. As for the "policy solutions" Jobbik is practically bringing up the typical measures connected to punitive populism. Aside from strengthening the police and raising its technical and training level, instead of their criminalization, Jobbik openly advocates the treatment of self-defense organizations, including the Hungarian Guard, as potential partners in resolving public safety issues. The government's attempts at tempering with crime statistics are brought up again. One section of the public safety program deals specifically with taking into account politicians holding office in the socialist era and in the past twenty-four years. As part of this agenda, Jobbik would publish the list of secret agents, ban "communist leaders" from public life and management positions in state-owned companies, and reclaim all assets once belonging to *Magyar Szocialista Munkáspárt* and later acquired illegally by MSZP. Slashing luxurious communist pensions would benefit small pensioners. With respect to the past twenty-four years, to hold political criminals accountable, Jobbik proposes the de-classification of information documenting MSZP and Fidesz corruption. The proposed package extends to major corruption-related scandals attached to Fidesz in the past four years: siphoning EU grants, fraud related to arable land, nepotistic tobacco shop tendering, and so on. In parliament, they would eliminate members' immunity and make representatives recallable. In an anti-Semitic gesture, the party demands that representatives' dual citizenship be made public. In connection to prison reform, they recommend "prisoner outsourcing," sending prisoners with over ten-year terms sentenced for serious crimes involving homicide primarily to facilities in the East.

In the party's rural development program, it is worth looking at proposals to hold accountable an "agricultural oligarchy" closely tied to Fidesz and MSZP, and an investigation of the clientele holding state-owned land. One of the Utopian items in the proposals is the introduction of "local cash substitutes" to promote local ecosocial farming, a "magic bullet" in the fight against multinational, global lobby groups.

Jobbik disagrees with a new small-district system and politically controlled government agencies put in place by recent reforms of the self-government system. The party's program would slash the excessive power of government agencies and, to restore the autonomy of local governments, it would transfer 8 percent of income tax and 100 percent of vehicle tax to municipalities. As opposed to centralization, it supports a multilevel public administration with real scope for action through the assistance of institutions with regional competence returned to county self-governments.

With respect to the energy sector, using the country's carbon dioxide quota to run coal-operated power plants is another creative idea from Jobbik. In addition, the party also recommends the elimination of the summer daylight saving time—which would bring the country closer to Eastern Europe. While the Hungarian governmental party Fidesz supported this initiative and it has been almost passed in the parliament in 2016, finally it was not put on final vote due to EU regulations that could not be modified by a national parliament.

In health care, the program would eliminate under-financing by reversing budget cuts amounting to thousands of billions. Jobbik promises health care workers to adjust wages and, to slow emigration, a new career model in health care.

With respect to education, the program raises the responsibility of both Fidesz and MSZP for reducing the educational budget relevant to the GDP and lowering the quality of education. Jobbik conceives of running schools as a cooperative effort between the state and local governments. It would raise compulsory education to age seventeen. In higher education, the party would increase the number of state-financed quotas, while it would also permit the simultaneous access to tuition-based and state-financed education. To facilitate planning, they propose that the number of students accepted for specific disciplines should be indicated two years in advance. With a review of the Bologna system, Jobbik would eliminate the system's anti-quality features. In respect of Roma, the party opposes artificial, politically motivated school integration and instead proposes offering parallel classes for "students with different abilities," as well as the establishment of boarding schools, as mentioned earlier. This is practically the institutionalization of school segregation—that practically started to be implemented after 2010 by the Fidesz-led governments.

In culture, aside from purges and a culture war aimed against liberal intellectuals, referred to in our opening remarks, the party plans to establish an Institute of Hungarian Prehistory to challenge the prevailing Finno-Ugric theory. To protect the Hungarian language, it proposes the creation of a "language act."

In church politics, Jobbik rejects Fidesz's 2011 Church Act, which made, according to their interpretation, the state's recognition of churches "subject to the whims of a political lobby." The new act would deny representatives the right to rate churches, although it fails to name an agency with the competence to make decisions on these issues in the future. Jobbik acknowledges and supports the extra rights of historical churches, and specifically denies the neoprotestant "Hit Gyülekezete" (Congregation of Faith), the title of historical church. And with respect to genuine historical churches, the party urges the signing of "Vatican treaty-type" documents and guaranteeing secure financing. As part of its church policy, in the program the party assigns a special role to historical churches in Roma integration with the creation of a Roma Mission Foundation. In addition, the party advocates the state recognition of church marriage.

Jobbik describes the media as the plaything of a dual political elite, establishing a media oligarchy and political media monopolies. Therefore, the party calls for the creation of genuine media pluralism and the establishment of a parity-based monitoring board. The program rejects the media's exclusive focus on viewer ratings and "extra profits." In the interest of quality content, the party would ban fortune telling and esoteric programs. The program would also limit the powers of Artisjus, on which it places accusations of criminalizing content users and entrepreneurs alike.

Jobbik would assist youth at the workplace, in home building and education, and so on. The proposal of "a network of youth case officers" is an interesting program item; it would serve to improve the conditions of young people and help to keep them in their communities. In addition to youth case officers, Jobbik would establish "youth houses" in settlements as a venue for community events and entertainment.

With respect to transportation, the program would ease congestion on public roads, improve traffic safety, stop the rampage of drivers posing a public threat, and would take action against crime endangering railroad transportation, for example, the theft of cables (another indirect reference to Roma, as they are thought to be behind the stealing of such cables).

In the area of sports, the party would change the negative, spectacle-driven representation of sports in the media. It also considers it important to end the practice of fan registration in the football courts, a measure criminalizing predominantly nationalist sports fans.

In national defense, Jobbik would work to improve the country's military capability relying on Hungarian industry and achieve independence from alliance systems (EU and NATO). The program would increase the number of military personnel, which would also include a 20,000–22,000-strong "heartland" defense force with the integration of the Hungarian Guard and the civil guard.

As part of its national policy program, the party would attach conditions to the EU accession of Ukraine and Serbia, demanding in return the broadest freedoms of self-representation for Hungarian minorities living in those countries. In addition, they would establish an independent ministry to manage the affairs of Hungarians living in neighboring countries, and by 2018 gradually increase their support to 0.5 percent of the annual budget.

The national policy section also includes the party's concepts about the Holy Crown doctrine and the historical constitution. The party traces the entire constitutional order to the Hungarian constitutional idea, the Holy Crown doctrine, and the fundamental laws. In its interpretation, the Holy Crown doctrine is a public law concept that simultaneously expresses the unity of Hungarian statehood, the constitutional inalienability of arable land and drinking water, and a Christian statehood. The program proposes the passage of a new fundamental act containing the fundamental principles of the Holy Crown doctrine, which is to be confirmed in a referendum. The party's constitutional proposals include a plebiscite with the power to dissolve parliament, as well as the disbanding of elected bodies. The program would also expand the powers of the state president and allow his direct election. Moreover, it would restore the institution of ministerial liability and an unlimited no-confidence motion against the government.

In connection to the EU, the program states that the EU is not identical with Europe and Jobbik stands for the Europe of Nations concept, significantly curtailing the scope of compulsory community acts. The program calls for an independent audit of the EU's financial balance sheet. If the Union continues down the path of a "Brussels-based empire building," the party would demand a referendum on EU membership. But this is already important, as shows that Jobbik is not a hard Euroskeptic party calling for leaving the EU anymore, but a soft Euroskeptic party.

As a counterpoint to the EU, Jobbik advocates an East-Central European alliance along the Polish-Hungarian-Croatian axis that may be expanded with Slovakia and Romania at a later stage. The party links the issue of Hungarians living in neighboring countries with the

EU, claiming that the predicament of the Hungarian minority has been "hushed up" at the European level, which means that the autonomy demands of these communities must be raised at EU forums.

The place of minorities in the program

As discussed earlier, the issue of the Roma minority returns practically in all parts of the 2014 program, with essentially no area where the Roma would not be described as part of the problem, an issue to be resolved or put in the role of a scapegoat. Homosexuality is referred to indirectly in the party's welfare program as a "deviant behavior pattern" threatening family life. In the eyes of Jobbik, the family is defined categorically as the legally defined cohabitation of a woman and a man. Jewry is only mentioned at the end of the program in the form of Israel, striving for global hegemony, and the problems with Zionism—fitting the party's standard conspiracy theory mind frame. In its program Jobbik also deals with its own minorities: it would not only decriminalize the Hungarian Guard but would also involve it in the performance of public safety and military defense duties, and would also exempt extremist sports fans from the obligation to register.

Jobbik's organizational background

The structural division of today's Hungarian far right

Just as in other countries, the far right is divided in Hungary. Based on the level of their integration into the political power field, there are three partly overlapping sets in this category: (1) political parties present in the political arena, (2) satellite organizations and groups affiliated to parties to different degrees, and (3) independent organizations and groups keeping their distance from far-right political parties.

In addition to extremist ideas, overlapping membership also creates a link between the various sets—especially between Jobbik and its traditional violent satellite organizations.

Of all the parties in the first set, Jobbik plays a prominent role and, following the fall of 2006, it has played an integrating role on the Hungarian far right. But groups in the second and third levels are also important from a political perspective, as they have connections to Jobbik and are traditionally integrated into Jobbik's structure as well. On the second level, one finds legally operating but also semi-legal and illegal (such as the already banned Hungarian Guard) organizations. These movements are important as they have laid down the foundation for the party's national network and recruitment. These include the Sixty-Four Counties Youth Movement (*Hatvannégy Vármegye Ifjúsági Mozgalom*, HVIM), which had even members in the parliament (such as Gyula Zagyva György) and has been receiving generous funding from the state-supported Jobbik party foundation in the past, the Outlaws Army with a long history of alliance with Jobbik—its leader, however, recently started to criticize Gábor Vona in a pro-governmental daily for not supporting the antiquota constitutional modification (24.hu, 2016b)[40]—or the already banned Hungarian Guard, and its still-operating, although eviscerated, successor organizations. The common feature of these organizations is that they have traditionally glorified violence and sometimes have also been involved in violent actions. For example, the leader of Outlaws' Army (*Betyársereg*) has even physically attacked the then vice president of the party, Előd Novák, after a controversy. These movements played an important role during and/or after the violent actions at 2006 autumn; therefore, their "heroes" have an important symbolic role in the far right. This explains the ambivalent relationship between these institutions and the moderating Jobbik: while they are more and more an obstacle to implementing the centrist shift, Gábor Vona has been trying to keep them close, being afraid that they can cause more harm if they turn against the party.

The third set is a collection of the ideologically most extreme—typically neo-Nazi (new Arrow Cross and Hungarist)—organizations, which, while carrying the potential for violence (the leader of such an organization shot down a policeman in 2016), are insignificant with respect to the power they bear on the political arena and, with respect to their public position, they are considered to be marginal. While

---

[40]   24.hu. (2016b). Csalódott a Jobbikban a Betyársereg vezetője. [online] Available at: http://24.hu/belfold/2016/12/21/csalodott-a-jobbikban-a-betyarsereg-vezetoj e/ [Accessed April 12, 2017].

through some individuals these groups may also have ties to political parties or their satellite organizations, in their case one cannot talk about institutional links. They have no ambition to play a political role, their growth is hampered by their hermetic operation, typically they define themselves as antiestablishment or outside any establishment, have no plans to join the system of political institutions, and look with disdain at all organizations and parties with such an agenda. They can pose a security risk, but their political relevance only lies in the fact that their extremist action can pose some reputational risk for the political far right, namely Jobbik.

In the second level of organizations, besides the Sixty-Four Counties Youth Movement, the Outlaws' Army, and Hungarian Guard successor organizations, the Football Ultras (hardcore fans of Ferencváros, Újpest, Debrecen) are also playing an important role. Given that some members of these fan clubs have strong political links, it is not accidental that as we could see, in the 2014 electoral program, Jobbik was calling for the abolition of the registration of the football fans—a step to exclude the most extreme elements. Football fans also played an important role during the "hot autumn" in 2006—that, as we have seen, play a very important role in the identity of the extreme right. The exact headcount of the most dangerous groups in the second and the third levels is unknown. Based on estimates, they may have a total membership of around 8,000–12,000 (Institute for Strategic Dialogue and Swedish Ministry of Justice, 2012).[41]

Jobbik's organization building and the Guard phenomenon

Jobbik's organizational strength lies in the fact that after 2006 it managed to extend its control over a large part of the highly diverse and divided far-right scene and created some sort of integrated network. Jobbik could efficiently use these organizations to consolidate and build its party organization. The best example for this is the Hungarian

---

[41]   Institute for Strategic Dialogue and Swedish Ministry of Justice, (2012). Preventing and Countering Far-Right Extremism: European Cooperation—Country Reports. [Online] Available at http://www.academia.edu/2301191/Prev enting_and_Countering_Far-Right_Extremism_European_Cooperation_Count ry_Reports [Accessed April 12, 2017].

Guard. The Hungarian Guard, a self-proclaimed paramilitary self-defense organization, is not an atypical feature in the region, though. In 2005–2007, in the Czech Republic, Bulgaria, and Hungary, the so-called self-defense guards formed almost simultaneously, with a similar outlook, similar slogans ("Gipsy crime," "Gipsy terrorism"), and similar objectives. First, a National Guard was born in Bulgaria, followed by the Hungarian Guard in Hungary and the National Guard in the Czech Republic. The Slovakian Brotherhood (*Slovenská pospolitost*) had a lot in common with these organizations.

The groups, often labeled incorrectly and in a simplifying manner as "neo-Nazi," shared some common features: they wear a uniform, they have a militant demeanor, they express the anti-Roma sentiment, and they build their politics on the promise of maintaining order and public safety instead of the incompetent and "political correct" law enforcement institutions. They also share some other features such as anti-Semitism, antiglobalism, as well as discriminatory and chauvinistic nationalism. They all have some connection to party politics. Their simultaneous formation suggests that the region's organizations, while showing only minimal signs of cooperation (the national chauvinism of these organizations in a region where the idea of territorial revisionism is still strong is a strong obstacle of their cooperation), respond to similar social concerns, and may also closely watch each other's activities to implement some "best practices."

For these organizations, violence and threatening and provocative posturing to taunt minorities have never been ends in themselves. These movements were exploiting the perceived, and real, incompetence of the state, especially in the countryside, in the poor rural areas with high Roma population. They promise of stepping into the gap created by powerless state enforcement agencies (the police and military) to provide "genuine protection" for citizens. And, of course, this position provides them a great popularity in some rural communities, in which citizens feel that they are totally abandoned by the state.

Often unwittingly, the Hungarian Guard and similar organizations typically follow party political objectives, that is, serve as a tool in the hands of far-right parties standing behind them. The Hungarian

Guard was created by Jobbik (Gábor Vona was the one who established the organization formally), the Czech National Guard (not identical to the banned Czech Workers' Party [Dělnická strana]) by the Czech National Party, and the Bulgarian National Guard by the Bulgarian National Union (Български национален съюз). Marian Kotleba, the ex-leader of the Slovakian Brotherhood, later, in 2010 formed its own party Our Slovakia. These organizations carry the potential of delivering a variety of political gains to a political party standing in the background.

First, they provided huge media coverage: organizations marching up and down in uniforms can always count on intense public attention both domestically and internationally. When the Hungarian Guard was formed in the summer of 2007 (with some prominent Fidesz supporters among the founders), it was followed by a huge moral panic, and brought the party an unprecedented publicity—that could have also contribute to their first electoral success in 2009. They also provide an opportunity to "outsource" extremism: political actions testing constitutional boundaries are performed not by political parties participating in the democratic process but by organizations of their making. It creates a comfortable distance, with which the party can distance itself from the organization, or just not claim responsibility for its statements and actions, if it wants to—but can harvest the political fruits of their activity as a party.

These organizations also help to improve the efficiency of recruitment of members: a campaign based on deteriorating public safety serves to increase the rural base and helps organization building. Presence in small settlements that are usually regarded to be too small for parties to penetrate creates opportunities for maintaining regular contact with the local population. And Jobbik could exploit the success of this organization later: in the last elections, Jobbik was more successful in collecting nomination slips and to run candidates on the some elections than the Socialist Party—with almost two decades political experience. It shows that they have well-functioning grassroots organizations (PCBlog.hu, 2014). These paramilitary organizations, as a form of political provocation, also helped in the mobilization of youth: for a young generation opposed to politics and disappointed in parties, radical organizations disguised in civilian clothing proved to be attractive.

From a political viewpoint, the activities of the guards were effective and productive. The Hungarian Guard's organizational structure, operation, and ideology—even in the face of statutory bans and despite their often apparent disorganization—could become a model for other organizations in the region as well.

Established by Jobbik, the Hungarian Guard effectively contributed to the development of Jobbik's popularity and organization. Jobbik intuitively understood the framework in which the majority of its fundamentally antiestablishment potential sympathizers are ready to act. As a result, it became easier to organize large numbers of supporters clearly demonstrated when, following the establishment of the Hungarian Guard, the number of newly formed Jobbik organizations increased by leaps and bounds. While Jobbik has rather shown a stagnation in terms of party organizations, after the formation of the Hungarian Guard, the local party cells started to proliferate in a huge pace. Hungarian Guard demonstrations and formation of organizations served as a good "hook" to recruit party members (see Figure 13).

Figure 13:   The impact of the Hungarian Guard on the recruitment capacities of Jobbik

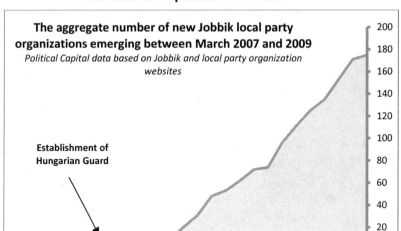

No doubt, the formation of the Hungarian Guard also contributed to the fact that Jobbik invested more time and energy in meeting with the electorate than other political parties. Party leaders and members, supporting Guard demonstrations, crisscrossed the country, often holding two or three town meetings a day. And this high level of activity continues to characterize the party's politicians to this day—and, for example, contributed to the victory of the first parliamentary seat from an individual constituency. The Hungarian Guard not only represents an organizational turning point in the history of Hungarian extremist political movements but has also become a unifying factor success-fully channeling in one direction a large number of supporters and members of hitherto competing smaller organizations.

With respect to the activities of the Hungarian Guard and its successor organizations, from the very start the biggest political risk for the whole nation was that an exacerbation of already existing eth-nic tensions between the Roma and non-Roma populations may lead to violence. The fear has been based primarily on the fact that the political strategy of the Hungarian Guard was aimed at provoking just

such incidents. Due to the failures of successive Hungarian governments and other political forces in the area of Roma integration, the
threat continued to escalate. Public figures left the public discourse of
the Roma issue to representatives of radical and extremist political
groups, offering them the opportunity to build a political strategy on the
conflict between the Roma and the non-Roma populations. This has
only deepened the problem, making rational discussion impossible,
strengthened extremists, and increased the likelihood of violent conflict. And in Gyöngyöspata, the political label of the extreme right, in
2011 Jobbik could successfully fuel ethnic conflicts via the Guard—
and then make its candidate elected to the place of the resigned
mayor.

Thanks to intense domestic and international media attention,
actions of the Hungarian Guard significantly undermined Hungary's
image abroad, especially with respect to assumptions about the country's stability and democratic development. As part of the reorganization of Hungarian far-right groups receiving increased attention and
new momentum after the fall of 2006, starting with the summer of
2007, a number of organizations defining themselves as "national self-
defense" clubs were formed in Hungary. Following the same script,
these groupings preferred to identify themselves as civic organizations, while openly advertising training for their members (in some
cases teaching the use of firearms) to perform disaster relief, national
defense, and law enforcement duties, often referring to the incompetence of the police, the military, and the state. The applied method
corresponded to a practice by which, taking advantage of society's
disaffection with politics and political parties, political aspirations are
couched in a civilian garb. In other words, emphasizing a civil origin
and the association format not only served to circumvent legal obsta-
cles in the way of registration, but it has also become part of these
organizations' political strategy. They could remain "clean" in the eyes
of many voters because they posed as real grassroots, civic organizations, and not as political parties that are generally regarded to be corrupt and selfish.

The actions of the Hungarian Guard also became a risk-increas-
ing factor with respect to neighborly relations. A number of neighboring

countries, such as Slovakia and Romania, referred to the Hungarian Guard as a potential source of threat, and ultra-nationalist political players in some neighboring countries justified their anti-Hungarian policies by referring to the emergence of the Hungarian Guard and revisionist extremism.

The Hungarian Guard established in 2007 by Jobbik (whose opening ceremony was attended by a number of politicians from Fidesz, today's governing party) was eventually banned in 2009 in a final court judgment. Subsequently, the Guard's successor organizations disappeared, continued to cooperate with Jobbik, or morphed into organizations breaking with the party. The process can be traced not only to stricter legal regulations passed by a Fidesz government recognizing the danger of the guards, but partly also to a lingering conflict developed between these successor organizations and Jobbik.

At the time of establishing the Hungarian Guard, the party hoped to have an easily mobilized and active base. Attracting media attention was another consideration. And the Hungarian Guard definitely fit the bill. However, following the 2010 election the paramilitary organization trying to establish its independence became "uncomfortable." Jobbik did nothing to close it down and hoped that its leadership would simply "wither of the vine."

Since then, the majority of the remaining guard members have turned their back on Jobbik. Three officially unlicensed organizations claimed to be successors to the Hungarian Guard banned in 2009. Of these the oldest is the István Dósa-led Protective Hungarian Guard Movement that split from a still legally active association in 2008. In an interview the leader of the "Protective Wing," Dósa, identified the cause of the split by saying that the party had used the Guard as a tool in getting votes and some of Dósa's anti-Semitic remarks "were unacceptable" for the leadership (indeed, at the time Jobbik used fewer anti-Semitic remarks than it does today).

Already after its dissolution, the officially not registered New Hungarian Guard Movement (*Új Magyar Gárda*) (which later changed its name to Hungarian National Guard [*Magyar Nemzeti Gárda*])

started its operations following the 2009 Szabadság Square demonstration electing as its leader Róbert Kiss, the "chief captain" of the
former Hungarian Guard. In 2010, following a power struggle within
the organization, Kiss resigned, Jobbik refused to accept the new
leader, and eventually, in December 2010, the tensions led to a further
split: the Hungarian National Guard established the self-styled Guard
Alliance that subsequently joined the anti-Jobbik Protective Hungarian
Guard Movement (Őrzők Nemzeti Gárda). The Hungarian National
Guard (whose members usually march in camouflaged pants and
green T-shirts) tends to cooperate with that Protective Guard and
other right-wing organizations even more radical than Jobbik, such as
the Hungarist Pax Hungarica Movement. In response, a number of
members left the organization and started a movement under the
name of New Hungarian Guard, distancing themselves from the Guard
Alliance. The New Hungarian Guard maintains the closest ties to Jobbik.

 After 2010, Jobbik developed the closest cooperation with the
Civil Guard Association for a Better Future (*Szebb Jövőért Polgárőr
Egyesület*, also disbanded in 2014) and while its name did not contain
the word "guard," based on its membership and operational style, the
association was rightly considered to be a successor of the Hungarian
Guard. In all likelihood, the size of successor organizations declined
drastically in the past few years. In 2007, the Hungarian Guard started
with fifty-six members and, based on documents leaked by WikiLeaks,
it had 1,500 members "within a short period of time," and in its heyday
the unified organization's membership was estimated to be around
2,000. In contrast, we estimate the combined membership of current
successor organizations no more than 1,000 nationwide.

 In the last few years, very little is heard about successor organizations. Jobbik's efforts to bring these organizations under party control have rather failed. While Gábor Vona symbolically keeps supporting the spirit of Hungarian Guard, and never said a word about
regretting establishing it, he let these organizations to slowly, gradually fade away. The conflict and split of these organizations was not
against Vona's interest, and he practically does not speak about the
Guard anymore. While they are present in some Jobbik rallies, and

leading politicians of Jobbik, such as János Volner, promise to boost their relevance if Jobbik becomes a governing party, the Guards, that once contributed a lot to Jobbik's success, have lost their political relevance for now. Vona created them, and Vona let them to fade into irrelevance.

Jobbik's subcultural background

Since the fall of 2006, the Hungarian far right can be described as the country's most dynamic, but at the same time the most self-enduring autonomous political community. In addition to the party's organizational skills described earlier, a strong far-right subcultural background played an important role here as well. In the section that follows, we aim to introduce the main features of this subcultural phenomenon.

Alternative politics—"Civil character"

In naming their own formation, all far-right opinion leaders are keen to avoid pejorative expressions alluding to unyielding categories that would block further expansion. In the Hungarian far right, in addition to terms like "national" and "radical," discussed earlier, one finds "civilian" as a very popular word used in self-definitions (as in "civilians" and "civil society"). On the one hand, this is mainly about hiding a radical political agenda behind civilian garb, while it also demonstrates the far right's antiparty and antipolitics attitude that, quite importantly, characterizes the vast majority of Hungarian society as well. So, in short, several political organizations actually consider and define themselves to be civilians. This is not accidental that Jobbik calls itself a "movement" instead of a "party"—as they know well that the latter sounds bad for most of the voters. But the "civic" self-definition also shows that the institution-based approach, only focusing on the role of specific individuals or organizations, is insufficient. The far right can manifest itself in multiple forms, not only as political parties or registered organizations but also as-cultures or, in many cases, simply fads closely tied to informal social networks. The subcultural milieu behind a party can strongly determine the party's ability to reach out and keep the electorate; therefore, it needs to be examined behind the parties (see for such approach, Minkenberg, 2015).

Thanks to the self-organizing networks the Hungarian far right has a number of cultural associations, motorcycle clubs, bookshops, community colleges, legal-aid organizations, and voluntary law enforcement units through which it can address social and political issues, keep contact with the voters, or intervene directly as a problem solver.

In other words, a viable community has sprung up around Jobbik whose foundation is based in part on recent experiences. And this community helped a lot for Jobbik in the political, and then electoral breakthrough. As suggested earlier, the demonstrations and riots in the fall of 2006, racist reactions to the incident in Olaszliszka also in 2006, and the emergence of the Hungarian Guard in 2007 demolished barriers in Hungarian public life that previously checked the open articulation of prejudices and blatant, often violent antiestablishment attitudes. All this has significantly expanded the far right's potential social base and its scope for political action in Hungary. The year 2006 was very important not only for Jobbik, but for the broader far-right community and subculture: the year of awakening. The proliferation, development, and institutionalization of the far-right subculture following the autumn of 2006 gave a very strong background for the party. From the point of the contemporary far right, 2006 must be considered to be as relevant as the 1920 Trianon decision. An article published in 2010 in Jobbik's paper, the weekly, *Barikád*, commemorating September 18, 2006, and the revelation of Ferenc Gyurcsány's Őszöd speech is a case in point: *Exactly four years ago we took each other's hand. We should never let it go because it represents a historic reawakening!*

This is not an exclusively Hungarian phenomenon. All over Eastern Europe far-right political movements owe their success (as the case may be) to having taken over and occupying civic organizations (Polyakova, 2013). In fact, pseudo-civilian far-right politics expressing antipolitical slogans and, in some cases, using human rights terminology as a self-defense weapon is a phenomenon known in the West as well. The English Defense League's mission statement, for example, starts out as a human rights declaration. The organization declared *the protection and promotion of human rights* as its top priority (Englishdefenceleague.org, n.d.). The appropriation and abuse of human rights rhetoric is a well-known phenomenon on the Hungarian far right as well: Tamás Gaudi-Nagy, former MP of Jobbik, and Krisztina Gaudi, the leader of the party's EP list in 2009 and 2014, have started their public career on the far right with the legal defense of the victims of the 2006 autumn police brutality. They frequently blamed the enemies of the far right for denying the human and political rights, such as freedom of speech and assembly, from the "national radicals," and to use double standards.

Alternative media

The success of the far right's "civilian" politics has been closely related to the unique far-right communication space mentioned earlier. Some sort of alternative political discourse evolved, thanks primarily to the fact that the application of modern communication technology has become a distinguishing feature of the far right.

Web sites carrying extremist content are interactive, the forums are well attended, and sympathizers are highly active. Not surprisingly the Internet—essentially uncontrollable, suitable for "home-based" editing and affording continuous up-to-the-minute information—became the number one channel. There are a large number of far-right-oriented Web sites and home, and social media pages. Of all these, Kuruc.info, HunHir.hu (a spinoff from a former music portal), and the Jobbik-affiliated alfahir.hu stand out. While kuruc.info, belonging to the sidelined ex–vice president Előd Novák, is not very supportive toward Jobbik leadership anymore, the wide variety of nationalist-extremist Web sites usually are. The radicals' radio station, "Szent Korona Rádió," is also available on the Internet as is the former "Árpádhír Televízió," and the "Nemzeti1" Internet-based television channel set up by Jobbik. However, materials carried by news portals and various social media and video-sharing sites have more relevance. Content on these platforms is not limited to news reporting and editorials, and their forums and announcements for various actions and events are also extremely important.

Net-based mailing lists played a key role beforehand. Messages are sent out continuously, in many cases covering daily political developments, that is, they also serve as news sources.[42] Right now, the social media plays a crucial role, where Jobbik, and the Hungarian far right, in general, has a huge advantage and very developed and well-exploited infrastructure (Jeskó, Bakó, and Tóth, 2012), partially as a consequence of that the far right, lacking first-hand access to mainstream media, was forced to find alternative ways to communicate with the voters. Jobbik's use of the media is strongly Internet centered, which was a necessity in the early period of the party's history. Jobbik is one of the best-organized Hungarian parties on Facebook (Bartlett et al., 2012). Pirro (2015, p. 70) calls them "the far-right party of the Facebook generation" and emphasizes that alfahir.hu is the official news portal of the party responsible for informing the moderate voters, while kuruc.info belongs to the radical fans. At the same time, according to Domonkos Sik, while the digital communication of the party definitely has a big impact, it rather only creates an imitated public sphere than a real one:

> comparative advantage to the far right using the virtual public sphere only for a pseudo-communication aimed at collective rituals, instead of communication oriented to mutual understanding (Sik, 2014, p. 23).

In short, one can confidently claim that of all domestic political players today the far right is the most adept at using tools based on the Web2 technology. At the same time, communication is not limited to the Internet; by now other venues for public discourse have emerged at different levels and channels. A variety of printed material is also available nationwide: The paper-based versions of Barikád, the weekly of Jobbik, and even more importantly, Hazai Pálya, the tabloid paper that is obviously connected to Jobbik and distributed for free in some households. But overall, they carry less weight than the Internet, and their primary goal is to reach and serve typically older sympathizers not in the habit of reading online content. Jobbik tries to compensate for the lack of strong audiovisual media background with boosting the

---

[42]   See, for instance, "Nemzeti Hírháló," http://www.nemzetihirhalo.hu/

audience of N1 Television, the online television of Jobbik. Also, Jobbik has more positive coverage in the mainstream media "HírTV," "Lánchíd rádió," and "Magyar Nemzet," the media that is belonging to Lajos Simicska, the ex-oligarch ally of Orbán who turned against him. This positive coverage led to a conspiracy theory, generally holding on the governmental side, that Jobbik has become Lajos Simicska's party.

Thanks, to a large extent, to new technologies, the far right built a mostly self-organizing alternative public space that naturally communicates an alternative and radical interpretation of reality to its public. This public space—as an indigenous, Hungarian media—is also important in a symbolic sense and its development is based primarily on the belief that the mainstream media is a manipulative tool in the hands of the powers that be, that is, it hides reality and keeps the public in ignorance.

Alternative culture

As has been shown earlier, in some segments of society and parallel to the process of disappointment in politics, a demand was born around 2006 for the creation of an antiestablishment and nationalist community that draws strong boundaries (i.e., prejudice and discrimination against certain minorities) to define Hungarianness. All this has led to the birth of a unique counterculture. Today's far right has surrounded itself with hugely popular bands (such as Hungarica, Kárpátia, and Romantikus Erőszak and also Ismerős Arcok, all leading the Hungarian toplist Mahasz charts), festivals (Magyar Sziget), brands (Hungarian Warrior, Büszke Botond, and earlier Turul, tied to ex–vice president of the party, Csanád Szegedi), and intellectual fellow travelers (writers, historians, linguists, physicists, and physicians).

In cultural and consumer networks, there is a proliferation of channels claiming to offer alternatives to "global demagoguery" and a "global consumer industry." A national network of bookstores (Szittya, Fehérlófia, Két Hollós, Magyar Menedék, etc.) selling not only new books but also reprints of classic far-right literature, and increasingly the same sphere takes over works expressing a folksy ideology. Small businesses specializing in the production of national costumes and everyday objects have taken off, increasingly they advertise and distribute their products through the Internet, and set up stands at various public events and fairs.

Similarly, an important role is played by businesses producing and selling specifically Hungarian foodstuff (sometimes also sold as "bio") trying to present even daily shopping as a political statement. This is a clear demonstration that increasingly business interests are not far behind developments helping the consolidation of the far right. Frequently, among the supporters and even leaders of various organizations one finds individuals with a vested interest in radicalism business.

Among the various centers and workshops, Magyarok Háza (the House of Hungarians) deserves special mention as it was one of the most important channels of the sale and distribution of the cultural/consumer products described earlier. However, it also provides and provided a venue for numerous forums: lectures, discussions, screenings, or as headquarters for some organizations. Workshops performing public information and educational activities are equally important. For instance, lectures by professors of "Nagy Lajos Király" Private University on prehistory, religion, and mythology are regularly presented at various public events, shaping radicals' intellectual-ideological orientation to a great extent. Also, one may mention the "Atilla Király" Community College directly tied to Jobbik.

The role of national rock should not be underestimated because for most young people the first encounter with radicalism is through an obsession with national rock. Musical events are mass events and vice versa: typically, political rallies end in a concert. The "top bands" of national rock culture are Hungarica, Kárpátia, Romantikus Erőszak, and also Ismerős Arcok, all were leading the Hungarian sales toplist Mahasz-charts. In the extremist subculture, bands such as Oi-kor and Magozott Cseresznye are also influential. Receiving increasing public attention and attracting large crowds, the Magyar Sziget festival was also held annually in Verőce is an alternative to the Budapest Sziget Festival considered by radicals to be the symbol of a "global loss of values." Produced by HVIM, Magyar Sziget and an HVIM youth re-cruitment camp feature the entire network of self-styled "national rad-ical" culture.

To sum up, the far-right ideology has also recast itself in the form of a subculture, manifested in music, dressing, and, of course, in a networking of friends and coevals. A similar process had already taken place with respect to skinhead movements. However, while the latter expressed their ideology primarily through a revival of Nazi sym-bols and ideology, the current trend, "national rock," stands more for a sort of hackney "super-Hungarian" patriotism and irredentism. The fact that the far-right subculture attracted a large number of young people, that cultural goods suffused with this ideology are more and more pop-ular, and, in fact, represent an increasingly profitable segment of the cultural market, can be traced to several factors.

1. **The transformation of higher education:** At the end of the 1990s Hungarian higher education started to be overrun by crowds of stu-dents, which, however, was not accompanied by genuine reform of the educational system, in increasing number of universities and colleges train students in fields with no market value.[43] Conse-quently, in many cases, university and college graduates find it dif-ficult to find employment: they fail to land jobs suited to their skills and expectations, or join the ranks of long-term job seekers. A fore-knowledge of difficult job and uncertain career prospects has a de-pressing effect on students throughout their university years (M. László, 2006). All this pushes some university students toward rad-ical behavior patterns; it is no accident that Jobbik also started its career as a university student organization. Radical right-wing or-ganizations and communities forming at universities find it easy to recruit young students entering higher educational institutions, and by joining students are not only offered a worldview but also circle of friends, contacts, and entertainment opportunities, and even of-ficial representation (see the links of most student self-govern-ments to Jobbik).

---

[43]   Among the many complex reasons, one also finds that an excessively theoretical training reflects little on practical aspects, the development of the curriculum lacks a user-friendly approach, and the objective of developing critical thinking is not given sufficient emphasis in high school and university education.

2. **The weak integrating ability and marginal appeal of main-stream parties:** The far-right youth subculture has extended beyond the walls of universities; it has seeped into high schools and among those with no college education. The main reason for this is an effective community-building force. Hungarian mainstream parties have been unable to address the general public, they failed to organize their voters into a political community, their youth organizations lack credibility, and they do not hold out the promise of political renewal. The distance of "traditional" parties from the population and their extreme unpopularity undermine youths' relationship to democratic institutions (membership in Hungarian political parties is low even by East European standards). In contrast, for all practical purposes the far right has emerged as the most successful youth community-organizing force, something that a number of radical organizations deliberately try to exploit. By steering the process of political socialization in a radical direction, the far right attempts to establish its future political heartland.

3. **Vacuum on the left:** Due to the lingering memory of existing socialism, in Eastern Europe the left lost its credibility in the eyes of young people who, as a consequence, cannot be addressed even by alternative left-wing movements. As a result, following the regime change in Hungary left-wing student organizations have never managed to regroup and leftist and liberal organizations have challenges in mobilizing a large number of students for a longer time[44]

4. **Strong and closed consumer culture:** Several East European countries are not simply characterized by the weakness of the radical left but also by a strong and closed consumer culture that among youths often leads to more severe apolitical attitudes than in Western Europe (Hunyadi et al., 2013). With some exaggeration one can state that in this region the economic socialization effects of free-market democratic systems went deeper (i.e., young people

---

[44]   In this area the emergence of Hallgatói Hálózat (Student Network) and other informal groups organizing to protest the Fidesz government's public and educational policy measures, made up for the most part by university students, may signal a shift. While these groups mostly represent leftist values, they do not necessarily consider themselves to be on the left and, in fact, avoid contact with the left's institutionalized political forces.

grew up to be "good consumers") while political socialization was an utter failure (it failed to create "good democrats").

The subcultural, movement-like background was very important for the emergence of Jobbik—but it gradually loses its relevance since Jobbik became an established party, and especially since the party tries to move towards the center since 2013.

Appropriation of the "Roma issue": "Taboo-breakers" against "Gipsy crime"

Jobbik's advance has been significantly facilitated by the appropriation of the issue of the Roma integration. More precisely, following 2006 the party managed to connect two topics holding special interest for the electorate: Roma and public safety (particularly in rural areas). Earlier research has shown that the Roma issue was the one area where social demand and political supply reinforced each other with the most efficiency. Far-right political rhetoric was built primarily on anti-Roma attitudes current in public opinion: the perceived parasitism of Roma ("aversion to work" and "vegetating on welfare benefits") and, related to that, predisposition for crime ("Gypsy crime"). Furthermore, the perceived rise in crime rate and "Gypsy crime" is felt despite any supporting evidence in crime research.

In the following passages, we shall present the proliferation of the concept of "Gypsy crime," with a special focus on the period between 2006 and 2009, from the emergence of the party until the main electoral success. Also, we will discuss its shifting meaning and the relevance of all this in public discourse. In the period under review the term "Gypsy crime" has become the symbol of expressing "the truth" for a wide segment of the population: Jobbik is posing as a taboo-breaker in an issue that mainstream parties are afraid to deal with due to "political correctness." The use of this term and openly racist language increasingly refers to not only prejudice, popularly called "personal experience"—not prejudgment, but post-judgment, in the far-right rhetoric—but also the concept of "Gypsy crime," which has become a reference point, a shared position on an otherwise highly diversified far-right scene: in fact, even beyond that because the utterance of the expression "Gypsy crime" has come to symbolize boldness in public discourse. Of course, while this development is not without its own history or social context, below we focus on the proliferation of the term "Gypsy crime" in public discourse and later the expression's shifting meaning.

The proliferation of the term "Gypsy crime"

Looking at quantitative criteria, in the past three or four years and compared to the period prior to 2006, two major changes can be observed in the public use of the term "Gypsy crime." First, in connection to certain incidents such as the Tatárszentgyörgy lynching and the Cozma murder (perceived as "sensational" by the public), the expression has on several occasions produced extremely high and steadily increasing usage; a considerably higher number of media outlets used it on significantly more occasions than before. Going beyond cases preoccupying the general public and becoming important national topics, the expression has become a recurrent and "standard" fixture of public discourse (see Figure 14). This is true even if some of the occurrences are due to objections to its use.

Figure 14:   The history of the term "Gipsy crime" in the Hungarian media, 2005–2009. Source: Political Capital's calculation based on Observer database

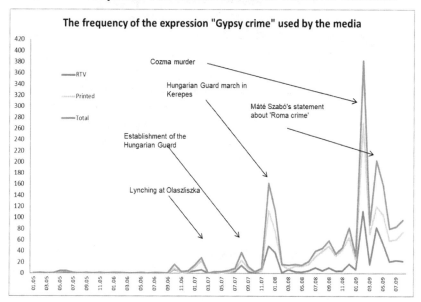

Of all incidents evoking the expression "Gypsy crime," the highest rate of media coverage was generated by the Hungarian Guard, a paramilitary movement of Jobbik, in the summer of 2007 following the lynching in Olaszliszka, and later the various events held by the movement, the Cozma murder case in Veszprém, [45] and ombudsman Máté Szabó's statement related to "Gypsy crime." In one month, some of these incidents generated several hundred mentions, setting the agenda not only for the media but for politics as well. At the same time, regardless of any event in specific, the expression "Gypsy crime" became common currency: even in the first months of 2010 the total number of daily occurrences moved between twenty and forty. Moreover, these data refer only to the mainstream media, and in the case of openly far-right, typically Internet-based media sources, such as ku-

---

[45]   On February 8, 2009, a nationally known handball player, Marian Cozma, was killed in a Veszprém bar following a brawl.

ruc.info, hunhir.hu, or barikad.hu, there is an even wider use. kuruc.info, the most popular far-right portal in Hungary, launched a special section on "Gypsy crime," updated several times a day, mentioning almost exclusively Gypsy suspects in connection to crime reports.

When describing matters of paramount importance as "sensational," we use the terminology introduced by Fokas Nikos, who studied the dynamics of the proliferation of specific topics in the media (aside from the media's "mandatory" topics) (Nikos, 2006). Nikos identified the categories of "evergreen," "sensation," and "pet peeve" that signify unique dissemination patterns, where "evergreen" topics have a relatively even presence in public consciousness, while "sensations" burst into public discourse and, following an initial intensive phase, they blow over and often join other "evergreen" topics. However, this is not the only difference; according to the findings of media dynamics studies, topics representing "sensation," after turning into a symbol, often function as an identity-forming tool generating mass emotions. In this case, Olaszliszka has become a reference point for the far right, or an occurrence justifying the introduction of the term "Gypsy crime." In a wider social context, the Olaszliszka incidence was turned into a symbol that is a constant reminder of a specific incident generating strong mass emotions, as well as it incorporates a number of opinions, connotations, and interpretations (Vörös, n.d.).

Following the events in Olaszliszka, the "Gypsy crime" expression became an almost constant component when reporting on conflicts between Roma and non-Roma. In the media, coverage of incidents similar to the Olaszliszka affair proliferated, invoking the memory of the murder case in connection to minor atrocities. However, the most media attention and the strongest public outrage were generated again by a homicide, the murder of Marian Cozma. This is where the use of the term "Gypsy crime" reached its peak: the incident generated a large number of tributes and commemorative events, and a movie was made about the murder within a few months, entitled *A Country Stabbed in the Heart*. The movie was premiered in front of 4,000 spectators in the Veszprém sports arena and, according to media reports, it incited anti-Roma sentiment in the audience. The loudest whistles swept through the arena when lawyer György Magyar said:

There is no Gypsy crime in Hungary, and when the EP representative, Viktória Mohácsi of Roma origin, appeared on the screen and said that she finds the disparaging of Roma unacceptable. Afterward, György Bárándy was quoted as saying that "in Hungary a large majority of those committing a crime are Gypsies"—a statement that was met with praise from the audience. On the whole, the audience regularly applauded people featured in the movie claiming there is Gypsy crime, and drowned out those denying it (Hajnal, 2009).

According to public opinion polls asking about incidents considered to be the most important by people, the conflict between Roma and non-Roma is no longer only on the media's agenda, but evidently provides discursive reference points to the audience consuming media content. A study by Gergely Karácsony and Dániel Róna (2011, pp. 61–92) concluded that the Cozma-murder case and the lynching at Olaszliszka were considered more significant by a greater number of people than the EP election. At the same time, although given wide coverage in the media, public discourse was not equally preoccupied with a series of murders committed in 2008 and 2009, targeting specifically Gypsies and claiming six lives. Becoming dominant public issues and taken together, deeply anti-Roma social attitudes, the murder cases in Olaszliszka and Veszprém generating strong mass emotions provided huge publicity for the "Gypsy crime" concept, as well as for Jobbik that, starting with the end of 2006, clearly used the expression as a campaign slogan, lending it new political meaning going well beyond the "Gypsy issue."

The shifting meaning of the term "Gypsy crime"

Following regime change, the expression "Gypsy crime" did not gain wide currency in the Hungarian public and it did not constitute part of the political discourse, although in the 1970s and 1980s it was already used in legal, criminology, and police circles and cropped up in some crime reports in the news.

After regime change the term started spreading in the first months of 2005, when blogger and provocateur Tamás Polgár, aka Tomcat, following the appearance on the Internet of a computer game,

Oláh Action, simulating the annihilation of Gypsies, engaged in an argument in Hungarian Television's "A szólás szabadsága" (Freedom of speech) ("A szólás szabadsága," 2005), with aesthete, Péter György, who considered legal action against the game, and when Tomcat posted the game on his blog. In the subsequent months, Tamás Polgár continued to express the view, for instance in connection to the so-called Mortimer affair,[46] that some segments of the Gypsy population are predisposed to crime and tried to justified his statements with statistics coming from criminologist Szilveszter Póczik. The affair generated public debate and the "Gypsy crime" expression started to spread throughout the far-right communication space, in various blogs, forums, and comments. This is when the first shift in meaning became apparent: the concept was removed from its earlier, more limited criminology-police context, became invested with political content in the public arena, and took on the function of supporting the anti-Roma attitudes of the participants in the discourse. Later, Tamás Polgár recalled this time as follows:

> At the time I was the first to talk in the national media about the facts of Gypsy crime, about representation in prison populations and crime statistics. My partners in the debate cannot challenge the statements supported by numbers (Bombagyar.hu, 2008).

The sentence written at the end of 2008 demonstrates that by that time the use of "Gypsy crime" was considered so important that claiming its first use became a matter of contention in far-right rivalry.

Tamás Polgár's primacy notwithstanding, the expression "Gypsy crime" became a visible political slogan only starting from December 2006 when Jobbik launched its "ciganybunozes.com" Web site, and systematically appropriated not only the expression itself but all topics related to the conflict and coexistence of the Roma and non-Roma populations, as well as their potential interpretation. This is

---

[46] On May 8, 2005, on a bus in Budapest a seventeen-year-old vocational school student, called by the nickname Mortimer, with a sword stabbed a fifteen-year-old passenger. The case generated huge media attention and antiracist demonstrations, because the victim was of Roma descent. However, later it turned out that the incident was not racially motivated and, in fact, the suspect was Roma as well.

when the next change in meaning took place: earlier stereotypes, communicated by the media and alluding to Gypsies' lack of intelligence, sloth, and petty crime, and essentially describing them as inoffensive, changed, and were replaced in the public mind by an aggressive, dangerous, and murderous image of the Gypsy. Starting in the summer of 2007, Jobbik-founded Hungarian Guard (subsequently disbanded in a final court decision) justified its own birth and provocative marches "in the defense of the majority" with this image of the Gypsy. In other words, after Jobbik exacerbated public fear of Gypsies and ethnic tensions with its "Gypsy crime" campaign, with the establishment of the Hungarian Guard it also offered some sort of "solution" for a symptom presented as a critical problem. With this the party initiated political action that simultaneously responded to a popular aversion to the Roma population, fears concerning public safety, and importantly to antiestablishment sentiment and a lack of confidence in state institutions.

Thus, while the Hungarian Guard (provoking conflicts) clearly only aggravated the situation, a large part of the public had the feeling that of all political players Jobbik was the only one looking for a solution for perceived problems, problems fueled by the term "Gypsy crime," put within a framework and invested with special meaning.

With the rise of Jobbik, the party's rhetoric started to include a growing number of interpretations about Gypsy crime. One of the extremes is represented by a speech by Jobbik's former vice president, Tibor József Bíber, delivered on April 13, 2008, where the politician stated the following:

> [...] Why is it that no political force in position of power has anything to say about Gypsy crime? How come they don't see that an ethnic-bomb is ticking in Hungary? Don't they see that the local Gypsy population is led by people subject to police investigation and those already condemned in court? Of course they do! However, presumably they have a vested interest in seeing the plan presented by Israeli president, Simon Peres, implemented where Hungary comes under total Jewish control. So, what is exactly Gypsy crime? Let's not fool ourselves: it's a biological weapon in the hands of Zionism [...] (Jobbsajoszentpeter.eoldal.hu, 2009).

In this interpretation, fitting the classic far-right conspiracy theory, Gypsies are simply unsuspecting tools in a conspiracy. The other extreme is represented by the party's written programs featuring the concept's original, criminological definition. The same definition is used in the party's 2009 EP election and its 2010 general election program. The letter document contains the following statement:

> Of course, the concept of Gypsy crime doesn't imply that every Gypsy is a criminal. In other words, it doesn't imply either racism or the collective labeling of the Gypsy community, for the phenomenon is not the consequence of genetic determinism but of a special socio-cultural background. This is a criminological concept according to which there are criminal practices tied to specific minorities (e.g., loan-sharking, knife attacks, brawls and the theft of nonferrous metals) requiring special treatment. The victims of Gypsy crime are often Gypsies themselves (Jobbik.hu, 2010b).

However, the text also sets the political context:

> In a historic breakthrough, Jobbik said and will continue to say what everybody knows but suppresses in the name of 'political correctness': Gypsy crime exists and, in fact, is spreading like wildfire in Hungary. And this must be stopped with strong measures. Jobbik is stigmatized for saying this by those who, through their extremist neoliberal economic policies, caused the loss of jobs on a scale where the upcoming generation of Gypsies no longer see work as a primary means of survival, and then with the deceitful terminology of 'subsistence crime' provide excuses for a variety of criminal activities (Jobbik.hu, 2010b).

The quotes cited here clearly show that in the far-right discourse Gypsies mentioned for the most part in a negative context are actually not seen as the enemy, but simply as one of the tools and symptoms in a wider conspiracy against Hungarians. In trying to identify the real enemy, overt and covert references (couched in antiglobalization language) are made to "big business" or directly to Israel's "colonizing intentions" that, in far-right interpretation, are manifested primarily in the ideology of liberalism and its representatives. In this perspective, Gypsies are either a dangerous weapon used by liberalism or its reviled victims. Which of the two is determined by the extremism of the wording? However, it is important to note that in a far-right narrative defining Gypsy crime, the image of the Gypsy is not the most important component. There is an even more important message shared by all narratives. This is none other than naming the act, emphasizing that while every other political player keeps quiet, Jobbik is the only one calling a spade a spade: "there is Gypsy crime." *This is not prejudice, this is personal experience, this is the truth. But there is a deep silence about this, and Jobbik and the Guard have a historical role in breaking through this wall of silence,* Gábor Vona said in an interview (Miklósi, 2009). *We're not in the habit of talking about statistics, but about reality,* he said in another interview (Plankó and Sálink, 2009). And he goes on: *The strongest weapon, truth is on our side* (Maxfm.hu), *The problem of Gypsy crime is no longer a taboo, and the majority of the people know what the truth is* (Alfahír.hu, 2009b), *Truth will always triumph* (Jobbikmedia, 2009). One could continue with a long list of similar quotations, for by now it would be difficult to find any statement where talk about Gypsy crime is not identified with truth saying. In that sense, the expression "Gypsy crime" gains its widest possible meaning and, utterly detached from its original subject, becomes a symbol of sincerity and credibility.

Of course, none of this would have happened if the use of the term "Gypsy crime" had remained exclusively within the far-right discourse. This was not the case, however. Other public figures defining their own position on the issue also used the term "Gypsy crime" as a point of reference. The media, opinion leaders, politicians from parliamentary parties, government officials, and other public figures all but unanimously confirmed the general assumption that the utterance of the term "Gypsy crime" is equivalent to letting "truth" rise to the surface.

In most cases, the various opinions and statements carried that meaning even as the use of the expression "Gypsy crime" was condemned. On January 3, 2009, at a news conference Miskolc police chief Albert Pásztor had the following to say when he reported on a spate of theft and robbery in the city:

> One can safely state that robbery on public property—a crime involving violence—is committed by people of Gypsy descent. To be honest, I have to say that in Miskolc whites at best rob financial institutions or gas stations, while all other robberies are done by them (Hírszerző.hu, 2009).

The police chief's dismissal by the minister of law enforcement caused a popular uproar and led to demonstrations in support of Albert Pásztor. Regardless of political affiliation, all Borsod County politicians lined up behind him. In a typical example, in her statement issued on January 31, 2009, SZDSZ Miskolc president, Ildikó T. Asztalos, stated:

> The liberals of Miskolc were shocked by the dismissal of Albert Pásztor. We are familiar with the police chief's professional accomplishments and respect his correct and honest attitude aimed at resolving, instead of hiding a problem. On a number of occasions the police chief has already talked about criminal practices rampant in Miskolc and their social dimension, although in our hypocritical world he received few answers or support from those who judge him today (Boon.hu, 2009).

Miskolc' socialist mayor, Sándor Káli, also came to the police chief's defense. The issue made the headlines when, on February 11, 2009, after a meeting with state president, László Sólyom, Viktor Orbán made the following statement in front of the Sándor Palace:

> While respecting the values of liberal democracy, at the meeting I made no secret of my position that certain facts must be made clear. The fact that, in respect to public safety, the proportion of Gypsy criminals committing serious crimes increases steadily every day, and this must be stated. Those refusing to talk about this close their eyes and make the situation worse. Things must be called by their proper name (Ildikó).

Not incidentally, this all happened around the time of the Cozma murder case.

In the debate over the use of the term "Gypsy crime," a statement by general ombudsman Máté Szabó represented the next phase; Szabó, on April 2, 2009, had the following to say in an interview:

> Not long ago I talked to a Gypsy self-government representative and a criminologist. The discussion resulted in the unmentionable: a profile of Gypsy crime. It represents specific categories of subsistence crime: the collection and theft of nonferrous metals, the theft of crops and tools, from bicycles through nuts and bolts. Also, in this context, crime is often committed by groups, and here we are talking about a collectivist society, an almost tribal group, in contrast to Hungarian society's high level of individualization. Collective violence creates a situation where responsibility completely disappears; everyone remembers the lynching in Olaszliszka. In my opinion, this kind of crime cannot be simply considered to be a data-protection or minority issue, and the state and law enforcement agencies also have the duty of crime prevention. Well, if we have a crime-prevention regime that we have all accepted, then, following the recognition of a criminal profile, we must warn the population, and the issue must be called by its proper name (Angyal, 2009).

Following the publication of the interview, Máté Szabó issued a statement indicating that his position has not been presented to the public in the proper context. However, by that time it was generally accepted that even the parliamentary commissioner for civil rights thought it necessary to "warn of Gypsy crime."

The recurring use of such phrases as "call a spade a spade" in reference to Gypsy crime laid the foundation where eventually the concept could become the symbol of truth itself. Responding to a question in a television morning news program, *Napkelte*, on June 6, 2009, MSZP president Ildikó Lendvai said: *Jobbik's success may be due to the fact that it may just pose real questions* (Atv.hu, 2009). Fidesz vice president Zoltán Pokorni said that *the party's success was due to the outing of the truth.* In his opinion, Jobbik *poses real questions,* and there's nothing wrong with that, although its proposed answers are unacceptable (Lanchidradio.hu, 2009). On June 21, 2009, in a statement sent to MTI (Hungarian News Agency), Prime Minister Gordon Bajnai expressed the following opinion: *In some cases Jobbik raises urgent questions, although the solutions it proposes are appalling and despicable* (168ora.hu, 2009).

A short detour: Developments after 2010

Before taking a closer look at the proliferation of the term "Gypsy crime" and its semantic changes, developments in the years after 2010 must be mentioned. This is all the more important because, based on Observer Media Monitor's database, empirical data presented in this study are available only through February 2010. After that date the Observer switched to a different methodology, that is, data fully comparable with that of the previous period are nonexistent. However, there is other research covering the period after 2010 that establishes a link between the Roma minority and crime in the public mind.

In 2011, Gábor Bernáth and Vera Messing performed a media content analysis of the Hungarian mainstream news media (Bernáth and Messing, 2013), which concluded that far-right rhetoric and agenda have become common currency in public discourse after 2010. Accordingly, on the one hand, the representation of the Roma topic in Hungarian media increased only slightly, with reporting involving the Roma on three out of four days on average, and 15 percent of in-depth coverage—compared to previous years (2000 and 1997). On the other hand, Roma image projected in various media formats was dominated by two core sets of topics: majority politics and crime with a significant rise from 50 percent to 100 percent, respectively, in the timeframe and report topics investigated.

The Roma minority's increasing criminalized media representation coincided with a sharp rise in general crime coverage in the mainstream media, as much as 37 percent of reports dealt with crime cases showing the highest rate since years, and the regime change.

However, a rise in crime reporting has not resulted in a more systematic or sensitive presentation of crime claiming Roma victims. A significant difference between the various media has been found: television news programs are more likely to criminalize the Roma population. In close to or more than half of these programs one finds reporting on crime committed by Roma.

Another important finding of the study is that while the most frequent media topic related to the Roma is crime, "only" one in ten Roma presented is a criminal. However, this is a contradiction only at first glance: instead of identifying specific individuals and cases, most crime reporting refer to "the Roma" of some towns and villages in the country, echoing public discourse on "Gypsy crime." The conflict that erupted in Gyöngyöspata coinciding with the research is a case in point. Paramilitary organizations affiliated with the far right appeared in the village and, under intense media attention, used the opportunity to talk freely about rising "Gypsy crime" and thus criminalize the entire Roma community living there.

Similar trends are indicated in a series of studies conducted since 2011 by the National Media and Infocommunications Authority (*Nemzeti Média—és Hírközlési Hatóság*, NMHH) under the title of *A study of the representation of social diversity in major news and general-interest programs in Hungary*. The reports covering six-month periods are based on the regular monitoring of news and political programs in nine public and ten commercial television and radio companies. The reports consistently show that for the most part, members of the Roma minority are presented in the news in the context of scandals and crime. Compared to other minorities, the Roma receive the most coverage in commercial news programs, mostly in the context of crime reporting. By 2012, in the programs reviewed by NMHH the percentage of crime-related Roma topics already accounted for 24 percent of total Roma representation (National Media and Infocommunications Authority, 2012). The most recent NMHH report covering the second half of 2013 (National Media and Infocommunications Authority, 2013) shows further deterioration regarding the perception of the Roma. According to the report, members of the Roma community are shown primarily (20%) in programs dealing with public scandal (for the most part, irregularities tied to by-elections in Baja) and continue to be relatively overrepresented in the coverage of other criminal cases (16.1%). In other words, 36 percent of the total coverage involving the Roma is clearly placed in a negative, criminalizing context.

As a result of far-right and mainstream media's interaction prejudiced statements are no longer limited to far-right actors, but have spread to a much wider circle than ever before. Moreover, in the opinion of Bernáth-Messing, by giving free rein to the regular use of statements referring to "crime committed by Gypsies" without offering counterarguments, the media is all but neglecting investigative reporting and making highly selective choices that contribute greatly to rising prejudice and fear of the Roma community. This has become a persistent trend in Hungarian public discourse, obviously closely related to a discursive shift on the perception of "Gypsy crime" preceding 2010. Below, we shall take a closer look at this phenomenon.

The politics of speaking out

By its very logic, in political discussion generated by the far right the expression "Gypsy crime" is a concept serving political ends, expressing the general consensus that there is a close, deterministic correlation between violent crime and Gypsy ancestry. In this context, the fight against crime is reduced to the Roma issue, creating a perfect overlap between the two sets of perpetrators and gypsies: the statements "every criminal is a Gypsy" and "every Gypsy a criminal" have become interchangeable. This is how the expression "Gypsy crime" has redrawn the Roma image in Hungary, although its effect on public discourse points beyond that—partly in a party political, but also in a much wider sense.

The proliferation of the expression "Gypsy crime" and its changed meaning is not free of the past few years' political developments, disputes, and relations. In the fall of 2006, following the publication of Prime Minister Ferenc Gyurcsány's Balatonőszöd's speech, and in the wake of its widely accepted interpretation (Gyulai, 2007, pp. 105–122), public discourse came to be defined primarily by the duality of truth and falsehood. Obviously, the political context had influenced the consolidation of the far right in the past few years to no small degree. For, while there were several reasons behind Jobbik's spectacular rise (Political Capital, 2009), one of the most crucial ones was that with its use of the expression "Gypsy crime" the party took the moral high ground with respect to other political players seen as liars. Moreover, this perception was further entrenched when outside players regularly responded to the challenge by saying unanimously and repeatedly: *Jobbik poses real questions, while its responses are inadequate.* This may have provided Jobbik the opportunity to move beyond the far-right camp and address a number of new voters without a firm political opinion or affiliation.

As demonstrated earlier, the party legitimizes its use of the expression with two arguments. On the one hand, it uses "rational" language claiming that the existence of "Gypsy crime" is based on facts and figures. On the other hand, and more importantly, using a symbolic argument, it emphasizes that the overwhelming majority of the population fully agrees with the Roma image presented by this interpretation, that is, the party simply states what everyone thinks. In the 2010 parliamentary election campaign, Jobbik not only used the expression "Gypsy crime" but also introduced the concepts of "Jewish crime," "multinational crime," "police crime," and "politician crime." The term "Gipsy crime," even if used less frequently in the communication of the party than before, remains a central concept for Jobbik, included in their 2014 manifesto as well (Jobbik.hu, 2014). In 2016–2017 party websites and politicians mentioned the term in the context of corruption issues of Roma politicians affiliated to Fidesz. And, in a broader sense, the proliferation and changing meaning of the term "Gypsy crime" was no longer relevant only in the campaign and party politics, but in the public space as well.

Political strategies against the far right

Lack of political strategies?

The rising far right, especially after 2009, puts a constraint on the Hungarian political players, media, and some social actors to respond. In this short section, we aim to give an overview of the counterstrategies that have been used against the rising far right in Hungary.

The problematic political and media strategies played an important role in the rise of the far right in Hungary. For years, the image of the far right established in public discourse has been defined by the mutual recrimination of opposing parties blaming each other for the resurgence of the extremists. The 2009 campaign before the EP elections has been the most diagnostic: Fidesz's politicians repeatedly claimed that each and every far-right incident serves the interest of MSZP, while MSZP, to feed their followers' Orbán-phobia, appeared to find the Fidesz president pulling the strings behind the far right. Moreover, the two smaller parliamentary parties also looked at the far right simply as a means to an end. The liberal SZDSZ tried to mobilize its camp with a constant reference to the "Árpád-striped" flag. In response, the conservative party MDF blamed SZDSZ for the rising strength of Jobbik. Finally, neither of these strategies worked: Jobbik performed much better than expected on the elections, while the liberal party was unable to pass the 5 percent threshold—and disappeared from the party landscape afterward.

The hesitance and lack of clear strategies created a favorable political climate for Jobbik. While we cannot claim that each parliamentary party bears the same responsibility—Fidesz's rhetoric amplifying the messages of the far right has been more important—one thing is clear: although in different ways and to different degrees, no parliamentary party took the far right seriously enough and looked at its resurgence only to make political gains.

All this had three major consequences on the general thinking about the far right. First, for a long time it appeared that the far right could not stand on its own feet because the left tied extremists to the

right, and the right to the left. Second, at several junctures the definition of the far right as a source of danger prevented a study of the far
right's political position and agenda, as well as the development of
counterarguments because, in this context, the demonstration of the
danger or its denial was the only objective. For instance, the institutional solutions promoted by MSZP (legislative ban, strict sanctions,
and restrictions) clearly pointed to the gravity of the problem, while
Viktor Orbán's promise made in 2007 to slap around Jobbik had the
opposite effect by trivializing the far right. Political arguments lined up
against the far right did not work on either side because, instead of
addressing the far right, the mainstream parties were essentially preoccupied with their own strategies developed against each other.

The 2009 EP election campaign demonstrated that while all parliamentary parties look at the far right as a challenge, none were able
to develop a real effective strategy to counter it. In fact, practically
every player helped the rise of the far right with different tools. And the
period following the election created an entirely new situation: the position of the far right changed in the political arena when, due to the
marginal position occupied by small parliamentary parties, Jobbik
came to be seen as relatively strong. Thanks to feeble support for
smaller parties, in the public eye Jobbik became the "third force" even
as a party outside parliament. Parliamentary parties were unable to
respond to the new situation and continued to engage the far right
along outdated and/or failed strategies. Essentially, this state of affairs
persisted throughout 2010 and up to the 2014 parliamentary and EP
election campaigns as well. In 2010, the pro-governmental media tried
to destroy the reputation of Jobbik with some scandals (e.g., publishing information about a porn star member of the Hungarian Guard),
with probably some, but definitely limited success. Before the 2014 EP
election, Fidesz tried to reduce the popularity of Jobbik with a well-
timed release of some information on a possible cooperation between
Russia and an MP of the Jobbik Party Béla Kovács—which could also
had some, but limited impact on Jobbik's popularity. At the time of fin-
ishing this book, at the end of 2016, Fidesz launched a huge, coordinated smear campaign against the leader of Jobbik—not focusing

mainly on the party's narratives, but only the person of the leader. The success of this strategy is unknown.

The Hungarian strategies (or lack of) from an international perspective

Effective social strategies against the radical right may be rated with respect to the various actors, be they political parties, government agencies, civic organizations, or the media (Bertelsmann Stiftung, 2009). When it comes to strategic responses given to extremist politics, we can distinguish between four categories with respect to parliamentary and non-parliamentary movements, in two dimensions (Widfeldt, 2003 p. 152). One dimension is cooperation: the political environment may strive for some sort of positive recognition (accommodation) or negative marginalization. In terms of responses, they may be directed specifically to the given organization or, more generally, to the wider public. In the Hungarian political landscape, all the responses appeared against Jobbik, but never in a systemic and strategic manner, rather by different periods and different players.

Of the two dimensions, four fundamental political response types can be developed (Widfeldt, 2003).

1. General acknowledgment: In this case, the goal is to influence public opinion and minimize certain negative tendencies by recognizing/co-opting some of the demands of extremists. For instance, the adoption of stricter immigration laws to ease anti-immigrant attitudes. Fidesz in power dominantly followed this strategy, and the general outcome, as we can judge it at the end of 2016, is the general shift of the whole political spectrum to a more extreme position, the legitimization of the far right's standpoint and, at the same time, keeping the support of Jobbik party on a controllable level (see Figure 15, indicating that when Fidesz's popularity is on the rise, Jobbik is on decline). This is the same outcome that what Grabow and Hartleb (2013) warn about in their study, analyzing the strategic responses of center-right parties to the radical-right challenge, and calling this approach "partial approximation." But as we will discuss in the closing chapter,

Fidesz's radical nationalist and authoritarian shift cannot be only explained on the basis of this strategy: the power grab is a goal in itself and not only and not dominantly a reaction to Jobbik's policies.

2. Specific acknowledgment: The inclusion of extremists into the government, decision-making, and sharing of political responsibility to unmask populist promises. Of course, as the case may be, the social environment doesn't really consider the extremists as being really radical. From the point of communication, in some sense debate over major political issues is part of the strategy. While there has been a huge debate in Hungary over the dialogue with extremists (Juhász et al., 2012), this debate has become rather outdated and theoretical for now, given that Jobbik, as an integral part of the political system, is involved in policy debates in every important issue. Right now only one opposition party, the left-wing Democratic Coalition keeps boycotting debates with Jobbik politicians. Far-right parties, though, have never been formal participants of Hungarian coalition governments (while MIÉP provided some help from the outside at the end of the first governmental period of Orbán, in 2001–2002).

3. General marginalization: The purpose of this strategy is to block the introduction of racist, xenophobic, and other extremist views into public discourse. These include regulations banning the use of totalitarian symbols and hate speech. In the public space, majority parties suppress standard extremist topics, and emphasize topics where they enjoy an advantage. While this was the official strategy of some parties against the far right for a while, it has never really worked. One reason might be that there was never a consensus between the left and the right over how to handle the far-right political players, and the blame game over who is responsible for their rise provides an obstacle for real cooperation.

4. Specific marginalization: Restrictions and prohibitions are aimed at specific groups or parties. One of the examples is the "cordon sanitaire" applied by otherwise rival democratic parties. At the same time, the elimination of extremists from political life may radicalize them and their supporters. Here, the same rule applies as in the previous point: the lack of consensus between the political players was always an obstacle of a real cordon sanitaire—even in the 2009–2012 period, it was only a "semi-permeable" cordon, to say the most.

Figure 15:   Support for Fidesz-KDNP, Jobbik, 2014–2016 (%, among all adults, IPSOS/ZRI)

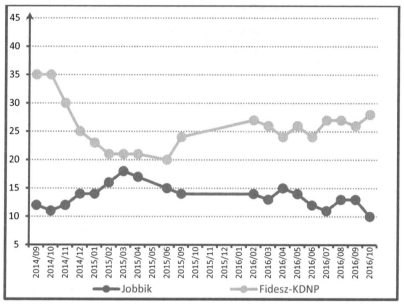

The crisis of the media in covering the far right

Even before the resurgence of the political far right, the Hungarian media had been characterized by a strong "passive prejudice," that is, the advocates of radical ideas had ample opportunities to propound their vulgar views directly and without counterarguments, making the far-right ideology "palatable" for the electorate. Moreover, "active prejudice" gained steady ground, and some media organizations started to publish intolerant, antiminority pieces, editorials, and essays generating ethnic tensions with increasing frequency. Of the two, commercial and tabloid news were characterized primarily by passive prejudice, while part of the political printed media by active prejudice as well.

It is commonly believed that media coverage favorable from the point of the far right is often closely tied to the responsibility of journalists and media companies in general. Put simply, it is tied to a normative approach defining topics, journalistic style and skills, and the context in which such issues can be presented to media consumers. A debate formulated around these and similar issues has had a strong presence in the Hungarian political discourse since the fall of 2006. The majority of the media has no idea what to do with the far-right phenomenon; it has no methodology or "language" for its presentation or interpretation and, for lack of anything better, it follows standard media strategies.

While it must be noted that there may be considerable differences in certain commercial media's sense of mission and strategy, it must also be recognized that infotainment is one of the foundations of commercial and tabloid media, something that cannot be ignored in connection to the far right's media presentation. The far right adjusted to the specific features of news entertainment, for they were well aware that, lacking a well-structured organization, they may reach the largest number of people the most effectively through the commercial media (mainly in foreign ownership, such as TV2 and RTL Klub). This is why one sees a large number of eye-catching communication techniques and often entertaining performances adapted to the stylistic requirements of popular news programs.

The additional features of commercial and tabloid media strategy are related to a changed cult of celebrity, seen in commercial media in the past few years. Reality-show-type programs created their own celebrities making a public spectacle of completely ordinary people and, following them with the camera, attaching an endless stream of new stories to their lives. The celebrities of the reorganizing far right (such as "Tomcat," the blogger, and Krisztina Morvai, a lawyer defending the players of the far right at that time) were born following a similar process. From this aspect, for commercial media the presentation of radical far-right opinion leaders has meant nothing more than inviting a rabble-rouser expected to drop a provocative and extremist statement on cue, likely to generate high viewer ratings. Here is where the interests of the media and far-right celebrities meet because, for reasons described earlier, with these media appearances radical opinion leaders hope to increase their credibility in their own camp and address new groups of potential followers. At the same time, in response to criticism for presenting radical celebrities, a large part of the entertainment media has become increasingly cautious in approaching this topic not to burn itself by the controversial topic.

As demonstrated by a series of media analyses in the past two years, the political media typically follows the strategies of political parties. For all practical purposes, three such strategies may be distinguished: *amplification, trivialization*, and *support.* The amplification (or hysterization) of extremism is typical of leftist and liberal media organizations. Over-dramatization not only amplifies the far-right phenomenon out of proportion and presents it as a much bigger threat than it really is, but it also provides extremists an excellent opportunity—even in the absence of genuine social demand—to promote their agenda. Trivialization (including the total ignorance of the threats posed by the far right-and "standardizing" the phenomenon—the antithesis of over-dramatization) is typical in right-wing media in thrall of Fidesz's communication, while support comes primarily from the far-right media empire, including such nationalist media as the daily *Magyar Hírlap* and "Echo Television," but even from some more radical members of Fidesz beforehand (see, for example, Barta, 2008). These strategies were clearly evident in the coverage of the murder of Roma citizens in Hungary by various media organizations. In typical fashion, one side of the political media tried to prove racist motivation, while the other tried to deny the same. Consequently, each print medium handled the case insofar as it supported its own preconceptions (Zsolt, 2008). Another typical example of the same phenomenon was the way the media interpreted the resurgence of Jobbik following the 2009 EP election; again, some media companies made every effort to reflect the position of the political side close to their heart (Zsolt, 2009).

The mainstream media and the mainstream political discourses may have unwittingly facilitated the communication of the far right also when they operated with the same set of topics, presented specific social problem in a simplified or stereotypical manner, or, taking an

extremely value-free position, submitted to the logic of political struggle and left the responsibility of dealing with racial issues and disputes
to politicians (Bernáth and Messing, 2013).

For all the aforementioned reasons, it is a common misconcep-
tion that media or political quarantine ever existed with respect to the
far right in Hungary. Of course, in many cases a quarantine against
the far right has been less than perfect in West European countries,
whose practices are often set up as a positive model in this context.
This policy worked faultlessly in Western Europe only in the period
immediately following World War II with the emergence of postfascist
parties—an era referred to as the first wave of the return of the European far right—against those with direct ties to the years preceding
World War II. The major differences between these parties and new,
far-right parties returning to Europe in several waves since the 1970s
are that the latter have appropriated topics where their position coincides with the majority opinion as a part of a "neopopulist" strategy.
The same is happening in Hungary when Jobbik seizes on topics—
such as the hatred of the Roma and the hatred of the politicians—
where it can claim to represent majority opinion. When part of the media or the other parties reacted to this by saying, "we refuse to talk to
them," that is, fail to offer a challenge, they relinquish the opportunity
of shaping social attitudes and, instead of Jobbik, they lock themselves into a quarantine.

Governmental strategies

In Hungary, as in most of the post-transitional countries, no general
strategic model has been developed on how to treat the threat of extremism—like the "militant democracy" in Germany, or the most liberal
Anglo-Saxon model. The practices of the law enforcement bodies and
the government have been oscillating between these poles—with governmental politicians often having the belief that everything can be
solved by legal tools.

An approach based on "legal fetishism," prevalent in Eastern
Europe, hopes to resolve all problems generated by the far right
through legislation and stronger action taken by the authorities. Aside
from the fact that this approach has resulted in unqualified failures in

Hungary, the Czech Republic, and Slovakia,[47] it completely ignores the fact that the far right is kept alive by a supportive social environment that is impervious to legislative and law enforcement measures. This is particularly the case in postsocialist countries where the conduct of law enforcement organizations is typically devoid of strategy, inconsistent and divided. Thanks to the fact that law enforcement organizations operate without established standards and practices and there are no consistent legal interpretations, and also to the lack of a deliberate strategic choice between various concepts of democracy (liberal vs. repressive approaches), that is, laws are applied haphazardly, balancing between the two rival concepts.

In turn, this helps the radical camp that, in many cases, can turn a climate of chaos and ambiguity to its own advantage and mock the constitutional order. In these countries, instead of more and more legislation, effective action against the far right would require just, consistent, and rigorously implemented law enforcement. However, the method applied must point beyond the world of law: while obviously official legal action against violent or potentially violent organizations is extremely important, the identification of adequate political and social tools would be a far more urgent task.

The seasonal rise and fall of far-right populist parties in the political arena is part and parcel of the democratic process. It is not realistic and, if we take the principles of political pluralism seriously, it is far from desirable that the state apply excessively repressive measures (e.g., banning) against political forces playing by the basic rules of democracy and enjoying widespread popular support.

Accordingly, the political, media, and social strategies marshaled against the far right may follow three objectives:

1. The policies of the far right and its electorate must be brought into the democratic mainstream.

---

[47]   In Hungary, the Hungarian Guard was dissolved only in name; in Slovakia, the interior minister's ban of the Slovak Brotherhood was eventually overruled by the High Court; and in the Czech Republic, the Workers Party banned after a lot of wrangling was reborn following the 2010 election.

2. Ethnocentric and antiminority positions and rhetoric must be local-
   ized to prevent their spread to the wider political community.
3. Ensure that rhetoric based on prejudice and hatred is not translated
   into violent action.

In this respect, the Hungarian political system can show up some partial success in the first case—but not so much at the second and the
third.

Possible strategies for the future

After analyzing the strategies so far, we would come up, based on a
former study of Political Capital, some recommendations as well—at
least for future political players.

1. **Emphasis on reducing demand:** With respect to the radical right,
   the standard repressive approach tends to strangle the supply side
   through legal means (banning extremist movements and rigorous
   law enforcement), a tactic the efficiency of which is highly questionable. On the one hand, it is far from evident that a repressive legal
   environment achieves more than simply pushing the problem "underground" as to make it invisible (see the German terrorist cell,
   the Nationalsozialistischer Untergrund)[48] and, on the other hand, in
   the lack of sufficient resources, the state cannot perform all the duties required to suppress extremists. Effective demand-reduction
   strategies, involving the cooperation of state and civic organizations, and the development of counter-narratives, along with education and community building, offer more than a palliative and,
   instead, may prevent the perpetuation of extremist attitudes. Particularly in Eastern Europe, the development of democracy-educa-
   tion and the stimulation of the debating culture are extremely important, for without these the public will become more receptive to
   far-right arguments and democracy will lose its immunity for a rhetoric aimed at undermining its institutional framework.

---

[48]   Between 2000 and 2006, members of the organization committed ten murders
       and fourteen bank robberies. German authorities "got to the" organization only in
       2011.

2. **Ridiculing instead of stigmatization and fear-mongering:** The far right lives and dies by provocation. As demonstrated by a number of examples (that of Jobbik in Hungary, the FN in France, or the Freedom Party in Holland), fear-mongering and diabolizing the far right may often backfire and could in fact increase the relevance and reach of these political organizations. For the far right gains its strength from the dual claim that they are the sole "champions" of truth and, in contrast to the mainstream political elite, they have the courage "to say it as it is," which also explains all the anger aimed at them. Moreover, some far-right organizations (such as the Hungarian Jobbik, British English Defence League, and the Greek Golden Dawn) become attractive in the eyes of young people thanks to their mobilizing subculture and the fads they generate. The "frightful" image of the far right painted by the political establishment also adds to the appeal of these organizations. Therefore, making their ideas the subject of ridicule (the far right's simplistic, bombastic, and single-minded ideology offer an excellent target) may be a much more effective strategy than all the efforts to sow fear. And here, along with mainstream politicians, investigative journalism also has a major role to play. Obviously, political forces are not expected to stand by idly as the written and unwritten rules of democracy are violated, although an appeal to such an attitude may be effective only in countries with strong democratic traditions. It is also essential that politicians and the media refrain from stigmatizing radical forces and radical voters ("Nazis") for this generic label usually makes it more difficult for these voters to return to the political mainstream.

3. **Close engagement with the electorate:** Extremist forces set up their own political base in opposition to a corrupt political elite alienated from the electorate. Typically they do this through strong grassroots movements and intense personal contact with their voters. This lends them a huge advantage over hide-bound political parties. A spreading aversion to representative democracies sweeping across Europe can only be checked if the electorate is made to feel that politics is about them and here personal contact plays a crucial role.

4. **The political mobilization of first voters:** Far-right parties are often blamed for their "populism," although in many cases this simply hides an envy of their rhetorical and political resourcefulness. Thus an appeal to emotions and political discourse based on simple and direct language are features of a broadly interpreted populism that should be acquired by all democratic political forces. If centrist parties could play "populist" politics in this sense (i.e., less technocratic), it would limit the appeal of far-right populism among the general population and young people alike. In a number of countries, such as Great Britain, Hungary, Italy, and Greece, new far-right movements appear to be well positioned to address politically passive or undecided youngsters and first voters with no or scarcely any political opinion. They use highly effective mobilizing techniques, clear and stunning symbols, loud campaigns drowning out all rivals, as well as easily understood and provocative messages simplified to the extreme. To make themselves attractive to young voters, traditional political parties must develop innovative organizational structures, communication platforms (with a strong emphasis on social media), and a new style of discourse.

Concluding remarks—Hungary: Taken hostage by the far right?

As the story of the Hungarian far right discussed reveals, what we could observe in the last few years is a very typical example of the *"one-sided polarization"* in politics, with the political right not only becoming more radical but dominating the political landscape, gaining two-thirds of the votes in the last elections. This situation usually creates a fertile breeding ground for the far-right forces—both the parties and the narratives, as it makes the extreme mainstream (see, for example, Ignazi, 2003).

Since 2010, we could see a gradual shift of Fidesz from a nationalist populist position toward the position of a genuine far-right party (see, for example, Mudde, 2015), characterized by authoritarianism, xenophobia, populism, and conspiracy theories in the heart of their ideology. In the general view, the reason for this radical shift is that Fidesz wants to hamper Jobbik's rise in the polls. Exploiting this belief, when Orbán speaks for an international audience, such as diplomats and journalists, he keeps using this argument, claiming that Fidesz is the guarantee of stopping the rise of the far right.

However, this tempting explanation is unfortunately too simple to be true. It seems that from the very beginning, Fidesz could consciously use Jobbik as an instrument to reach its political goals to transform the system in Hungary (Krekó and Mayer, 2015). Jobbik has been serving Fidesz as a "pioneer" to mark out new pathways ideologically and politically. In this way, so far, Fidesz has rather instrumentalized Jobbik than vice versa. While Jobbik definitely had an impact on the governance of Fidesz, as the latter implemented their policy proposals, it would be a mistake to assume that the governmental line was set this way because of Jobbik. For five years, Fidesz could govern with a two-third constitutional majority, without any need to adapt its policies to receive votes from the opposition. Furthermore, in politics there is no such thing as copyright: it was Fidesz, and not Jobbik, that could capitalize on the implementation of radical policy measures originally initiated by Jobbik, such as Trianon commemoration day and extra taxes on multinational companies.

Following the shocking experience of losing governmental power in 2002, it has become obvious that Orbán thinks the only way to hold on to power against the networks of postsocialist and international elites is to eliminate their power via a complete transformation of the institutional system. And Orbán was not shy to tell this to the public: in his speech in Băile Tuşnad in 2014, he talked about the importance of building up an "illiberal" system to keep the "national" forces in power. Jobbik played some role in this process as a source of inspiration (ideologically, culturally, and politically speaking), and as the pioneer, broadening the limits of politics and even changing the reference points of where the mainstream ends and the extreme begins. But Orbán wanted to go this direction anyway, and this infamous speech was mainly inspired by his political advisor Gyula Tellér (2014). Orbán really believes the postliberal "brave new world", and his hopes are that the the presidency of Donald Trump is proof for the beginning of a new era in western politics. With the emergence of nationalist forces in Europe, Orbán does not even need Jobbik as a pioneer anymore. The ideological foundations upon which Orbán has built his politics are not new, and they were already present even before Jobbik emerged on the scene. Orbán's goals to build up the "illiberal state" serves his own, and not Jobbik's, political interests.

Orbán, while mainstreaming the extreme and extreming the mainstream, was able to instrumentalize Jobbik's politics. Orbán himself did a great deal to radicalize a part of his electorate with harsh anticommunist, antiliberal, anti-Western, and pro-Eastern (mainly pro-Russian) rhetoric. Orbán also knows he benefits from the political presence of Jobbik: it makes the opposition to his regime divided between two poles: the left and the far-right. And Orbán's ideology and politics are intertwined in serving his long-term strategic goal of establishing a consolidated illiberal system—they have been not just reactive steps to counter Jobbik's rise. Orban does not need a radical nationalist ideology to challenge Jobbik, but rather to justify the illiberal system he is building up.

The interesting thing is that while the extremization of Fidesz and mainstreamization of Jobbik led to a convergence between the ideology and policies of these parties, their political relations were poisoned. Fidesz's main ideological enemy has ben traditionally the left-liberal side. Between 2009 and 2015, Fidesz was mainly fighting with the left and liberals ideologically, and just occasionally (before elections) paid some, but not too much, attention to Jobbik. Fidesz, while in government, implemented several measures that Jobbik proposed (Deconspirator.com, 2015). Jobbik adopted a position similar to the government's on many issues and behaved as the "most pro-governmental opposition party": it supported the most governmental bills at the beginning of their first parliamentary cycle (Political Capital, 2010). In this situation, a possible future coalition between Fidesz and Jobbik was easy to imagine. At the same time, the left have rather treated Jobbik as an archenemy, an even more evil version of Fidesz.

We can see a totally different picture at the end of 2017. Conflicts started to intensify between Fidesz and Jobbik by 2015, when the conflict between a former supporter of Orbán, media mogul Lajos Simicska, and the Prime Minister escalated publicly, and Simicska started to give more media space to Jobbik. This process reached a new level after the failed EU referendum of the government on the refugee quota system in October 2016. Vona asked for the resignation of Viktor Orbán after the failed referendum, and Jobbik rejected to support Viktor Orbán's constitutional modifications to prevent the "forced immigration" to Hungary afterwards, referring to the hypocrisy of Fidesz and a corruption scheme behind Fidesz's policy of granting citizenship for wealthy foreign individuals. After this move, the leader of Jobbik could experience a personal smear campaign against him that not even the most hated left-wing politician experienced beforehand. The pro-governmental media blamed Gábor Vona for, among others, being gay, also, referred to his shady family origin, hinting to Slovakian and even Jewish ancestors (his original name was Gábor Zázrivecz). Furthermore, pro-governmental media started to write about the extremist links of Jobbik—that they did not care about before—and governmental politicians even referred to the possibility of banning Jobbik

(Civishir.hu, 2016) because of its pro-extremist links. A pro-governmental quasi-NGO started a smear campaign, in which Ferenc Gyurcsány, the most hated politician on the right, and Gábor Vona are shown together as the ones who welcome the refugees in Europe. Viktor Orbán blamed Vona in the parliament for cooperating with oligarch Lajos Simicska, and for serving Brussels' and Washington's instead of Hungarian interests: *you are people under others' control, a party that is bought up.* This unprecedented attack, aims to weaken Jobbik and remove its leader can be explained with four main reasons: (1) the need for a scapegoat after the failed referendum for Orbán, (2) the theory that Jobbik is cooperating with Lajos Simicska, who became a hated enemy for Fidesz from a pro-governmental oligarch, (3) the conspiracy theories that see pro-Western, anti-governmental plot behind every political attack on Orbán, and (4) Fidesz's attempt to weaken and discredit Jobbik as its rival on the right.

On a similarly strange development, and as an indication of the radicalization of the Hungarian political system, on the left-liberal side there are more and more calls for cooperating with Jobbik. Miklós Haraszti, a well-known intellectual on the Hungarian liberal side, and an ex–liberal politician, said that without Jobbik and the left-wing parties joining forces, Fidesz could remain on power forever (ATV.hu, 2016); therefore, some cooperation on the next elections (in 2018) is inevitable. Ferenc Kőszeg, prominent ex–liberal politician and human rights activist, raised a similar idea (Panyi, 2016). Ferenc Gyurcsány, ex–prime minister, the leader of Democratic Coalition Party (*Demokratikus Koalíció*) that called for a total boycott against Jobbik for years (including having public debates with Jobbik), and kept calling it a neo-Nazi party, referred (Soline.hu, 2016) to the opportunity of some kind of cooperation with Jobbik, saying that the voters can force opposition forces to join and create an alliance above the "central power field" of Fidesz, and cooperate in order to demolish the two-third regulations of Fidesz. This approach is not completely new: Gergely Karácsony, then a politician of the green LMP party, raised the possibility of a "technical coalition" between the left and Jobbik to change such regulations back in 2011. But since the beginning of 2016, the idea of a possible parliamentary and/or election cooperation between the left and Jobbik is becoming an increasingly popular idea. Péter Medgyessy, another ex–prime minister of the left, also urged the left to cooperate with Jobbik (Fábián, 2016). At the same time, results of the interim elections and polls both suggest that voters of left-wing opposition parties and voters of Jobbik are becoming less hostile against each other's parties and shows increasing willingness to support an opposition force that has the most chance to defeat Fidesz. At the same time, polls in autumn 2017 suggest that the left-liberal side simply does not have enough supporters to defeat Fidesz in the elections—which would also make some kind of cooperation with Jobbik logical. Taking all this into consideration, we can observe a "Ukrainization" tendency in Hungarian politics: with nepotistic, corrupt, and illiberal tendencies are becoming mainstream on the governmental side, some elements of the democratic and the radical opposition of the government seem increasing willingness to cooperate in order to sweep Orbán out of power—as it happened with the temporary cooperation of democratic opposition parties with the far-right Svoboda and Pravyi Sektor to replace Yanukovych from power. With this parallel, we do not refer to a scenario that there will be a revolution against the government in Hungary—just claiming that in the context of increasing polarization, the extranormal practices of the government can lead to extranormal alliances on the opposition.

At the same time, while Fidesz has become increasingly radical (Euroskeptic, nativist, and illiberal), especially since the refugee crisis, Jobbik is showing a more moderate face than ever—at least on the surface. As a sign of the end of the era of anti-Semitism, Gábor Vona and Ádám Mirkóczki have written Chanukah greetings for a chief Rabbi in Hungary at the end of 2016 (Medvegy, 2016). The party that was burning EU flags a few years ago is calling for a "wage union" within the EU member states, reflecting an increasingly pro-integrationist approach. Jobbik has more moderate policy proposals and rhetoric regarding the refugee crisis than the governmental party. Party leaders are more and more reluctantly using the term "Gipsy crime." Vona has gotten rid of his more radical consultants and continues the centrist shift. While Jobbik still has some radical proposals (e.g. withdrawing the voting rights for the ones who have not finished elementary school—a subtle proposal exploiting the anti-Roma prejudices—compared to what they represented a few years ago (e.g. "resocialization camps" for the Roma), they underwent a very important transformation. But the question is how the party will be able to keep its identity. Jobbik has traditionally defined itself as "national radical." But as a consequence of the moderate shift, both of the fundamental terms of the party's definition have been questioned: But the party is not radical anymore—compared to the mainstream of politics—and not distinctively nationalist on the Hungarian political scene. While Jobbik does not have serious allies among European parties, they seem to start to break out from the diplomatic isolation, with diplomats from more than forty countries (including Western European EU countries) were participating on a meeting organized by the party for diplomats in mid-2016.

Jobbik and Fidesz are changing places. While Fidesz is becoming a genuine far-right party and shifting more extreme, Jobbik is heading toward the center. Ten years ago, these moves in opposite directions would have most likely predicted the strengthening of Jobbik and a popularity loss for Fidesz. But times are changing, and so does the international context and political norms. The fate of these parties will depend largely on how well they feel the political "Zeitgeist." Vona plays the political game according to the rules of the establishment yesterday, while Orbán thinks he plays according to the rules of the establishment tomorrow. While Vona thinks the "old" international elites are strong enough to keep the mainstream alive—and tries to adapt the party to their perceived demands—Orbán is betting on the collapse of the Western, liberal, pro-EU mainstream as we know it, and the rise of a "new," illiberal, nationalist, and Euroskeptic mainstream. Paradoxically, Vona is interested in the survival of the traditional Western elites, while Orbán is interested in the failure and collapse of these elites. Time will decide who is right.

Appendix

Detailed methodology of the DEREX index

Political Capital designed the Demand for Right-Wing Extremism (DEREX) index using its own theoretical model and data from the European Social Survey (ESS), a biannual study that tracks changes in societal attitudes and values in more than thirty countries in Europe and the Middle East. Our risk analysis division developed the model, chose the questions, determined subject groupings, and set the criteria over the course of roughly one year.

We took both inductive and deductive approaches to constructing the DEREX index. We began with a theoretical model, relying on the ESS questionnaire and correlations between variables to create the subindices.

We developed the methodology in four steps: (1) building the theoretical model; (2) choosing the appropriate questions to include from the ESS; (3) deciding how to qualify the respondents' answers to the survey questions; and (4) assigning numerical values to the answers, which allowed us to calculate scores for DEREX and its sub-indices. At the end of the process we also tested the model's reliability and validity.

Step 1—Building the theoretical model

Our hypothesis was that demand for right-wing extremism could be divided into four basic categories. We took care to ensure that these four categories describe the concept of "extreme right wing," both in everyday language and in the language of previous academic studies on far-right extremism. They are as follows:

1. Prejudice and welfare chauvinism
2. Antiestablishment attitudes
3. Right-wing value orientation
4. Fear, distrust, and pessimism

Our definition of right-wing extremism is thus based upon both ideological and psychological elements. The first three subindices (prejudice and welfare chauvinism, right-wing value orientation, and antiestablishment attitudes) are inherent parts of extreme right-wing ideology according to practically every author who studied the subject. The fourth (fear, distrust, and pessimism) includes emotional factors that typically fuel the first three component. Right-wing extremism is therefore defined by these four qualities; however, we define an individual as a potential right-wing extremist if his answers to the ESS questions evince attitudes and ideas that meet the criteria for at least three of the four categories.

Step 2—Choosing the questions

The questionnaires of ESS consist of permanent and rotating modules. The 2009 round included as many as 285 questions, all of which were multiple choice.

The DEREX model includes only those questions that ESS surveyors asked in all four rounds. This is the only way to ensure that index values for different years can be compared with one another.

We chose the following twenty-nine questions based upon the criteria outlined earlier:

Complete list of ESS questions used in the DEREX Index

1. All things considered, how satisfied are you with your life as a whole nowadays?
2. Apart from special occasions such as weddings and funerals, about how often do you attend religious services nowadays?
3. Do you think that most people would try to take advantage of you if they got the chance, or would they try to be fair?
4. How much like you is this person? He believes that people should do what they're told. He thinks people should follow rules at all times, even when no-one is watching.
5. How much like you is this person? It is important to him always to behave properly. He wants to avoid doing anything people would say is wrong.
6. How much like you is this person? It is important to him that the government ensures his safety against all threats. He wants the state to be strong so it can defend its citizens.
7. How much like you is this person? It is important to him to live in secure surroundings. He avoids anything that might endanger his safety.
8. How much like you is this person? Tradition is important to him. He tries to follow the customs handed down by his religion or his family.
9. How safe do you – or would you - feel walking alone in your local area or neighbourhood after dark?
10. How you feel about your household's income nowadays?
11. In politics people sometimes talk of "left" and "right". Where would you place yourself on a scale, where 0 means the left and 10 means the right?
12. Is [country] made a worse or a better place to live by people coming to live here from other countries?
13. On the whole how satisfied are you with the present state of the economy in [country]?
14. On the whole, how satisfied are you with the way democracy works in [country]?
15. Please tell me on a score of 0-10 how much you personally trust politicians.
16. Please tell me on a score of 0-10 how much you personally trust the [country]'s parliament.
17. Please tell me on a score of 0-10 how much you personally trust the European Parliament.
18. Please tell me on a score of 0-10 how much you personally trust the legal sytem.
19. Please tell me on a score of 0-10 how much you personally trust the police.
20. Please tell me on a score of 0-10 how much you personally trust the United Nations.
21. Regardless of whether you belong to a particular religion, how religious would you say you are?
22. Thinking about the government, how satisfied are you with the way it is doing its job?
23. To what extent do you agree or disagree with the following statement: Gay men and lesbians should be free to live their own life as they wish?
24. To what extent do you think [country] should allow people from the poorer countries outside Europe to come and live here?
25. To what extent do you think [country] should allow people of a different race or ethnic group as most [country]'s people to come and live here?
26. Would you say it is generally bad or good for [country]'s economy that people come to live here from other countries?
27. Would you say that [country]'s cultural life is generally undermined or enriched by people coming to live here from other countries?
28. Would you say that most of the time people try to be helpful or that they are mostly looking out for themselves?
29. Would you say that most people can be trusted, or that you can't be too careful in dealing with people?

These questions are divided into the four categories described earlier (based on "face validity" and correlational data).

Prejudice and welfare chauvinism (six questions)

Antiestablishment attitudes· (eight questions)

Right-wing value orientation· (eight questions)

Fear, distrust, and pessimism (seven questions)

These groupings make it possible to examine the different aspects of the attitudes that make up right-wing extremism. We can therefore identify country-specific qualities and characteristics in each of the four categories and develop country groups using cluster-analysis techniques.

Step 3—Determining the criteria

After choosing the DEREX questions and dividing them up among the four subindices, we determined the criteria that would qualify an individual as a right-wing extremist. This process had two levels:

Item level: We determined the answer—or range of answers—to each question that would indicate right-wing radical views.

Category level: We then established categories, deciding how many of the above answers a respondent had to give, and in what combination, to qualify as a potential right-wing radical voter.

After categorizing the questions and establishing the criteria, we refined each of the four groups through a qualitative examination of the answers' correlations with each other, as well as the range of possible answers for each criterion. This was based on a subjective assessment by the analysts who developed the index.

Step 4—Calculating index values

Using the criteria outlined, we determined how many respondents over the age of fifteen belong to each of the four subindices in each country. We then divided the total number of respondents in each country by the number of respondents in each of the four groups. This gave us a numerical value for each subindex in each of the thirty-three countries in ESS.

A country's DEREX score is determined by the rate of respondents who belong to at least three of the four categories: for example, respondents who express anti-immigrant sentiments, antiestablishment attitudes, and right-wing values all at once. Using these strict criteria, the DEREX index examines the percentage of people whose extremist views could destabilize a country's political and economic system—if these views continue to gain credence.

Reliability of the model

Although DEREX is an index, not a scale, we examined the model's consistency using Cronbach's alpha statistic, a scientific indicator that measures reliability using correlational data. All of DEREX's subindices significantly exceed a rate of 0.6 that can be regarded as acceptable, the overall index has a rate of 0.868, demonstrating a strong consistency between the items that compose the index. In other words, both the individual categories in the model and the DEREX index as a whole can be regarded as psychological constructs.

	# of items	Cronbach's Alpha
Prejudice and Welfare Chauvinism	6	0.806
Anti-Establishment Attitudes	8	0.896
Right-Wing Value Orientation	8	0.644
Fear, Distrust and Pessimism	7	0.759
DEREX Index	29	0.868

Bibliography

24.hu. (2016a). *Orbán: nemzeti egység hozhat csak eurót.* [online] Available at: http://Orbán: nemzeti egység hozhat csak eurót [Accessed April 12, 2017].

24.hu. (2016b). *Csalódott a Jobbikban a Betyársereg vezetője.* [online] Available at: http://24.hu/belfold/2016/12/21/csalodott-a-jobbikban-a-bet yarsereg-vezetoje/ [Accessed April 12, 2017].

168ora.hu. (2009). *Bajnai: A Jobbik borzasztó, gyalázatos megoldásokat javasol.* [online] Available at: http://www.168ora.hu/itthon/bajnai-a-jobbi k-borzaszto-gyalazatos-megoldasokat-javasol-38539.html [Accessed November 18, 2016].

"A szólás szabadsága". (2005). [video] Available at: https://www.yout ube.com/watch?v=xXfXdkw92oA&NR=1 [Accessed April 12, 2017].

Ablonczy, B. (2007). Trianon-problems. *Kommentár,* 2007(4).

Ablonczy, B. (2015). *Jobbik és iszlám—Egy csodálatos barátság ér végét a szemünk előtt?* [online] Valasz.hu. Available at: http://valasz.hu/itthon /jobbik-es-iszlam-egy-csodalatos-baratsag-veget-latjuk-114354 [Accessed April 12, 2017].

Adorno, T. W., Frenkel-Brunswik, E., Levinson, D. and Sanford, N. (1950). *The Authoritarian Personality.* New York: Harper and Row.

Alfahír. (2012). Vona: *"Ha az anyaföldünket bántják, akkor azt megvédjük."* [online] Available at: http://alfahir.hu/vona_ha_az_anyafoelduenket_bant jak_akkor_azt_megvedjuek-20120315 [Accessed April 12, 2017].

Alfahír.hu. (2009a). *Vona Gábor: A holokausztigenlőkről még nem esett szó (Rend, Jólét, Ébredés—31. rész).* [online] Available at: http://alfahir.hu/n ode/28493 [Accessed April 12, 2017].

Alfahír.hu. (2009b). *A cigánybűnözés után a politikusbűnözésre összpontosít a Jobbik: a Fidesz jelöltjeinek négyötöde álláshalmozó.* [online] Available at: http://alfahir.hu/node/42902 [Accessed April 12, 2017].

Alfahír.hu. (2011). *Izrael Törökbálinton is teret hódít.* [online] Available at: http://alfahir.hu/izrael_t%C3%B6r%C3%B6kb%C3%A1linton_teret_h% C3%B3d%C3%ADt-20110406 [Accessed April 12, 2017].

Alfahír.hu. (2012). *Megfontolások a Jobbik ideológiai alapvetéséhez.* [online] Available at: http://alfahir.hu:8081/megfontolasok_a_jobbik_ideologiai_a lapvetesehez-20120225 [Accessed April 12, 2017].

Alfahír.hu. (2014). *Küszöbön a harmadik világháború?* [online] Available at: http://alfahir.hu/kuszobon_a_harmadik_vilaghaboru [Accessed April 12, 2017].

Altemeyer, B. (2006). *The Authoritarian Specter.* Cambridge, MA: Harvard University Press.

Altemeyer, R. (1981). *Right-wing Authoritarianism.* Winnipeg: University of Manitoba Press.

Anderson, C. J. (1996). Economics, politics, and foreigners: Populist party support in Denmark and Norway. *Electoral Studies,* 15(4), pp. 497–511.

Angyal, Á. (2009). *Szabó Máté: figyelmeztetni kell a cigánybűnözésre.* [online] 24.hu. Available at: http://www.fn.hu/belfold/20090401/szabo_mate_fig yelmeztetni_kell/ [Accessed April 13, 2017].

Arendt, H. (1951). *The Origins of Totalitarianism.* New York: Harcourt, Brace and World.

Arendt, H. (1963). *Eichmann in Jerusalem: The Banality of Evil.* New York: Viking Press.

Arzheimer, K. (2009). Contextual factors and the extreme right vote in Western Europe, 1980–2002. *American Journal of Political Science,* 53(2), pp. 259–275.

Arzheimer, K. (2012). Working Class Parties 2.0? Competition between centre left and extreme right parties. In: J. Rydgren, ed., *Class Politics and the Radical Right.* Oxford: Routledge, pp. 107–121.

Arzheimer, K. and Carter, E. (2006). Political opportunity structures and right-wing extremist party success. *European Journal of Political Research,* 45(3), pp. 419–443.

Ásotthalom Nagyközségi Önkormányzat Képviselő-testülete, (2016). Ásotthalom Nagyközségi Önkormányzat Képviselő-testületének 25/2016.(XI.23.) önkormányzati rendelete közösségi együttélés alapvető szabályairól szóló 12/2014. (IV.30.) önkormányzati rendeletének módosításáról. Ásotthalom.

Atlatszo.hu, L-Monitor, Politcal Capital and Transparency International. (2015). [online] Available at: https://dkehg2m1ads8n.cloudfront.net/wp-content/uploads/2015/02/PC-Atlatszo-TI-KM_ASzegenyekVoksaKozmu nkaEsAValasztasTisztasaganakKockazatai_150219-1.pdf [Accessed April 12, 2017].

ATV.hu. (2009). *Lendvai: A Jobbik valódi kérdéseket tesz fel, de gyilkos választ ad rájuk.* [online] Available at: http://atv.hu/belfold/090608_le ndvai__a_jobbik_valodi_kerdeseket_tesz_fel__de_gyilkos_valaszt_ad_ rajuk.html [Accessed April 13, 2017].

ATV.hu. (2013). *Vona: "az iszlám az emberiség utolsó reménye."* [online] Available at: http://www.atv.hu/kulfold/20131108-marokkoi-lap-a-magya r-szelsojobbos-partvezeto-szerint-az-iszlam-az-emberiseg-utolso-reme nye [Accessed April 24, 2017].

ATV.hu. (2016). *Haraszti: Együtt kell működnie a baloldalnak a Jobbikkal.* [online] Available at: http://www.atv.hu/belfold/20160528-haraszti-eg yutt-kell-mukodnie-a-baloldalnak-a-jobbikkal [Accessed April 13, 2017].

Az európai liberalizmus Európa sírásója. [European liberalism is Europe's gravedigger]. (2015). [video] Available at: https://jobbik.hu/videoink/vo na7-az-europai-liberalizmus-europa-sirasoja [Accessed April 12, 2017].

Bálint, F. (2014). *Tanítani fogják a Jobbik stílusváltását—interjú Vona Gáborral.* [online] Origo.hu. Available at: http://www.origo.hu/valasztas2 014/20140403-valasztas-2014-interju-vona-gaborral-a-jobbik-elnokeve l.html [Accessed April 12, 2017].

Barta, J. (2008). *A szélsőjobboldali tematika kezelése a magyar médiában (Médiakutató).* [online] Mediakutato.hu. Available at: http://www.mediaku tato.hu/cikk/2008_04_tel/05_szelsojobb_a_magyar_sajtoban/ [Accessed April 13, 2017].

Bartlett, J., Birdwell, J., Krekó, P., Benfield, J. and Gyori, G. (2012). *Populism in Europe: Hungary.* London: Demos.

Bernát, A. (2010). Idegenellenesség Magyarországon és a visegrádi országokban. In Hárs, Á. and Tóth, J., ed., *Változó migráció—változó környezet.* Budapest: MTA Etnikai-nemzeti Kisebbségkutató Intézete., pp. 268–269.

Bernát, A. (n.d.). *Leszakadóban: a romák társadalmi helyzete a mai Magyarországon.* [online] Tarki.hu. Available at: http://www.tarki.hu/adat bank-h/kutjel/pdf/b333.pdf [Accessed April, 12, 2017].

Bernat, A., Juhász, A., Krekó, P. and Molnár, Cs. (2012). A radikalizmus és a cigányellenesség gyökerei a szélsőjobboldal szimpatizánsai körében. In *Társadalmi Riport 2012.* Budapest: Tárki, pp. 355–376. English translation: http://citeseerx.ist.psu.edu/viewdoc/download?doi=10.1.1.42 3.2311&rep=rep1&type=pdf

Bernát, A., Juhász, A., Krekó, P. and Molnár, Cs. (2013). *The Roots of Radicalism and Anti-Roma Attitudes on the Far Right.* [online] Tarki.hu. Available at: http://www.tarki.hu/en/news/2013/items/20130305_berna t_juhasz_kreko_molnar.pdf [Accessed April 12, 2017].

Bernáth, G. and Messing, V. (2013). *Pushed to the Edge Research Report on the Representation of Roma Communities in the Hungarian Mainstream Media, 2011.* 1st ed. [ebook] Budapest: Centre for Policy Studies. Available at: https://cps.ceu.edu/sites/cps.ceu.edu/files/cps-working-pap er-pushed-to-the-edge-2013_0.pdf [Accessed April 13, 2017].

Bernath, G., Miklosi, Z. and Mudde, C. (2005). Hungary. In: Mudee, C., ed., *Racist Extremism in Central Eastern Europe.* New York: Routledge.

Bertelsmann Stiftung, ed., (2009). *Strategies for Combating Right-wing Extremism in Europe.* Gütersloh: Bertelsmann Foundation Publishers.

Betz, H. G. (1993). The new politics of resentment: Radical right-wing populist parties in Western Europe. *Comparative Politics,* 25(4), pp. 413–427.

Bíró, N. A. and Róna, D. (2011). Tudatos radikalizmus. A Jobbik útja a Parlamentbe, 2003–2010. In Lánczi, A., ed., *Nemzet és radikalizmus,* Budapest: Századvég, pp. 242–283.

Bíró, N. A., Boros, T. and Varga, Á. (2012). *A szélsőjobboldal Magyarországon.* Budapest: Policy Solutions.

Bombagyar.hu. (2008). [online] Available at: http://www.bombagyar.hu/inde x.php?post=1728 [Accessed October 12, 2016].

Boomgaarden, H. G. and Vliegenthart, R. (2007). Explaining the rise of anti-immigrant parties: The role of news media content. *Electoral Studies,* 26(2), pp. 404–417.

Boon.hu. (2009). *A miskolci SZDSZ is kiáll Pásztor Albert mellett.* [online] Available at: http://www.boon.hu/hirek/magyarorszag/cikk/a-miskolci-szdsz-is-kiall-pasztor-albert-mellett/cn/news-20090131-06100424 [Accessed April 12, 2017].

Boross, Zs. (2014). *Nem ma kezdték—a rendszerváltás utáni magyar szélsőjobb orosz kapcsolatai.* [online] PCblog.hu. Available at: https://pcblog.atlatszo.hu/2014/11/24/nem-ma-kezdtek-a-rendszervalta s-utani-magyar-szelsojobb-orosz-kapcsolatai/ [Accessed April 12, 2017].

Bozóki, A. (2010). A Fidesz radikális, liberális, alternatív szervezet. In: Bába, I., ed., *Felgyorsult Történelem,* Budapest: Demokratikus Átalakításért Intézet, pp. 357–369.

Brückner, M. and Grüner, H. P. (2010). *Economic Growth and the Rise of Political Extremism: Theory and Evidence*. Accessible at: http://www.unikassel.de/fb07/fileadmin/groups/w_030515/WS1011/growth-extremis m.pdf.

Bumm.sk. (2009). *A trianoni határok ledöntése a Jobbik célja*. [online] Available at: http://www.bumm.sk/archivum/2009/06/13/30368_a-triano ni-hatarok-ledontese-a-jobbik-celja [Accessed April 24, 2017].

Bustikova, L. (2015). The democratization of hostility. In: Minkenberg, M., ed., *Transforming the Transformation?: The East European Radical Right in the Political Process*. New York: Routledge, pp. 59–80.

Canovan, M. (1981) *Populism*. London–New York: Harcourt Brace Jovanovich.

Canovan, M. (2004). Populism for political theorists? *Journal of Political Ideologies*, 9(3), pp. 241–252.

Cappoccia, G. (2002). Anti-system parties: A conceptual reassessment. *Journal of Theoretical Politics*, 14(1), pp. 9–35.

Carter, E. L. (2005). *The Extreme Right in Western Europe*. Manchester: Manchester University Press.

Central Statistics Office, (n.d.). *Az államháztartás hiánya (–) és többlete (+) (2004–2015)*. [online] Available at: https://www.ksh.hu/docs/hun/eurost at_tablak/tabl/teina200.html [Accessed April 12, 2017].

Civishir.hu. (2016). *Kósa Lajos felvetette a Jobbik betiltását*. [online] Available at: http://civishir.hu/kosarlabda/2016/11/kosa-lajos-felvetette-a-jobbik-betiltasat [Accessed April 13, 2017].

Coffé, H. (2013). *The Gender Gap in Radical Right Voting Behavior: Introducing Personality Traits and Support for Strict Migration Policies*. European Conference on Politics and Gender Barcelona, March 21–23, 2013.

Csepeli, Gy., Fábián, Z. and Sik, E. (1998). "Xenofóbia és a cigányságról alkotott vélemények." In: Kolosi, T., Tóth István, Gy. and Vukovich, Gy., ed., *Társadalmi Riport 1998*. Budapest: TÁRKI, pp. 458–489.

Political Capital (2015). *Jobbik's policy proposals realized by Fidesz: A summary in 10 points*. [online] Available at: http://deconspirator.co m/2015/05/15/jobbiks-policy-proposals-realized-by-fidesz-a-summary-in -10-points/ [Accessed April 13, 2017].

Dennison, J. and Goodwin, M. (2015). Immigration, Issue Ownership and the Rise of UKIP. *Parliamentary Affairs*, 68 (suppl. 1), pp. 168–187. Available at: http://pa.oxfordjournals.org/content/68/suppl_1/168.full [Accessed March 30, 2016].

Doty, R. M., Peterson, B. E. and Winter, D. G. (2006). Threat and authoritarianism in the United States: 1978–1987. In: Jost, J. and Sidanius, J., ed., *Political Psychology: Key Readings*. New York: Taylor and Francis.

Drábik, J. (2005). *1956, a magyarok harmadik útja: kiút a kommunizmus és a pénzuralom zsákutcájából*. Budapest: Gold Book.

Dupcsik, Cs. (2009). *A Magyarországi cigányság története: történelem a cigánykutások tükrében, 18902008*. Budapest: Osiris Kiadó.

Eco, U. (1998). *Öt írás az erkölcsről*. Budapest: Európa Kiadó.

Englishdefenceleague.org. (n.d.). *Mission Statement*. [online] Available at: http://englishdefenceleague.org/mission-statement [Accessed April 12, 2017].

Enyedi, Z. (2005). *A voluntarizmus tere. A pártok szerepe a törésvonalak kialakulásában*. Budapest: Századvég. Századvég, 15(3), pp. 3–27.

Enyedi, Zs. (2004). Érték, értelem, érzelem. Politikai pszichológia Bibó nyomán. *Politikatudományi Szemle*, 12(4), pp. 5–18.

Enyedi, Zs. (2005) A voluntarizmus tere. A pártok szerepe a törésvonalak kialakulásában. In: Gombár, Cs., ed., *Két Magyarország?* Budapest: Osiris-Korridor.

Enyedi, Zs., Fábián, Z. and Tardos, R. (2014). Parties and voters, 2002–2014. In: Kolosi, T., and Tóth, Gy. I., eds., *Social Report 2014*. Budapest: TÁRKI.

European Policy Center. (2016). *Europe's Troublemakers: The Populist Challenge to Foreign Policy*. [online] Available at: http://www.epc.eu/pu b_details.php?cat_id=17&pub_id=6377 [Accessed April 12, 2017].

Evola, J. (2012). *Jobboldali fiatalok kézikönyve*. 1st ed. Debrecen: Kvintesszencia Kiadó.

Fábián, Z. (1999). *Tekintélyelvűség és előítéletek*. Budapest: Új Mandátum Kiadó.

Fábián, T. (2016). *Medgyessy: A baloldal csak a Jobbikkal összefogva győzheti le Orbánt*. [online] Index.hu. Available at: http://index.hu/bel fold/2016/12/28/medgyessy_a_baloldal_csak_a_jobbikkal_osszefogva_ gyozheti_le_orbant/ [Accessed April 13, 2017].

Falter, J. and Schumann, S. (1988, April). Affinity towards right-wing extremism in Western Europe. *West European Politics,* 11(2), 96–110.

Filippov, G. (2011). A név kötelez. *Politikatudományi Szemle,* 20(3), pp. 133–153. [online] Available at: http://epa.oszk.hu/02500/02565/00067/pdf/ EPA02565_poltud_szemle_2011_3_133-154.pdf. [Accessed April 13, 2017].

Ford, R. and Goodwin, M. (2014). Understanding UKIP: Identity, Social Change and the Left Behind. *The Political Quarterly,* 85(3), pp. 277–284. [online] Available at: http://onlinelibrary.wiley.com/doi/10.1111/1467-923X.12099/citedby [Accessed April 13, 2017].

Fromm, E. (2002). *Menekülés a szabadság elől.* Budapest: Napvilág Kiadó. (Original in German published in 1941.)

Gábor, M. (2009). *Amit látunk, az szervezett provokáció.* [online] Index.hu. Available   at: http://index.hu/belfold/2009/06/30/amit_latunk_az_szervezett_provokaci o/ [Accessed April 12, 2017].

Gerő, A. (2010). *Nemzeti Bolsevizmus.* [online] 168ora.hu. Available at: http://www.168ora.hu/velemeny/gero-andras-jobbik-bolsevizmus-szelso jobb-nacizmus-zsidesz-52225.html. [Accessed April 13, 2017].

Glick, P. (2002). Sacrificial Lambs Dressed in Wolves' Clothing. Understanding Genocide.

Golder, M. (2003a). Electoral institutions, unemployment and extreme right parties: A correction. *British Journal of Political Science,* 33(3), pp. 525–534.

Golder, M. (2003b). Explaining variation in the success of extreme right parties in Western Europe. *Comparative Political Studies,* 36(4), pp. 432–466.

Grabow, K., and Hartleb, F. (2013). Exposing the demagogues: Right-wing and national populist parties in Europe. *European View,* 12(2), p. 329.

Grajczjár, I. and Tóth, A. (2009). Miért olyan sikeresek a radikális nemzeti-populista pártok nagy társadalmi-gazdasági átalakulások, válságok idején? *Politikatudományi Szemle,* 18(3), pp. 7–29.

Grajczjár, I. and Tóth, A. (2010). Válság, radikalizálódás és az újjászületés ígérete: a Jobbik útja a parlamentbe. In: Enyedi, Z., Szabó, A. and Tardos, R., ed., *Új képlet. Választások Magyarországon.* Budapest: Demokrácia Kutatások Magyar Központja Alapítvány, pp. 57–92.

Grajczjár, I. and Tóth, A. (2012). *A nemzeti radikalizmus. A jobboldali radikalizmus negyedik hulláma Magyarországon.* [online] Available at: http://politologia.tk.mta.hu/uploads/files/archived/6055_I_04_Toth_G rajczjar_Nemzeti_radikalizmus.pdf [Accessed March 30, 2016].

Győr, Á. and Katona, M. (2016). *Diplomatákkal egyeztetett a Jobbik.* [online] Mno.hu. Available at: https://mno.hu/belfold/diplomatakkal-egyeztetett-a-jobbik-1344030 [Accessed April 13, 2017].

Gyulai, A. (2007). "About truth and falsehood understood in the sense of a discursive strategy." *Politikatudományi szemle*, 2, pp. 105–122.

Gyulai, A., Juhász, A., Krekó, P., Somogyi, Z. and Szabados, K. (2006). *Gyurcsány vagy Orbán?* Budapest: Political Capital Könyvek.

Gyurgyák, J. (2007). *Mivé lett Magyar hazátok.* Budapest: Osiris Kiadó.

Hagtvet, B. (1994). Right-wing extremism in Europe. *Journal of Peace Research*, 31(3), pp. 241–246.

Hajnal, H. (2009). *4000 embert szúrtak szíven Veszprémben.* [online] Index.hu. Available at: http://index.hu/kultur/cinematrix/ccikkek/2009/05/08/4000_embert_szurtak_sziven_veszpremben/ [Accessed April 12, 2017].

Hetek. (2014). *Vona Gábor tíz éve képviseli az iszlám érdekeket.* [online] Available at: http://www.hetek.hu/belfold/201404/vona_gabor_tiz_eve_k epviseli_az_iszlam_erdekeket [Accessed April 24, 2017].

Hetek.hu. (2014). *Sneider Tamás élete és kora.* [online] Available at: http://www.hetek.hu/belfold/201405/sneider_tamas_elete_es_kora [Accessed April 12, 2017].

Hírszerző.hu. (2009). *Minden elkövető cigány volt—állítja a főkapitány.* [online] Available at: http://www.hirszerzo.hu/cikk.minden_elkoveto_ci gany_volt_-_allitja_a_fokapitany.96014.html [Accessed April 13, 2017].

Horváth, B. (2015). *Tapolcai Jobbik-jelölt: a cigányok a zsidók biológiai fegyvere.* [online] 24.hu. Available at: http://24.hu/belfold/2015/02/14/tapolcai-jobbik-jelolt-a-ciganyok-a-zsidok-biologiai-fegyvere/ [Accessed April 24, 2017].

Huber, J. D. (1984). Values and partisanship in left-right orientations: Measuring ideology. *European Journal of Political Research*, 17(5), pp. 599–621.

Hunyadi, B., Juhász, A., Krekó, P., Molnár, Cs. and Szitás, K. (2013). *Lelkes fogyasztók, el nem kötelezett demokraták: Tanulmány a fiatalok demokráciához fűződő viszonyáról.* 1st ed. [ebook] Heinrich Böll Stiftung. Available at: http://http://www.osztalyfonok.hu/files/Lelkes_fogyasztok_e l_nem_kotelezett_demokratak.pdf [Accessed April 12, 2017].

Hunyady, Gy. (1996). *Sztereotípiák a változó közgondolkodásban.* Budapest: Akadémiai.

Hunyady, Gy. (2000). *Nemzetkarakterológiák.* Budapest: Osiris kiadó.

Hvg.hu. (2016). *Toroczkai odacsap a bevándorlóknak: megtiltják a mecsetépítést Ásotthalmon.* [online] Available at: http://hvg.hu/itthon/20 161124_toroczkai_asotthalom_muszlim_tiltas [Accessed April 12, 2017].

Ignazi, P. (1992). The silent counter-revolution. Hypotheses on the emergence of extreme right wing parties. *European Journal of Political Research*, 22(1), pp. 3–34.

Ignazi, P. (2003). *Extreme Right Parties in Western Europe.* Oxford: Oxford University.

Ildikó, C. (n.d.). *Orbán Viktor: cigánybűnözés nincs, cigány bűnözők vannak.* [online] NOL.hu. Available at: http://www.nol.hu/belfold/orban_viktor__c iganybunozes_nincs__ciganybunozok_vannak [Accessed April 12, 2017].

Index.hu. (2002). *Orbán: "...ha mozdulnunk kell, együtt mozdulhassunk."* [online] Available at: http://index.hu/belfold/var0507/ [Accessed April 12, 2017].

Inglehart R. (1987). "Extremist political positions and perceptions of conspiracy: Even paranoids have real enemies." In: Graumann, C. F. and Moscovici, S., ed., *Changing Conceptions of Conspiracy.* Berlin: Springer, pp. 231–244.

Institute for Strategic Dialogue and Swedish Ministry of Justice, (2012). *Preventing and Countering Far-Right Extremism: European Cooperation—Country Reports.* [Online] Available at http://www.acad emia.edu/2301191/Preventing_and_Countering_Far-Right_Extremism_ European_Cooperation_Country_Reports [Accessed April 12, 2017].

Ivarsflaten, E. (2008). What unites right-wing populists in Western Europe? Re-examining grievance mobilization models in seven successful cases. *Comparative Political Studies*, 41(1), pp. 3–23.

Jackman, R. W. and Volpert, K. (1996). Conditions favoring parties of the extreme right in Western Europe. *British Journal of Political Science*, 26(4), pp. 501–522.

Jeskó, J., Bakó, J. and Tóth, Z. (2012). A radikális jobboldal webes hálózatai. *Politikatudományi Szemle*, 21(1), pp. 81–101.

Jesuit, D. K., Paradowski, P. R. and Mahler, V. A. (2009). Electoral support for extreme right wing countries: A sub-national analysis of Western European elections. *Electoral Studies*, 28(2), 27–52.

Jobbik.hu. (2007). *Bethlen Gábor Program*. [online] Available at: https://jobbik.hu/rovatok/bethlen_gabor_program/bethlen_gabor_progra m [Accessed April 12, 2017].

Jobbik.hu. (2009). *Magyarország a magyaroké!*. [online] Available at: https://jobbik.hu/sites/jobbik.hu/down/Jobbik-program2009EP.pdf [Accessed April 12, 2017].

Jobbik.hu. (2010a). *A Jobbik derecskei alapszervezetének önkormányzati választási programja*. [online] Available at: http://derecske.jobbik.hu/s ites/default/files/images/JMM%20Derecskei%20Alapszervezetenek%20 Onkormanyzati%20valasztasi%20programja.pdf [Accessed October 2, 2016].

Jobbik.hu. (2010b). *Radikális változás: A Jobbik országgyűlési választási programja a nemzeti önrendelkezésért és a társadalmi igazságosságért.* [online] Available at: https://jobbik.hu/sites/default/files/jobbik-program20 10gy.pdf [Accessed April 12, 2017].

Jobbik.hu. (2012). *Vona Gábor: El innen, rablók! (videóval)*. [online] Available at: https://jobbik.hu/rovatok/orsz%C3%A1gos_h%C3%ADrek/vona_g% C3%A1bor_el_innen_rabl%C3%B3k_vide%C3%B3val [Accessed April 12, 2017].

Jobbik.hu. (2013). *Irániakkal találkozott Vona Gábor.* [online] Available at: https://jobbik.hu/hireink/iraniakkal-talalkozott-vona-gabor [Accessed April 12, 2017].

Jobbik.hu. (2014). *Kimondjuk. Megoldjuk. A Jobbik országgyűlési választási programja a nemzet felemelkedéséért*. [online] Available at: https://job bik.hu/sites/default/files/cikkcsatolmany/kimondjukmegoldjuk2014_netre .pdf [Accessed April 12, 2017].

Jobbik.hu. (2015). *Köszönjük!*. [online] Available at: https://jobbik.hu/hirein k/koszonjuk [Accessed April 12, 2017].

Jobbikmedia, (2009). *Jobbik TV—"Az Igazság mindig győzni fog!"—Új Magyar Gárda avatás Kerepesen*. [video] Available at: https://www.you tube.com/watch?v=KNU5PuKQNYE [Accessed April 13, 2017].

Jobbsajoszentpeter.eoldal.hu. (2009). *A cigánybűnözés a cionizmus biológiai fegyvere.* [online] Available at: http://www.jobbsajoszentpeter.eoldal.hu/c ikkek/ebredj-s-vigyazz_/a-ciganybunozes-a-cionizmus-biologiai-fegyver e.html [Accessed April 12, 2017].

Johnson, D. B. (1999). Közösségi döntések elmélete. Budapest: Osiris Kiadó.

Jost, J. T., Glaser, J., Kruglanski, A. W. and Sulloway, F. (2003). Political conservatism as motivated social cognition. *Psychological Bulletin*, 129, 339–375.

Juhász, A. (2010a). *A "cigánybűnözés" szó politikai karrierje.* Anblokk, 2010(4) Available at: http://www.politicalcapital.hu/blog/?p=1937578 [Accessed April 24, 2017].

Juhász, A. and Szabados, K. (2006). *A populizmus éve. Magyarország Politikai Évkönyve 2005-ről.* Budapest: Demokrácia Kutatások Magyarországi Központja Közhasznú Alapítvány.

Juhasz, A., Krekó, P. and Molnár, Cs. (2012). *Attitűd-szélsőségesek Magyarországon—nemzetközi kontextusban.* Budapest: Political Capital. Available at: http://www.politicalcapital.hu/wp-content/uploads /fes_derex_20120229.pdf [Accessed: April 13, 2017].

Juhász, A., Győri, L., Krekó, P. and Dezső, A. (2015). *"I am Eurasian."* 1st ed. [ebook] Budapest: Political Capital. Available at: http://politicalca pital.hu/wp-content/uploads/PC_SDI_Boll_study_IamEurasian.pdf [Accessed April 18, 2017].

Juhász, A., Krekó, P., Molná, C. and Róbert, L. (2012). *Politikai stratégiák a szélsőjobboldallal szemben.* 1st ed. [ebook] Political Capital. Available at: http://www.riskandforecast.com/useruploads/files/politikai_strategiak _a_szelsojobboldallal_szemben.pdf [Accessed April 13, 2017].

Karácsony, G. and Róna, D. (2011). The secret of Jobbik. Reasons behind the rise of the Hungarian radical right. *Journal of East European and Asian Studies*, 2(1), pp. 61–92.

Keller, T. (2009). *Magyarország helye a világ értéktérképén.* Budapest: Tárki. Available at: http://www.tarki.hu/hu/research/gazdkult/gazdkult_wvs_kell er.pdf [Accessed Ápril 13, 2017].

Kessler, A. E. and Freeman, G. P. (2005). Support for extreme right-wing parties in Western Europe: individual attributes, political attitudes, and national context. *Comparative European Politics*, 3(3), pp. 261–288.

Knigge, P. (1998). The ecological correlates of right-wing extremism in Western Europe. *European Journal of Political Research*, 34(2), pp. 249–279.

Kocsis, A. (2014). *Egy futóbolond lett Putyin és a Jobbik ideológusa?—Alexandr Dugin és az Eurázsiai Birodalom.* [online] hvg.hu. Available at: http://hvg.hu/vilag/20140527_Alexandr_Dugin_eurazsiai_birodalom [Accessed April 12, 2017].

Koopmans, R. and Muis, J. (2009). The rise of right-wing populist Pim Fortuyn in the Netherlands: A discursive opportunity approach. *European Journal of Political Research*, 48(5), pp. 642–664.

Kopasz, M., Fábián, Z., Gábos, A., Medgyesi, M., Szívós, P. and Tóth, I. (2013). *Growing inequalities and its impacts in Hungary.* [online] Gini-research.org. Available at: http://gini-research.org/system/uploads/448/o riginal/Hungary.pdf?1370090544 [Accessed April 12, 2017].

Kopecky, P and Mudde, M. (2002). The two sides of Euroscepticism—party positions on European Integration in East Central Europe. *European Union Politics.*, 3(3), pp. 297–326.

Kornhauser, W. (1960). *The Politics of Mass Society.* London: Routledge and Kegan Paul.

Kovarek, D.; Róna, D.; Hunyadi, B.; Krekó, B. (in press). *Scapegoat-Based Policy Making in Hungary: Qualitative Evidence on How Jobbik and its Mayors Govern Municipalities.* Intersections (accepted: 29 August 2017).

Kovács, B. (2016). *Alkotmánybíróság: Nem nevezhetik szélsőjobboldalinak a tévében a Jobbikot.* [online] Index.hu. Available at: http://index.hu/kul tur/media/2016/12/08/alkotmanybirosag_nem_nevezhetik_szelsojobbol dalinak_a_teveben_a_jobbikot/ [Accessed April 12, 2017].

Krekó, P. (2011). *Jobbik needs Jews to run the world.* [online] Budapesttimes.hu. Available at: http://budapesttimes.hu/2011/05/15/job bik-needs-jews-to-run-the-world/ [Accessed April 12, 2017].

Krekó, P. (2012). A tekintély színe és fonákja. In: Fülöp, M. and Szabó, L., ed., *A Pszichológia mint társadalomtudomány—a 70 éves Hunyady György tiszteletére.* Budapest: Elte Eötvös Kiadó, pp. 245–260.

Krekó, P. and Győri, L. (2016). *OpEd: Part of a Pattern.* [online] Tol.org. Available at: http://www.tol.org/client/article/26521-oped-part-of-a-patte rn.html [Accessed April 12, 2017].

Krekó, P. and Juhász, A. (2014). *A Jobbik és Irán.* [online] Szombat Online. Available at: http://www.szombat.org/politika/a-jobbik-es-iran [Accessed April 24, 2017].

Krekó, P. and Mayer, G. (2015). Transforming Hungary-together? An analysis of the Fidesz–Jobbik relationship. In: Minkenberg, M., ed., *Transforming the Transformation? The East European Radical Right in the Political Process*. London: Routledge, pp. 188–206.

Krekó, P., Juhasz, A. and Szabados, K. (2015). Fidesz und Nationalpopulismus in Ungarn. In: Hillebrand, E., ed., *Rechtspopulismus in Europa: Gefahr für die Demokratie?* Berlin: Dietz Verlag, pp. 96–106.

Krekó, P., Juhász, A. and Molnár, Cs. (2011). A szélsőjobboldal iránti társadalmi kereslet növekedése Magyarországon. *Politikatudományi Szemle*, 2011(2), pp. 53–79.

Krekó, P., Kovács, M. (2016). Tesztoszteronpárt-e még a Jobbik? In Kovács, M.; Szabó, M. (Ed). Társadalmi nemek: elméleti megközelítések, kutarási eredmények. Budapest: ELTE Eötvös Kiadó

Kuruc.info. (2015). *Bakay Kornél: a harmadik muszlim invázió főszervezői az amerikai zsidók.* [online] Available at: https://kuruc.info/r/34/152126/ [Accessed April 12, 2017].

Kurtán, S. (2007). A Szabadság Párt (Ausztria). *Politikatudományi Szemle,* 2007/1, pp. 23–44.

Lanchidradio.hu. (2009). [online] Available at: http://www.lanchidradio.hu/nod e/72435/ [Accessed November 7, 2016].

Látlelet 2009. (2009). *Research Summary on Reasons Behind the Resurgence of the Hungarian Far-right.* 1st ed. [ebook] Political Capital. Available at: http://www.politicalcapital.hu/letoltes/20091028_PC_Latlel et_2009.pdf [Accessed December 13, 2016].

Lipset, S. M. (1981) *Political Man: The Social Bases of Politics.* Expanded ed. Baltimore, MA: The Johns Hopkins University Press.

Lubbers, M., Gijsberts, M. and Scheepers, P. (2002). Extreme right-wing voting in Western Europe. *European Journal of Political Research,* 41(3), pp. 345–378.

Lucassen, G. and Lubbers, M. (2012). Who fears what? Explaining far-right-wing preference in Europe by distinguishing perceived cultural and economic ethnic threats. *Comparative Political Studies,* 45(5), pp. 547–574.

M.Ferenc, L. (2006). "Radical behaviour patterns have increasing appeal" (Kálmán Gábor, youth researcher). *Magyar Narancs.*

Magyar, B. (2016). *Hungarian Octopus—Post-communist Mafia State.* 1st ed. Budapest: Noran.

260 THE HUNGARIAN FAR RIGHT

Magyar, K. (2015). *Hangfelvételen rántja le a leplet a cukiságkampányáról a Jobbik alelnöke, aki lecigányozza Orbán édesanyját.* [online] Magyarnarancs.hu. Available at: http://magyarnarancs.hu/kismagyarors zag/hangfelvetelen-rantja-le-a-leplet-a-cukisagkampanyarol-a-jobbik-al elnoke-aki-leciganyozta-orban-viktor-edesanyjat-94078 [Accessed April 24, 2017].

Mandiner.hu. (2015). A Jobbik üdvözli az iráni atomprogramról szóló megállapodást. [online] Available at: http://mandiner.hu/cikk/20150715 _a_jobbik_udvozli_az_irani_atomprogramrol_szolo_megallapodast [Accessed April 24, 2017].

Mannheim, K. (1994). *A konzervativizmus.* Budapest: Cserépfalvi Kiadó.

Marketing Centrum (2011). *Zárótanulmány. Roma társadalom—2010.* [online] Available at: http://84.206.8.166/dokumentum/A%20kutatas%20MC%2 0roma%20zárótanulmány_s.pdf [Accessed: October 15, 2016].

Máthé, Á. (2013). *Green Bolshevism—the forgotten precursor of the Communist dictatorship.* Kommentár, 2013(4).

Median.hu. (2007). *Matricás önkifejezés.* [online] Available at: http://www.med ian.hu/object.cb63b3e1-8fc4-43e2-a7b2-ebbb81ea84b2.ivy [Accessed April 12, 2017].

Medvegy, G. (2016). *Vona Gábor túl akar jutni a "keresztény-zsidó ellentéten."* [online] 24.hu. Available at: http://24.hu/belfold/2016/12/28/vona-gabor-tul-akar-jutni-a-magyar-zsido-ellenteten/ [Accessed April 13, 2017].

Meijerink, F., Mudde, C. and Van Holsteyn, J. (1998). "Research Note." *Acta Politica,* 33 (Summer), pp. 165–178.

Minkenberg, M. (2000). The renewal of the radical right: Between modernity and anti-modernity. *Government and Opposition,* 35(2), pp. 170–188.

Minkenberg, M. (2009). The radical right in Europe: Challenges for comparative research. In: Bertelsmann Stiftung, ed., *Strategies for Combating Right-Wing Extremism in Europe.* Gütersloh: Bertelsmann Stiftung., pp. 13–28.

Minkenberg, M. (2015). *Transforming the Transformation? The East European Radical Right in the Political Process.* Abingdon: Routledge.

Minkenberg, M. and Perrineau, P. (2007). The radical right in the European elections 2004. *International Political Science Review,* 28(1), pp. 29–55.

Molnár, Cs., Barna, I., Bartlett, J., Győri, L., Juhász, A. and Krekó, P. (2015). *Measuring Political Violence*. 1st ed. [ebook] Budapest: Open Society Foundations. Available at: http://www.politicalcapital.hu/wp-content/upl oads/PC_ISEC_political_violence_study_eng_web.pdf [Accessed April 13, 2017].

Molnár, Cs. and Krekó, P. (2010). *Államfetisiszták-e a magyarok? Magyarország Politikai Évkönyve 2010-ről*. Budapest: DKMKA, pp. 30–31.

Mudde, C. (1996). The war of words: Defining the extreme right party family. *West European Politics*, 19(2), pp. 225–248.

Mudde, C. (2000). *The Ideology of the Extreme Right*. New York: Manchester University Press.

Mudde, C. (2007). *Populist Radical Right Parties in Europe*. Cambridge: Cambridge University Press.

Mudde, C. (2010). "The intolerance of the tolerant." In: Mudde, C., ed., *Racist Extremism in Central and Eastern Europe*. London: Routledge.

Mudde, C. (2015). *Is Hungary Run by the Radical Right?* [online] Washington Post. Available at: https://www.washingtonpost.com/news/monkey-cag e/wp/2015/08/10/is-hungary-run-by-the-radical-right/?utm_term=.5b1bd bbd16a7 [Accessed April 13, 2017].

Muižnieks, Preface to Mudde, C. (eds.) (2005). *Racist Extremism in Central and Eastern Europe*. London: Routledge.

National Media and Infocommunications Authority (2012). A study of the representation of social diversity in major news and general-interest programs in Hungary (2012/2).

National Media and Infocommunications Authority (2013). A study of the representation of social diversity in major news and general-interest programs in Hungary (2013/2).

Nikos, F. (2006). "Evergreen, sensation and the rest." *Jel-Kép*.

Norris, P. (2005). *Radical Right: Voters and Parties in the Electoral Market*. Cambridge: Cambridge University Press.

Oesch, D. (2008a). Explaining workers' support for right-wing populist parties in Western Europe: Evidence from Austria, Belgium, France, Norway, and Switzerland. *International Political Science Review*, 29(3), pp. 349–373.

Oesch, D. (2008b). The changing shape of class voting: An individual-level analysis of party support in Britain, Germany and Switzerland. *European Societies*, 10(3), pp. 329–355.

Oesch, D. (2012). The class basis of the Cleavage between the new left and the radical right: An analysis for Austria, Denmark, Norway and Switzerland. In: Rydren, J., ed., *Class Politics and the Radical Right.* London: Routledge.

Origo.hu. (2013). *Keresi a Jobbik holdudvarát Vona.* [online] Available at: http://www.origo.hu/itthon/20130126-keresi-a-jobbik-holdudvarat-vona.html [Accessed April 12, 2017].

Paksa, R. (2009). Far-right movements in the 1930s. In: Romsics, I., ed., *Hungarian Rightist Tradition, 1900–1948.* 1st ed. Budapest: Osiris.

Paksa, R. (2012). A magyar szélsőjobboldal története. Budapest: Jaffa Kiadó

Paksa, R. (2013). *Hungarian National Socialists.* Budapest: Osiris—MTA BTK TTI.

Panyi, Sz. (2015). *Vona ideje akkor jöhet el, ha Orbán kiszállt.* [online] Index.hu. Available at: http://index.hu/belfold/2015/10/26/vona_ideje_ak kor_johet_el_ha_orban_kiszallt_jobbik_fidesz_menekultvalsag_1_resz/ [Accessed April 12, 2017].

Panyi, Sz. (2016). *Kőszeg Ferenc: Orbán ellenében még Vona Gáborra is lehet szavazni.* [online] Index.hu. Available at: http://index.hu/belfold/2 016/10/07/koszeg_ferenc_orban_elleneben_meg_vona_gaborra_is_leh et_szavazni/ [Accessed April 13, 2017].

PCBlog.hu. (2014). *Felemás eredményt hozott a Jobbik számára az önkormányzati választás.* [online] Available at: https://pcblog.atlatszo.h u/2014/10/13/felemas-eredmenyt-hozott-a-jobbik-szamara-az-onkorma nyzati-valasztas/ [Accessed April 12, 2017].

Pirro, A. (2014). Digging into the breeding grounds: Insight into the electoral performance of populist radical right parties in Central and Eastern Europe. *East European Politics*, 30(2), pp. 246–270.

Pirro, A. (2015). *The Populist Radical Right in Central and Eastern Europe: Ideology, Impact, and Electoral Performance.* Abingdon: Routledge.

Plankó, G. and Sálink, G. (2009). *"Nem remegne meg a térdünk"—interjú Vona Gáborral, a Jobbik elnökével.* [online] Origo.hu. Available at: http://www.origo.hu/itthon/20090630-vona-gabor-a-jobbik-elnoke-inter ju.html [Accessed April 12, 2017].

Political Capital (2009). *Reasons behind the resurgence of the far-right in Hungary.* [online] Available at: http://www.riskandforecast.com/post/hu ngary/reasons-behind-the-resurgence-of-the-far-right-in-hungary-_30 7.html [Accessed April 13, 2017].

Political Capital (2012). *Available on Demand. Demand for Right-wing Extremism.* Budapest: Political Capital.

Political Radical. (2014). *A Jobbik és Irán kapcsolata.* [online] Available at: http://politicalradical.cafeblog.hu/2014/03/31/a-jobbik-es-iran-kapcsola ta/ [Accessed April 24, 2017].

Political Capital. (2010). *A Jobbik a legkormánybarátabb ellenzéki párt.* [online] Available at: http://www.politicalcapital.hu/blog/?p=1937263&u tm_source=mandiner&utm_medium=link&utm_campaign=mandiner_20 1612 [Accessed April 13, 2017].

Polyakova, A. (2013). *Let's Stop Blaming the Economy.* [online] Eurozine. Available at: http://www.eurozine.com/articles/2013-01-30-polyakova-en.html [Accessed April 13, 2017].

Putnam, R. D. (1995). Bowling alone: America's declining social capital. *The Journal of Democracy*, 1995, 6(1), pp. 65–78.

Pytlas, B. (2015). *Radical Right Parties in Central and Eastern Europe: Mainstream Party Competition and Electoral Fortune.* Abingdon: Routledge.

Róna D. (2014). *A Jobbik-jelenség. A Jobbik Magyarországért Mozgalom népszerűségének okai.* [online] Available at: http://phd.lib.uni-corvi nus.hu/824/1/Rona_Daniel.pdf [Accessed April 13, 2017].

Róna, D. and Sőrés, A. (2012). *A kuruc.info nemzedék—Miért népszerű a Jobbik a fiatalok között?* [online] Available at: https://kuruc.info/ga leriaN/egyeb/kuruc.info_nemzed%C3%A9k.pdf [Accessed: April 13, 2017].

Rudas, T. (2010). A Jobbik törzsszavazóiról. In Kolosi, T. and Tóth, I. Gy., ed., *Társadalmi Riport 2010.* Tárki: Budapest.

Rydgren, J. (2002). Radical right populism in Sweden: Still a failure, but for how long? *Scandinavian Political Studies*, 25(1), pp. 27–56.

Rydgren, J. (2007). The sociology of the radical right. *Annual Review of Sociology*, 33, pp. 241–262.

Rytkó, E. (2008). "National Referenda in Hungary[online] Available at http://www.aceeeo.org/sites/default/files/PDF/presentation_of_conferen ce/2008/Referenda%20in%20Hungary_english.pdf [Accessed April 13, 2017].

Saari, S. (2011). Putin's Eurasian Union Initiative: Are the Premises of Russia's Post-Soviet Policy Changing? Ulbrief, [online] (9). Available at: http://www.ui.se/upl/files/65793.pdf [Accessed April 12, 2017].

Sales, S. M. (1973). Threat as a factor in authoritarianism: An analysis of archival data. Journal of Personality and Social Psychology, 1973(28), pp. 44–57.

Schwartz, S. H. (2003). Univerzáliák az értékek tartalmában és struktúrájában. Elméleti előrelé—pések és empirikus próbák húsz országban. In: Váriné, Sz. I., ed., Az értékek az életben és a retorikában. Budapest: Akadémiai Kiadó, pp. 105–154.

Shekhovtsov, A. (2017). Tango Noir—Russia and the Western far-right. London: Routledge.

Sidanius, J. and Pratto, F. (2005). A társadalmi dominancia. Budapest: Osiris Kiadó.

Sik, D. (2014). The imitated public sphere: The case of Hungary's far right. In: Druxes, H. and Simpson, P., ed., Far Right Media Strategies Across Europe and North America: Extreme Persuasion. New York: Lexington Books.

Simon, L., Greenberg, J., Harmon-Jones, E., Solomon, S., Pyszczynski, T., Arndt, J. and Abend, T. (1997). Terror management and cognitive-experiential self-theory: Evidence that terror management occurs in the experiential system. Journal of Personality and Social Psychology, 72(5), pp. 1132–1146.

Soline.hu. (2016). Gyurcsány Ferenc: nehéz évek előtt áll Orbán Viktor. [online] Available at: http://www.sonline.hu/somogy/kozelet/gyurcsany-ferenc-nehez-evek-elott-all-orban-viktor-662901/?utm_source=mandine r&utm_medium=link&utm_campaign=mandiner_201612 [Accessed April 13, 2017].

Solt, O. (1992). A skinheadtalány. Beszélő, 4/46. http://beszelo.c3.hu/ci kkek/a-skinheadtalany [Accessed May 13, 2017].

Spiegel Online. (2007). *Cat Fight on the Far Right: Mussolini's Romania Comments Split Extremist MEP Group.* [online] SPIEGEL ONLINE. Available at: http://www.spiegel.de/international/europe/cat-fight-on-the-far-right-mussolini-s-romania-comments-split-extremist-mep-group-a-51 6407.html [Accessed April 12, 2017].

Stent, A. (2008). Restoration and revolution in Putin's foreign policy. *Europe-Asia Studies*, 60(6), pp. 1089–1106.

Stenner, K. (2005). *The Authoritarian Dynamic.* Cambridge: Cambridge University Press.

Stratfor. (2015). *The Kremlin Connections of the Hungarian Far-Right.* [online] Available at: https://www.stratfor.com/the-hub/kremlin-connections-hung arian-far-right [Accessed April 18, 2017].

Sum, P. E. (2010). The radical right in Romania: Political party evolution and the distancing of Romania from Europe. *Communist and Post-Communist Studies,* 43(1), 19–29.

Szabó, A. (2013). *Political Orientations, Values and Activities of Hungarian University and College Students.* Prague: Heinrich Böll Stiftung.

Szabó, A. (2015). *Exit, Voice, Loyalty and Neglect—Political attitudes of Hungarian University and College Students.* Prague: Heinrich Böll Stiftung.

Szabó. I. (2005). Rendszerváltás és a nemzet. *Politikatudományi Szemle,* 14(2), pp. 89–110.

Századvég. (2012). *A Jobbik szavazói nem a Fidesztől jöttek.* [online] Available online: http://szazadveg.hu/ld/l5f1g6r0s9s3h5b6s2a7_pressrel ease_20121114.pdf [Accessed April 13, 2017].

Szazadveg.hu. (2012). *Századvég.* [online] Available at: http://szazadveg.hu /ld/l5f1g6r0s9s3h5b6s2a7_pressrelease_20121114.pdf [Accessed April 12, 2017].

Szilágyi, A. (2009). *A jobboldal mint tömegkultúra.* Mozgó Világ. 2009(4).

Tamás Gáspár, M. (1999). *On Post-Fascism: How citizenship is becoming an exclusive privilege.* Boston Review. [online] Available at: http://new.bost onreview.net/archives/BR25.3/tamas.html [Accessed April 13, 2017].

Tamás Gáspár, M. (2015). *A politikai helyzet Magyarországon.* [online] Available at: http://hvg.hu/velemeny/20150319_TGM_A_politikai_helyze t_Magyarorszagon [Accessed April 13, 2017].

Tamás, P. (2007). Neopopulizmus és nemzeti radikalizmus 1-2. *Kritika*, 2007. October–November.

Tárki (2013). *Értékek.* Budapest, 2013 október,

Tellér, Gy. (2014). *Született-e Orbán rendszer 2010 és 2014 között?* [online] Available at: http://www.nagyvilag-folyoirat.hu/2014-03_beliv_OK.pdf [Accessed October 13, 2016].

Tóka, G. (1998). "Választói magatartás." In: Kolosi, T., Tóth, I. Gy. and Vukovich, Gy., ed., *Társadalmi riport 1998.* Budapest: TÁRKI, pp. 391–411.

Tomkins, S. (1963). Left and right: A basic dimension of ideology and personality. In R-W. White (eds.), *The Study of Lives.* New York: Atherton.

Tóth, C. (2009). *Demokrácia, kirekesztés, lócitrom.* [online] NOL.hu. Available at: http://nol.hu/velemeny/20091105-demokracia__kirekesztes__locitro m-414661 [Accessed April 12, 2017].

Tóth, Cs. (2014). *Full text of Viktor Orbán's speech at Băile Tuşnad (Tusnádfürdő) of 26 July 2014.* The Budapest Beacon. [online] Available at: http://budapestbeacon.com/public-policy/full-text-of-viktor-orbans-sp eech-at-baile-tusnad-tusnadfurdo-of-26-july-2014/ [Accessed April 12, 2017].

Ungváry, K. (2004). Kik voltak a nyilasok?—egy szocialista tömegpárt. Rubicon, 2004(11).

Ungváry, K. (2012). *The Horthy Regime in the Balance—discrimination, Social Policy and Anti-Semitism in Hungary.* Budapest: Jelenkor Kiadó.

Van Der Brug, W., Fennema, M. and Tillie, J. (2005). Why some anti-Immigrant parties fail and others succeed. *Comparative Political Studies,* 38(5), pp. 537–573.

Varró, Sz. (2009). *"A Jobbik mint harmadik erő."* Magyar Narancs [online] Available at: http://oknyomozo.hu/varro_jobbik [Accessed: November 12, 2012].

Vejvodova, P. (2014). A Thorny Way to Find Friends: Transnational Cooperation and Network-building amongst Right-wing and National Populist Parties. In Hartleb, F and Grabow, K., ed., *Exposing the Demagogues.* Brussels: Martens Centre, 2015. pp. 373–396.

Vona, G. (2012). Előszó. In: Evola, J., ed., *Jobboldali Fiatalok kézikönyve.* Debrecen: Kvintesszencia.

Vona, G. (2013). *Fontos könyv lesz.* [image] Available at: https://www.faceb ook.com/vonagabor/photos/a.10150160184994623.341499.247920204 622/10151628159059623 [Accessed April 12, 2017].

Vona, G. (2016a). *Hová tűnt a Jobbik lelke? (Tabu 8. rész).* [online] Available at: https://www.facebook.com/vonagabor/posts/10154513327879623:0 [Accessed April 12, 2017].

Vona, G. (2016b). *Milyen a jó magyar politikus? (Tabu 9. rész).* [online] Jobbik.hu. Available at: https://jobbik.hu/hireink/vona-gabor-milyen-jo-magyar-politikus-tabu-9-resz [Accessed April 12, 2017].

Vörös, A. (upcoming). *Symbol-forming processes in the media—Olaszliszka.*

Vs.hu. (2016). *Szélsőjobbos cicaharc az iszlám védelmében.* [online] Available at: http://vs.hu/mind/osszes/szelsojobbos-cicaharc-az-iszlam-vedelmeben-1128 [Accessed April 12, 2017].

Widfeldt, A. (2003). The diversified approach. In: Eatwell, R. and Mudde, C., ed., *Western Democracies and the New Extreme Right Challenge.*

Zágráb, N. (2006). *A hazai kiskereskedelem védelmében.* [online] Jobbik.hu. Available at: https://jobbik.hu/rovatok/politika/a_hazai_kiskereskedele m_vedelmeben [Accessed April 12, 2017].

Zakaria, F. (2014). *The Rise of Putinism.* [online] Washington Post. Available at: http://www.washingtonpost.com/opinions/fareed-zakaria-the-rise-of-putinism/2014/07/31/2c9711d6-18e7-11e4-9e3b-7f2f110c6265_story.ht ml?utm_source=mandiner&utm_medium=link&utm_campaign=mandine r_hungarianglobe_201501 [Accessed April 13, 2017].

Zsolt, P. (2008). *Romaáldozatok és a média.* 1st ed. [ebook] Méltányosság Politikaelemző Központ. Available at: http://www.meltanyossag.hu/file s/meltany/imce/doc/ny-mediarepr-081201.pdf [Accessed April 13, 2017].

Zsolt, P. (2009). *A sorok között: a Jobbik az országos napilapokban.* 1st ed. [ebook] Méltányosság Politikaelemző Központ. Available at: http://ww w.meltanyossag.hu/files/meltany/imce/ny-asorokkozott-090624.pdf [Accessed April 13, 2017].

***ibidem*-**Verlag / *ibidem* Press**
Melchiorstr. 15
70439 Stuttgart
Germany

ibidem@ibidem.eu
ibidem.eu